Ted Egan was born in N̶ sixteen years there, descri̶

Since 1949 he has lived and worked in the Northern Territory, now based in Alice Springs, performing, writing, singing and recording his own songs, and collecting those of others.

He speaks two Aboriginal languages, and often lectures on Aboriginal language and issues. He is an inaugural Life Member of the Australian Stockman's Hall of Fame. In 1991 he was awarded the Order of Australia for 'services to the Aboriginal People, and for an ongoing and significant contribution to Australia's literary heritage through song and verse'. He was at one time a member of the Prime Minister's National Reconciliation Council.

Author of numerous books, his last was *Justice All Their Own*, an account of the clash of cultures when Aboriginals speared a group of Japanese fishermen and a white policeman to death in the early 1930s.

Sitdown Up North

TED EGAN

Ted Egan [signature]

K
KERR

First published 1997
Kerr Publishing Pty Ltd
176 Illawarra Road
Marrickville 2204
Australia
Telephone International + 61 + 02 9564 0064
Facsimilie International + 61 + 02 9564 0422

© Ted Egan 1997

This book is copyright. Apart from fair dealing for the purposes of private study, research, criticism or review, as permitted under the Copyright Act, no part may be reproduced by any process without the written permission of Kerr Publishing Pty Ltd or the recording of copying for Copyright Agency Ltd under their rules for use.

Cover artwork Susan Driemeyer, Hall & Jones, Brisbane
Cover photograph Carmel Sears, Alice Springs
Inset cover photograph Northside Photographics, Melbourne
Typeset in 12/15 Century Schoolbook by DOCUPRO, Sydney
Printed by McPhersons Print Group, Maryborough Vic
Printed by Australian Print Group, Maryborough Vic
Printed by Pirie Printers Pty Ltd, Canberra

Distributed by TOWER Books nationally
Distributed in New Zealand by Nationwide Book Christchurch

National Library of Australia
cataloguing-in-publication data:

Egan, Ted. 1932
  Sitdown up north.

Includes index.
  ISBN 1 875703 23 3.

  1. Egan, Ted. 2. Country musicians—Australia—Biography.
  3. Entertainers—Australia—Biography. 4. Northern
  Territory—Social life and customs. 5. Northern Territory
  —Description and travel. I. Title.

781.642092

Contents

1	Like Beer, Just Passing Through	7
2	Misspent Youth? What, Me?	28
3	You'll Learn, Son	45
4	St Mary Kamwari	65
5	Who's Protecting Who?	81
6	The Great Loo Debates	97
7	Bullocky's Joy and Jesus	116
8	Desert Rat	138
9	The Brunette	159
10	Mean Bugger Egan	171
11	Desk Jockey	185
12	Chalkie Ted	201
13	War Games	217
14	The Way of Wuyal	230
15	Poor Bugger Me	248
	Index	267

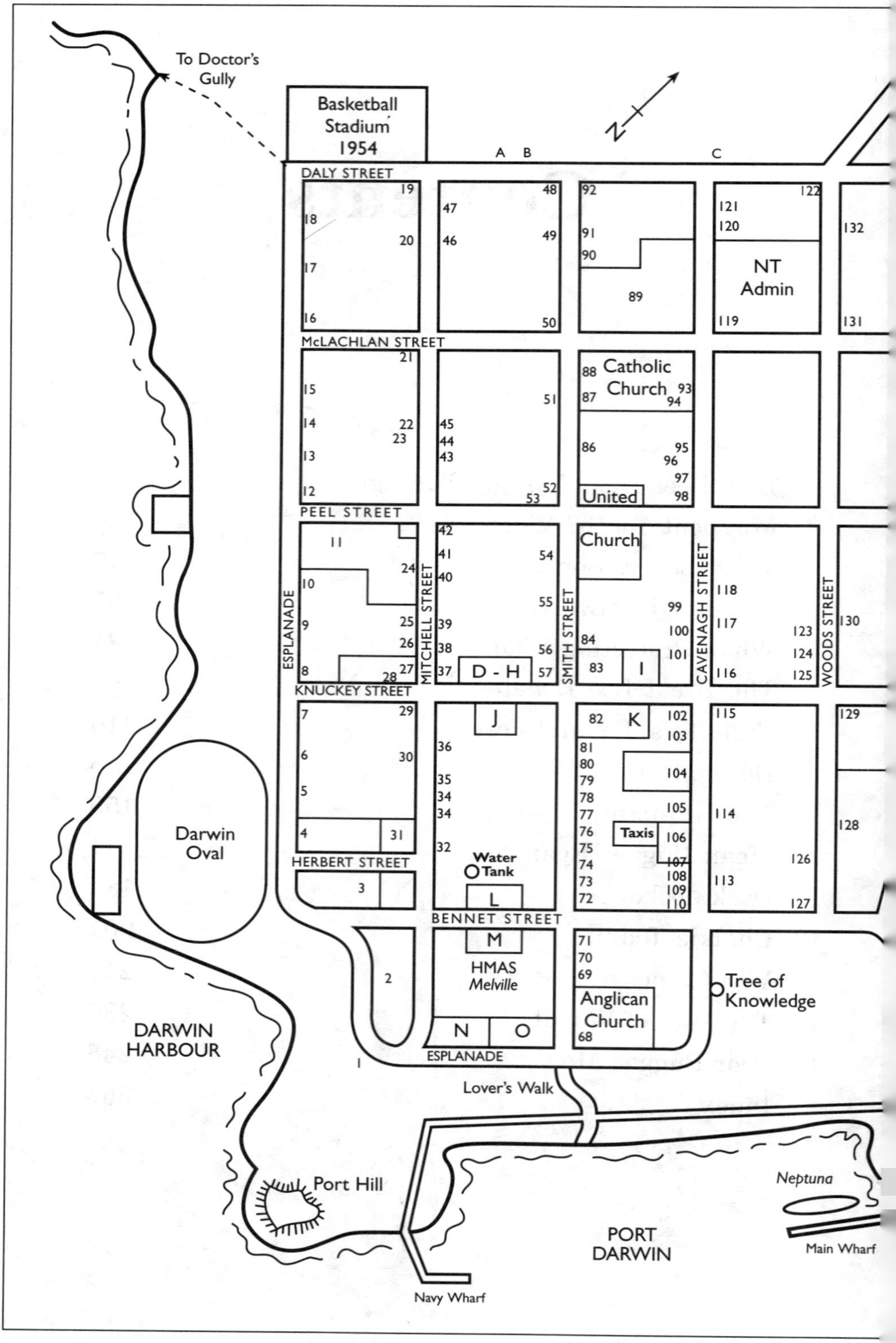

To Doctor's Gully
Basketball Stadium 1954
N
A
B
C
DALY STREET
McLACHLAN STREET
PEEL STREET
KNUCKEY STREET
HERBERT STREET
BENNET STREET
ESPLANADE
MITCHELL STREET
SMITH STREET
CAVENAGH STREET
WOODS STREET
NT Admin
Catholic Church
United Church
D - H
I
J
K
L
M
N
O
Taxis
Water Tank
HMAS Melville
Anglican Church
Tree of Knowledge
Darwin Oval
DARWIN HARBOUR
Lover's Walk
Port Hill
PORT DARWIN
Neptuna
Main Wharf
Navy Wharf
1
2
3
4
5
6
7
8
9
10
11
12
13
14
15
16
17
18
19
20
21
22
23
24
25
26
27
28
29
30
31
32
34
34
35
36
37
38
39
40
41
42
43
44
45
46
47
48
49
50
51
52
53
54
55
56
57
68
69
70
71
72
73
74
75
76
77
78
79
80
81
82
83
84
86
87
88
89
90
91
92
93
94
95
96
97
98
99
100
101
102
103
104
105
106
107
108
109
110
113
114
115
116
117
118
119
120
121
122
123
124
125
126
127
128
129
130
131
132

NORTHERN TERRITORY

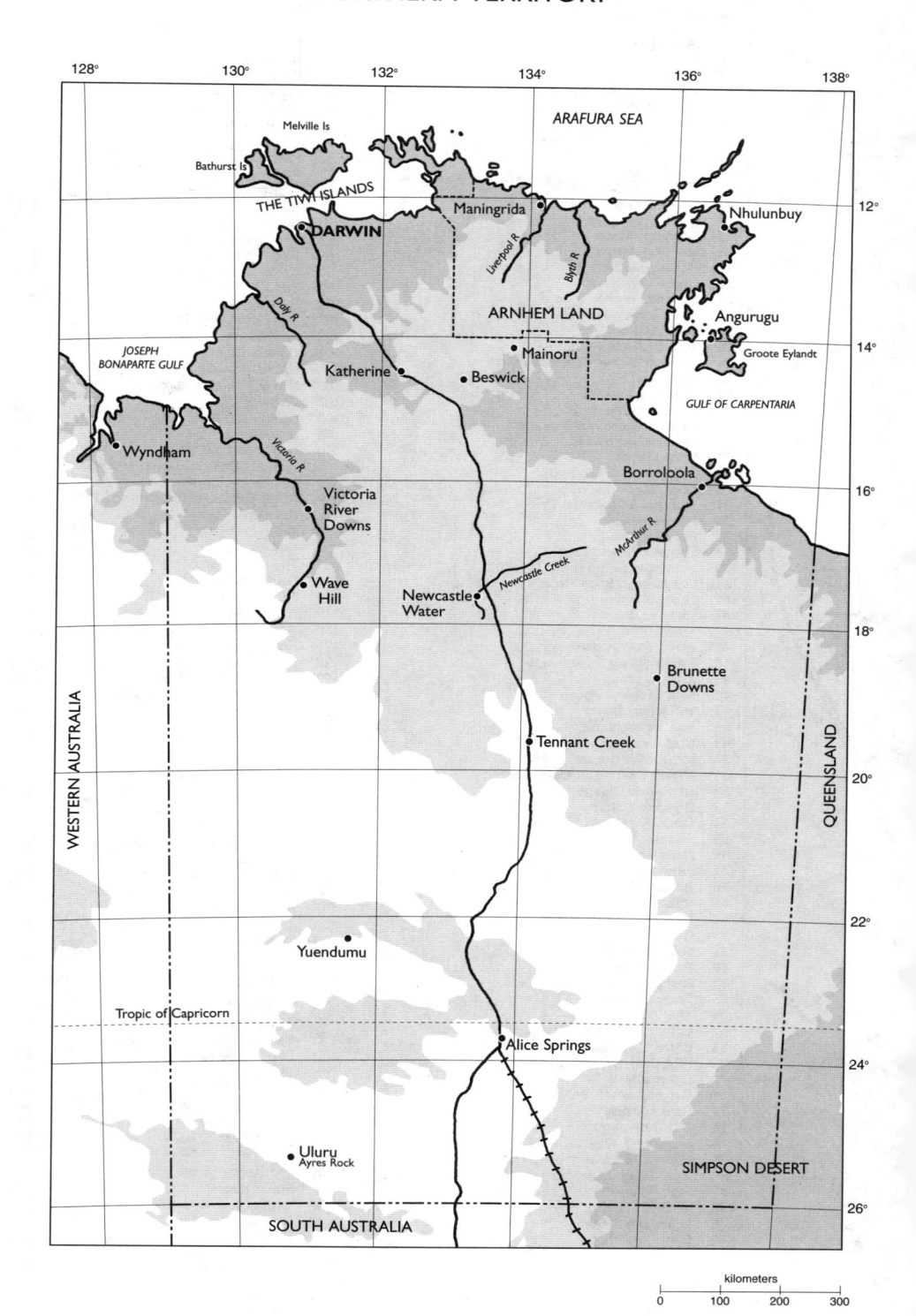

DARWIN CENTRAL BUSINESS DISTRICT 1948–1954

1. Government House
2. Old Post Office ruins
3. Jim Henry (BAT House)
4. Hotel Darwin
5. Public Library
6. Eric Izod House
7. Admiralty House (1953)
8. Tiger Lyons (BAT House)
9. Judge Wells
10. Court Buildings
11. Peel Street Mess (1954)
12. Seaspray Flats x 4
13. Jess Chardon
14. Bill Lauder (Auditor)
15. Gerry Gray (Municipal)
16. Burns Philp House
17. Doug Lockwood
18. Marrenah House
19. Bundey Butchery
20. Captain Wells
21. Macrides house
22. Felix Spain Hairdresser
23. Darwin Club
24. Mitchell Street Mess
25. J Schombacher/ Customs House
26. Alan Ford
27. Methodist mission
28. Methodist Church
29. Murray Johnston Motors
30. Masonic Temple
31. Hotel Darwin
32. Dept Works & Housing
33. Post Office
34. Weedon & Lawrence store
35. Poinciana Cafe
36. Roberta Library
37. Burnett's Newsagency
38. Sion House
39. Les Heaven Shoe Repairs
40. Graham house
41. Ramirez house
42. Albert Chan house
43. Albert Fong house
44. Rex & Nancy Eddy house
45. Canaris house
46. Nick Paspaley house
47. Yorky Peel house
48. Tom Harris house
49. Cashman house
50. Mrs Cook's house
51. Allwright & Fraser/ Ossie Jensen
52. Drysdale's Garage
53. Drysdale's Store
54. Clape & Paspalis houses
55. Henry & Bayley Electrical
56. Robertson & Walsh Bakery
57. Astoria Cafe
58. Burns Philp
59. Millers & Sandover
60. Mick Paspalis betting shop
61. George Hopkins 'Coolibah'
62. Valmae Frocks
63. Roslyn Court (N Paspaley)
64. Rendezvous Cafe
65. Snow E Bryant
66. The Vic
67. Commercial Bank
68. Christ Church ruins
69. ESA Bank (*NT News* 1953)
70. Brown's Mart
71. Commonwealth Bank
72. Bank of NSW
73. C J Cashman store
74. Koolpinyah Kool Store
75. Canaris Milk Bar
76. Tiger Lyons (upstairs)
77. Star Pictures
78. W G Chin & Co
79. Lorna Lim & Sons
80. Sam Calvi shop
81. Tahranoff's Dress Shop
82. Jack Sweetman shop
83. RSL Club
84. A E Jolly (Eddy Caffery)
85. Harry Chan Store
86. United Church Club
87. Keetley's Taxis (1954)
88. Bishop's 'Palace'
89. St Mary's Church
90. 'Belsen' Camp
91. Postmaster (J Marks)
92. Police flats x 2
93. Police barracks
94. Convent
95. Catholic Palais
96. Surveyor (A James)
97. PMG (Wag Graham)
98. Dept Works (J Sweeny)
99. Native Affairs (G Sweeney)
100. Sue Wah Chin & Eric Chin, tailor
101. Eastern Cafe
102. Don McKinnon's Bikes
103. Sun Cheong Loong
104. Oriental Cafe
105. NAWU stadium
106. Paddy Hickey, auctioneer
107. Worker's Club
108. Chin Loong Pak
109. D X Bakery
110. Bob Steel Fruit Shop
111. Gordon's Don Hotel ruins *later* Abbott House
112. Zero in the Tropics ruins
112. Albert Fong's Don Hotel
113. Chin Mook Sang
114. Ted D'Ambrosio
115. Izod Motors
116. Thomas Brown & Son
117. Darwin Public School
118. NT Administration
119. Harry Chan house
120. John Coleman house
121. George Chin
122. Allan Masters house
123. James Yuen house
124. Darwin Aerated Waters factory
125. Mrs Wu house
126. Joss house
127. Woods Street Flats
128. NAWU office
129. Jim Gonzales, pearler
130. Les Sadler house
131. T H Pierssene 1947–52
132. 'Noondi' Haritos
133. Fong Yuen Kee soft drink factory
134. Steam Laundry & RAOB lodge
135. Shell Oil Co. Mess
136. Railway houses
137. Railway station
138. Town Mess
139. Bond shed

CROSS STREETS

A. Dick Ward house
B. St George's Club (T H Pierssene house)
C. Haritos store
D. Charlie See Kee
E. Saunders Jewellers
F. Lilian Dean Photography
G. Mrs Wehr's Cakeshop
H. Ah Toy's Store
I. Les Heaven Shoes
J. CWA hall
K. Ted Davies Sports
L. Police Station
M. Dept Labour & Nat Service
N. Old Administration
O. Old Courthouse

Darwin Central Business District 1948-1954

1. Government House
2. Old Post Office Ruins
3. Jim Henry (BAT House)
4. Hotel Darwin
5. Public Library
6. Eric Izod house
7. Admiralty House (1953)
8. Tiger Lyons (BAT House)
9. Judge Wells house
10. Court Buildings
11. Peel Street Mess (1954)
12. Seaspray Flats x 4
13. Jess Chardon
14. Bill Lauder (Auditor)
15. Gerry Gray (Municipal)
16. Burns Philp House
17. Doug Lockwood
18. Marrenah House
19. Bundey Butchery
20. Captain Wells
21. Macrides house
22. Felix Spain hairdresser
23. Darwin Club
24. Mitchell Street Mess
25. J Schombacher/Customs House
26. Alan Ford
27. Methodist Missions House
28. Methodist Church
29. Murray Johnston Motors
30. Masonic Temple
31. Hotel Darwin bars
32. Dept. Works & Housing
33. Post Office
34. Weedon & Lawrence
35. Poinciana Cafe
36. Roberta Library
37. Burnett's Newsagency
38. Sion House
39. Les Heaven shoe repairs
40. Graham house
41. Ramirez house
42. Albert Chan House
43. Albert Fong House
44. Rex & Nancy Eddy house
45. Canaris house
46. Nick Paspaley house
47. Yorky Peel house
48. Tom Harris house
49. Cashman house
50. Mrs Cook house
51. Allwright & Fraser/Ossie Jensen
52. Drysdale's Garage
53. Drysdale's Store
54. Clape & Paspalis house
55. Henry & Bayley Electrical
56. Robertson & Walsh Bakery
57. Astoria Cafe
58. Burns Philp
59. Millers & Sandovers
60. Mick Paspalis betting shop
61. George Hopkins 'Coolibah'
62. Valmae Frocks
63. Roslyn Court (Nick Paspaley)
64. Rendezvous Cafe
65. Snow E Bryant
66. The Vic
67. Commercial Bank
68. Christ Church Ruins
69. ESA Bank (NT News 1953)
70. Brown's Mart
71. Commonwealth Bank
72. Bank of NSW
73. C J Cashman Store
74. Koolpinyah Kool Store
75. Canaris Milk Bar
76. Tiger Lyons (upstairs)
77. Star Pictures
78. W G Chin & Co
79. Lorna Lim & Sons
80. Tahranoff's Dress Shop
81. Jack Sweetman shop
82. RSL Club
83. A E Jolly/Eddy Caffery garage
84. Harry Chan Store
85. United Church Club
86. Keetley's Taxis (1954)
87. Bishop's 'Palace'
88. St Mary's Church
89. Belsen Camp
90. Postmaster (J Marks)
91. Police Flats x 2
92. Police Barracks
93. Convent
94. Catholic Palais
95. Surveyor house (A James)
96. PMG house (Wag Graham)
97. Dept Works house (J Sweeny)
98. Native Affairs house (G Sweeney)
99. Sue Wah Chin & Eric Chin, tailor
100. Eastern Cafe
101. Don McKinnon bike shop
102. Sun Cheong Loong
103. Oriental Cafe
104. NAWU Stadium
105. Paddy Hickey, Auctioneer
106. Workers Club
107. Chin Loong Pak
108. DX Bakery
109. Bob Steele fruit shop
110. Chin Loong Tang
111. Gordon's Don Hotel ruins later Abbott House
112. Zero in the Tropics ruins
113. Albert Fong's Don Hotel
114. Chin Mook Sang
115. Ted d'Ambrosio
116. Izod Motors
117. Thomas Brown & Son
118. Darwin public school
119. N T Administration
120. Harry Chan House
121. John Coleman house
122. George Chin
123. Allen Masters house
124. James Yuen house
125. Darwin Aerated Waters soft drinks
126. Mrs Wu house
127. Joss House
128. Woods Street Flats
129. NAWU Office
130. Jim Gonzales, pearler
131. Les Sadler house
132. T H Pierssene 1947-1952
133. George 'Noondi' Haritos
134. Fong Yuen Kee soft drinks
135. Steam Laundry/RAOB Lodge
136. Shell Oil Co. Mess
137. Railway houses
138. Darwin railway station
139. Town Mess
140. Bond Store

CROSS STREETS

A. Dick Ward house
B. St George's Club (T H Pierssene house)
C. Haritos Store
D. Charlie See Kee Radolectrics
E. Saunders Jewellers
F. Lilian Dean Photography
G. Mrs Wehr's cake shop
H. Ah Toy's Store
I. Les Heaven's shoe store
J. CWA Hall
K. Ted Davies Sports Store
L. Police Station
M. Dept Labour & National Service
N. Old Administration
O. Old Court House

Erratum Pages 4 & 5

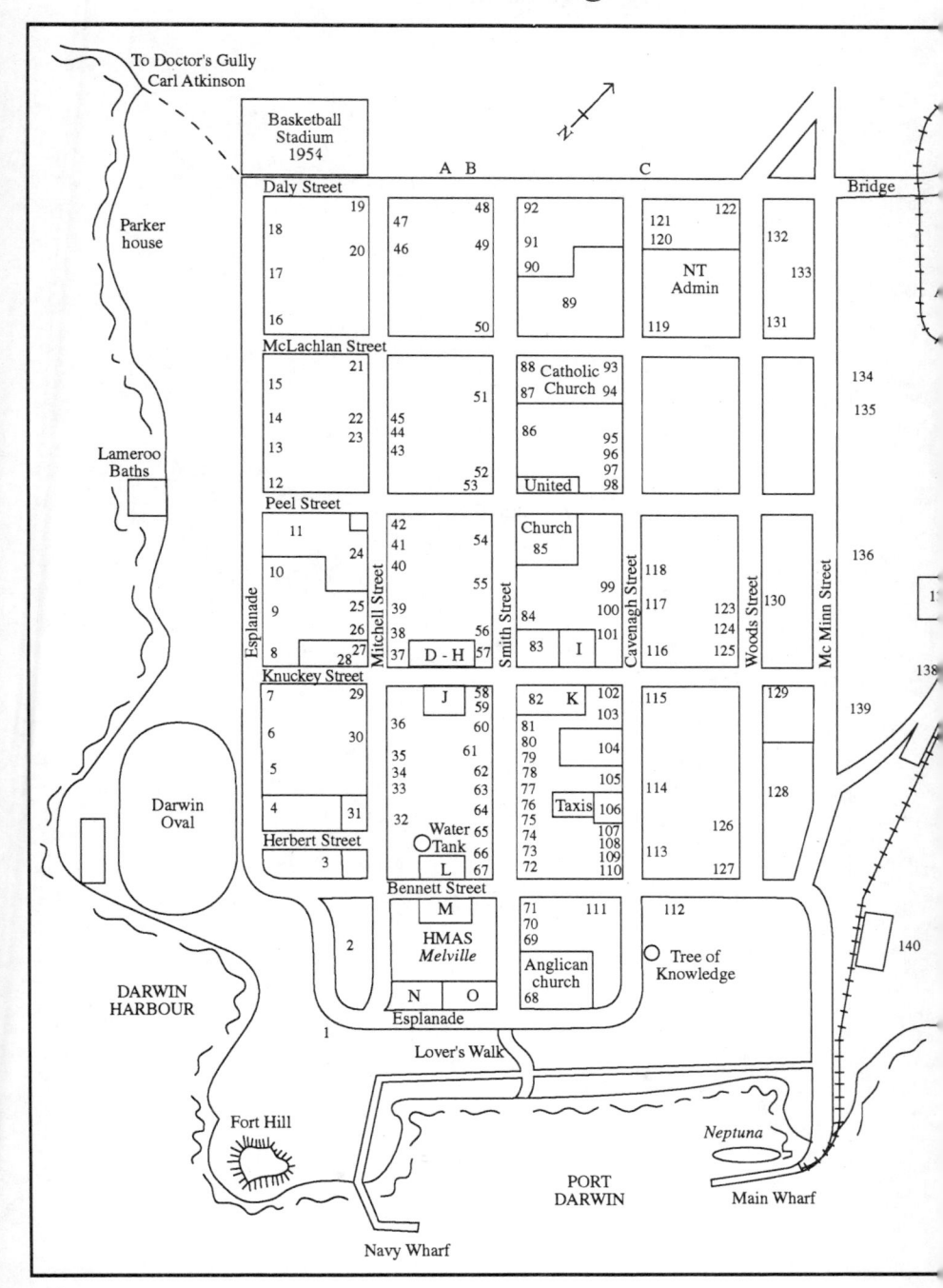

Map of Darwin showing:

- To Doctor's Gully / Carl Atkinson
- Basketball Stadium 1954
- Parker house
- Bridge
- Daly Street
- A B C
- 19, 18, 47, 48, 92, 122, 121, 120, 132
- 20, 46, 49, 91, NT Admin, 133
- 17, 90
- 89, 119, 131
- 16, 50
- McLachlan Street
- 15, 21, 88 Catholic 93, 134
- 14, 22, 45, 51, 87 Church 94, 135
- 13, 23, 44, 86
- Lameroo Baths
- 12, 43, 52, 95, 96, 97
- 53, United, 98
- Peel Street
- 11, 42, 54, Church 85
- 24, 41, 118, 136
- 10, 40, 55, 99, 117, 123, 130
- 9, 25, 39, 84, 100, 124
- 26, 38, 56, 101, 116, 125
- 8, 28, 27, 37, D - H, 57, 83, I
- Esplanade / Mitchell Street / Smith Street / Cavenagh Street / Woods Street / McMinn Street
- Knuckey Street
- 7, 29, 58, 82, K, 102, 115, 129
- 59, 103, 139
- 6, 30, 36, 60, 81, 80
- 35, 61, 79, 104
- 5, 34, 62, 78, 105, 114, 128
- 33, 63, 77, Taxis, 106
- Darwin Oval
- 4, 31, 32, 64, 76, 75, 107, 126
- Water 65, 74, 108
- Herbert Street, Tank, 66, 73, 109, 113, 127
- 3, L, 67, 72, 110
- Bennett Street
- M, 71, 111, 112
- 70
- 2, HMAS *Melville*, 69, Anglican church, Tree of Knowledge, 140
- DARWIN HARBOUR
- N O, 68
- 1, Esplanade
- Lover's Walk
- Fort Hill
- *Neptuna*
- PORT DARWIN
- Navy Wharf
- Main Wharf

Erratum Pages 4 & 5

1
Like Beer, Just Passing Through

George Fortiades, owner of Darwin's Rendezvous Cafe, ran his eye over me. He'd seen drifters before.

'What'll it be, son?'

'Six penn'orth of bread and butter, thanks.'

He weighed up the two of us, as he cut some thick slices of bread. He put down the bread knife, and slowly spread the butter. A generous man, I noted.

'Any work around town?' I asked. Nonchalant. Worldly.

'What can you do?'

'Anything.'

'Got a trade?'

'Er . . . no,' I said. 'Ouch.'

A sharp, shut-up kick in the ankle. Smithy took over.

'Both very willing, though.'

George handed us our bread and butter, wrapped in a greaseproof lunchwrap.

'Darwin's a tough town, boys. And it is Good Friday, you know. You won't get any sense out of anybody until Tuesday.'

I gave him the sixpence and we walked into the miserable glare of Darwin's empty Smith Street. Tuesday. Ye Gods. Four days.

I was seventeen and Smithy, Ron Smith, was nineteen. We had been at school together in Melbourne, and it was Ron who suggested we go up north to Darwin. He told me there was big money up there. The plan was to stay in Darwin three months, get a bankroll together, and head for, well . . . Brazil, we reckoned, to become cowboys. I had six months experience on a station in Queensland. Smithy was obviously destined to be one of the great horse-handlers. He'd put the horse's collar on upside-down when we were 'carting in' the buckets for grapepickers at Mildura on our way to Darwin. Breathless Brazilians were undoubtedly awaiting the arrival of the two great *vaqueros* from suburban Melbourne. They're still waiting.

We weren't broke. We both had a few quid in the bank, but we'd lobbed in Darwin at 7 pm on the Thursday before Good Friday. The bank would open at 10 am next Tuesday. We had two bob and a tin of sardines between us.

We'd been introduced to the free-spending attitudes Up North as we travelled by train for four days from Adelaide to Alice Springs on the old Ghan, and then four more days on Bond's motor coach from Alice to Darwin. It was red, arid and pristine around Alice Springs. My first ghost gums. Magnificent. Under the clean, bare, bronze mountains their starkly smooth white trunks and gnarly limbs twisted into the bluest sky I'd ever seen. But after we passed through the hills north of The Alice the country was featureless, brown and boring.

We were only apprentice beer drinkers, and hadn't expected beer to be six bob a bottle along The Track, which was what we discovered locals called the narrow, one vehicle-width stretch of bitumen that provided a thousand-mile link between the two main Territory towns. Overnight stops at Banka Banka, Daly Waters and Mataranka were great fun, with boisterous drinking and singing at each place. The most memorable night was at Mataranka, where we stayed at the Homestead and swam in the warm thermal pool. Phosphorescent, silky-warm, crystal-clear water, surrounded by pandanus palms. Magic.

Our coach driver, Jack Day, led the fun at each place, and encouraged us to 'spend up big'. 'Come on, you young jokers, hit the kick. We're here for a good time, not a long time,' he roared. 'Get that grog into yer. And sing us a song, young Egan.'

What had happened to that Confirmation vow of mine, the solemn oath sworn at age nine, that I would, 'under the pain of mortal sin, abstain from alcohol until I was twenty-five'? Ho-hum. Another beer? Thanks. Archbishop Mannix and my Mum both seemed a long way away, back in my childish past. I was heading up north. You little beauty. Sing, did you say, Jack? The problem was not how to start me, but how to stop me.

> An old cowpoke went ridin' out
> One dark and windy day,
> Upon a ridge he rested
> As he went along his way . . .

Yippy-i-yay. Some of our daytime stops were lengthy. Coach travel in those days was a casual business, and we often had to wait for Jack Day to have his 'Christmas drink' with his mates before we resumed our journey north. It was March. Nobody on the coach seemed to mind the delays, and, as some of Jack's friends were the coppers at the bush stations, his only concern about 'drink-driving' was if he couldn't get a drink. We had beer on ice in the coach, and Jack swigged from a long-neck bottle as he organised the community singing, driving along at a sedate 40 miles an hour. We passed about six vehicles each day.

I expected that the final day's travel, through Katherine, on to Darwin, would take us into Tarzan country, jungle, and was disappointed to find it was dry, sterile-looking savannah scrub. Locals told us it had been a 'dry wet'. Already they were burning-off the long rank speargrass, flattened, this particular year, by very meagre 'knock-em-down' rains. That signalled the end of the summer, The Wet, and introduced the other season, The Dry.

Placenames were often given an affectionate *The* as a prefix by the locals. *The* Alice. *The* Daly. *The* KathRine, as the locals pronounced Katherine. A couple of old prospectors we met at the Pine Creek pub told us we were going 'down' to Darwin. You still get a few old Territorians who say that. None of your 'up north' for them. They stick to the old rule that if you live inland you go 'down' to the sea, even if you're going north. And I quickly realised that, as in Queensland, lots of Territorians along The Track tacked 'eh' on the end of their sentences. Or even a single word.

'Hot, eh?' That was the weather.

'Pretty good, eh?' That was the beer.

'Time to let the red steer go in this long grass, eh?' said the 'yardy' at the Mataranka Homestead. I had no idea what he was talking about until he nonchalantly chucked a lit wax Vesta match into a patch of flattened dry speargrass. The boy from Melbourne watched in amazement. Nobody else took any notice or seemed the least concerned that he started this incredible bushfire. The diving hawks, which locals told me were called 'kites', had a great time as they rode the thermals on the fiery boundaries, checking out lunch. Spectacular, eh?

Daylight was fading quickly when we arrived in Darwin. The coach stopped at the Darwin Hotel. Jack Day looked at our small suitcases.

'Got somewhere to stay, boys?'

'Yeah, Jack. We're right.'

I lied. I've always been stupid like that. I feel sure now that if I'd mentioned our plight he'd have looked after us. Smithy gave me a filthy look. I felt I should do something positive, so I said:

'Come on. There's the Starlight Hotel. We'll camp there.'

In the fading light I could see the grandstand of the Darwin Oval silhouetted against my first, unforgettable, tropical sunset. We camped there for the four days. It was perfect weather, and there were not too many mosquitoes. There was a shower in the change rooms, and a Flaming Fury dunny made from a forty-four gallon drum. Over the Easter break it was deathly quiet in Darwin, so we had the chance to explore the tiny town. From my days as a paper-boy I knew Darwin had been flattened in 1942, but it was a shock to find that the wrecked buildings in the town centre had not been restored in any way. There was the old Post Office, the Bank of New South Wales, Gordon's Don Hotel, a derelict cafe called Zero in the Tropics — all devastated. Many of the buildings in Chinatown, the old Administration buildings between Bennett Street and the foreshore, the ES&A Bank, the town hall, the Anglican church, were crumbling pock-marked reminders of the extent of the bombing. And the otherwise magnificent harbour was scarred by the jagged outlines of the many ships sunk by the Japanese on 19 February

1942. In that brutal first raid, when the Japanese concentrated with pinpoint accuracy on the Darwin Harbour and the RAAF airstrip, the huge underground oil tanks were eliminated and huge fires raged for days, 250 people were killed, Australian and American ships sunk, the wharf wrecked, the airstrip and the pathetic squadron of Australian Wirraways devastated, 400 injured. So accurate was the Japanese bombing the Allied officers came to believe local opinion that the Japanese had been mapping the town and the local waters for years prewar, when hundreds of Japanese were employed in Darwin in the pearling industry. It was held that the Japanese intended to use the recently completed Darwin Hotel as their headquarters when they invaded. The Darwin Hotel was unmarked, right in among the other flattened buildings, and invasion seemed only weeks away. It never came to pass, and we are forever grateful, for the Japanese invaded New Guinea instead, but it is not widely known that there were sixty subsequent air raids on Darwin, the last late in 1943.

There seemed to be more Chinese than any other race of people, for we didn't get too far past Smith Street and Cavenagh Street in the first few days. Most of the shops in those streets were owned by Chinese. Lorna Lim and Sons and W G Chin were in Smith Street, Chin Mook Sang, Chin Loong Pak, Sue Wah Chin, Sun Cheong Loong, and Wu's Oriental Cafe were in Cavenagh Street. Some of the old Chinese women wore the traditional silk pyjamas, but most men of all different races wore smart, tailored white clothes, and everybody seemed friendly and very relaxed. Race didn't seem to matter much..

There wasn't the lush, green look that prevails in Darwin today. There were no lawns at all in Darwin until 1956. Darwin Oval, where we camped, looked like a gravel pit. There were straggly coconut trees here and there, turpentine mango trees, and some big calophylums around the few lovely, spacious old bungalows that had survived the bombing. Those old houses certainly looked appropriate for the place, built on stilts to catch the breeze through their slatted walls and shuttered windows. Two other things about Darwin were very tropical. The weather — it was searingly hot by day and stickily warm at night —

and the strange, new (to me anyway) exotic smell of frangipanni, which seemed to thicken the already syrupy evening air. It was immediately addictive, and I inhaled great, heady gulps. All very romantic.

If you weren't hungry, that is. We ate our sardines the first night, and, in the realisation that our two bob cash had to last four days until the banks opened, we rationed ourselves to 'sixpence worth' of bread and butter each day.

Tuesday came, and we hadn't starved. We got an injection of funds from the Commonwealth Bank, and I went straight to Chin Loong Pak's shop in Cavenagh Street, where I had seen people buying amazing-looking drinks. I had one. Mr Pak squeezed fresh limes into a huge glass, added lemonade, and then shaved ice from a big block with an instrument like a spokeshave. It was unforgettable. Then Smithy and I went to the Rendezvous Cafe for a slap-up feed of steak, two eggs and onions. George Fortiades gave us a big wink.

'In the money, eh boys? Got a tip for you. If you want a job, whip round to the Works and Jerks, Mitchell Street, next to the post office. Ask for a bloke named Alan Jones.'

It was too easy. Alan Jones, the personnel officer for the Department of Works and Housing, gave us jobs as base-rate-clerks in five minutes flat. I think Alan was more impressed by our expressed interest in playing cricket for Works and Jerks than our suitability as clerks. We both stated our ages as twenty-one. 'Of course,' said Alan Jones, so our wages were seven pounds ten shillings (£7/10/-) a week each, the adult rate. My dad back in Melbourne was getting five pounds a week working on the wharf as a shipping clerk. And we were provided with full board and lodging for just £3/10/- a fortnight. Talk about rich.

That night Ron and I had a couple of beers at The Vic, local name for the Victoria Hotel. So began my appreciation of the sordid, steamy, no-hoper flavour of Darwin, where Jack seemed a cut above his master, the weather was kind, nobody asked you too many questions about your background, and almost everybody, ourselves now included, seemed to have a good quid. All these years later I still haven't made it to South America. I now

Like Beer, Just Passing Through

live in Alice Springs, and love it. My first fifteen years of life were spent in Melbourne. But Darwin is the place I get nostalgic about. Many years later I wrote a song called 'She's on again in Darwin':

> There's a place where I misspent my youth
> Darwin is its name
> The old town's getting bigger now
> But the life is just the same
> There's plenty of time for meeting
> Your mates around the town
> With the famous Darwin greeting:
> 'Do you reckon you could keep one down?'

We moved into No. 3 Hostel, on the site of today's St Mary's Cathedral, between Smith and Cavenagh Streets. No. 3 Hostel was perversely known locally as Belsen Camp, or just Belsen, after the German concentration camp of the same name. It was an old army camp where the nurses had been billeted during the war, so it had had a huge barbed wire fence around it in earlier days. Belsen was a total misnomer, for it was a pleasant camp, only five minutes walk from the town centre, consisting of sixty little fibro huts, with communal showers and toilets, a large dining hall called 'the mess' — everything still worked to military terminology in Darwin — and a large recreation hut, which was the centre of the town's social life. The old Darwin Town Hall had been bombed.

Some of the older Belsenites had a hut to themselves, but the majority, and certainly all the young fellows like us, were two to a hut. We fitted in straight away, as everything was easy-going. Darwin was just so friendly. Our hut, about three metres square, had four army beds, a cupboard and an electric fan. Ron and I had two army stretcher beds each, one on top of the other, like the double-decker bunk beds of today. We slept on the top bunks and the bed underneath was our storage shelf. Fibro shutters were open at all times, as you never had to worry about privacy or security and it was never cold.

There was a fascinating mixture at the all-male Belsen. There were quite a few young fellows, slightly older than us, and we quickly got to know Rolly Dunn, Bertie Garrett, Charlie O'Dwyer, Jacky Maher, Peter Fogarty — called Fogue — and the garrulous Ron Bridgett, who was quick to take us for a drink, tell us he was a Queenslander and thereby a superior being, and challenge to 'bet you a quid' on any topic we dared to raise. We called him Cuddles because he had chubby cheeks, like the great old character actor S Z 'Cuddles' Szakall.

There was another group we mixed with a lot, even though they were much older, the Razzle Gang. They were all ex-servicemen. Some were around sixty and had been in both World War I — which we still called the 'Great War' — and World War II. They all drank up big at the RSL Club. There was Colonel Frank Annear, Gibby, Jack Riordan, Norm Haines, Reg (Burlington Bertie) Moss, Sandy McKay and quite a few others, and they used to go to the club every Saturday morning, an immaculate platoon. Darwin Rig — the local term for formal dress — for men in those days was tailor-made long white trousers, long-sleeved white shirt, black or white shoes and socks, and a tie. Shirts and trousers were starched and ironed, with knife-edged creases.

The old chaps drank at the RSL — the Razzle as it's known — all through Saturday, and at 10 pm, after closing, they marched drunkenly back to Belsen, singing the old army songs, ties either awry or cut short. Tie-cutting was a favourite Darwin 'trick'. People engaged you in earnest conversation, and suddenly they produced scissors and snipped your tie short. The old diggers didn't know or care about the tomato sauce, gravy and beer stains on their shirts and trousers or the skidmarks on their Y-Fronts as they reeled back to Belsen. On a few occasions, late on Saturday nights, we watched in amazement as Colonel Frank Annear stripped naked and climbed a tree, from which vantage point he conducted a full regimental parade of the old diggers.

'Sergeant Riordan! Strength, Number 3 Hostel Platoon?'

'Number 3 Hostel Platoon, strength 16, 14 on parade. Sir!'

'Thank you, sergeant. Number 3 Hostel platoon, at–ten–shun! Move to the right in column of route. Right turn! By the left, quick march!'

Round and round the old chaps marched, until thirst vanquished their zest for the old routines. On Sunday mornings Frank and the other old diggers would be a bit subdued, but this did not prevent them from 'getting a case' and drinking through the day. They were never anything other than good fun around Belsen, although you got the impression most of them were in Darwin because that was as far as they could get from whatever it was they sought to escape.

Gibby was a good example. He was employed as a mere timekeeper with Works and Jerks, lowest of the low, yet when a new judge, Martin Kriewaldt, was appointed to Darwin we discovered Gibby had been Judge Kriewaldt's law lecturer at Adelaide University before the war. Eventually Gibby got the sack from Works and Jerks, and he had a great chortle when he read aloud to us the letter that some jumped-up clerk had written to advise that the erstwhile professor was, henceforth, deemed 'copiously redundant'. Now that's some degree of redundancy. It was probably a good thing for the old chap, for I understand he was reunited with his family after he left Darwin, where the booze had a pretty solid hold on him. Frank Annear was another mystery man. He was a full Colonel in the war, but now a menial clerk, as quiet as a mouse during the week, but paid due deference as the CO by the other old diggers on weekends. I guess a lot of blokes in Darwin would have had tales to tell about failed marriages, and other reasons why they had chosen to spend the rest of their days in that remote spot, but one of the unwritten laws of the place was 'no names, no packdrill'.

Everybody had plenty of money at Belsen, and there seemed no point in saving it. We didn't have to outlay much money on clothes. We were getting full board at ridiculous rates. So 'getting a case' was a common occurrence. We just had to phone one of our taxi driver mates, Keith Jessop, Norm Jones, or Doug Lawrie, and they'd get the beer, some ice and deliver it. A 'case' was a wooden crate, containing four dozen big bottles of beer. Each bottle was wrapped in straw. Most people in Darwin had what were called 'hotboxes', ex–army insulated portable icechests that would hold 'a case' packed in ice. If Jack 'Boorie'

Hales was in a good mood ice was available from the Koolpinyah Kool Store in Smith Street. If there was no ice you drank faster, and wrapped your bottle in newspaper to keep it 'Kimberley cool'. Somebody just had to say 'Let's get a case' and she'd be on. Everybody would kick in with some money, and anybody who came along was welcome to share the beer. Darwin was definitely that sort of place. Provided there was beer in town.

There was very little road freight in those days, and Darwin depended on ships which arrived, alternately, from 'the eastern states' or 'from the west'. Shipping companies learned to stow the beer in the bottom of the hold, for in earlier days the wharfies would unload the beer, then go on strike for some reason or other, and get stuck into the grog. When the ship came from the west we drank Swan Lager. It was Foster's, Victoria Bitter (VB) or Abbot's when it came from the east. Beer cost four shillings and sixpence a big bottle. When the town was out of 'ship beer' people either drank cheap wine or spirits, and, occasionally, a truckload of some strange beer found its way by road to Darwin. 'Overland beer' was always very expensive, usually six bob a bottle. A road consignment might be Ballarat Bitter, Mac's from Rockhampton, Hannan's from Kalgoorlie, Mudgee beer, or the dreaded Springfield. Springfield beer was a shocker, and it used to have the most profound effects on people. A popular Darwin poet, Bill Armbrust, wrote regularly for the local newspaper, *The Northern Standard*. Here's Bill's opinion of Springfield:

> There's a fight in every bottle
> There's a brawl in every case
> You can tell he's been on Springfield
> By the blood upon his face.

There was a saying in those days that the ships brought to Darwin empty public servants and full beer kegs, and the town's only exports were full public servants and empty beer kegs. A local brewery operated for a while, when a bloke named Ellis-Kells produced beers named Darwin Lager, Palmerston Dinner Ale, and Buffalo Bitter. The word quickly got around that there was 'a horn in every bottle' of Buffalo Bitter but that was probably the brewer's boast as an alternative to brewer's droop. We were unanimous: the local beer was pathetic.

My clerical job, making entries in the Stock Ledgers at Works and Jerks, was not very challenging, and 'work' was merely the wherewithal for getting the money to enjoy the wonderful new freedom of Darwin. Belsen boys were all sport-mad, and there was intense competition among the younger blokes, spurred on by some hefty interstate prejudices, particularly over different codes of football. As Victorians Smithy and I were quickly reminded that Aussie Rules was definitely a game for girls, and was known in the more manly states of Queensland and New South Wales as 'aerial ping-pong' or 'cross-country ballet'. We returned the fire by telling the Rugby fans their game was strictly for brainless thugs and was called 'mobile wrestling' or 'sniffy bum' by more genteel Australians. I didn't even know there were two Rugby codes: that's how isolated and parochial the different states of Australia were in those pre-TV times.

Football was months away. The Darwin footy season runs through The Wet, starts in October, ends in March. Prewar and into the 1950s that was when the grassless Darwin Oval was softer. Nowadays they have lovely grassed ovals in Darwin, but they haven't changed the dates, a legacy of those times when gravel rash was the most common injury incurred in football matches. Cricket is played in The Dry, between May and September. Smithy and I both joined the Works and Jerks cricket club. Ron Smith had been a great batsman at school and was a big bonus to Works and Jerks. I bowled leg spinners and slogged a bit with the bat. Alan Jones was skipper and a classy batsman. We played tennis, and I also started playing basketball, a game I'd never heard of before I went to Darwin. But all other sports were merely to fill in the time until football started.

A bloke named Frank Whiteman, a Victorian, said he was anxious to get a 'Works and Jerks' Australian Rules team into the local competition, for there were only three local teams. I was keen, so all through the dry season of 1950 we kicked a ball around most afternoons, getting ready for the footy season.

The old Catholic church was across the road from Belsen camp, and we used to kick 'end to end' on the area of land on which the Catholic cathedral was eventually built. There were usually quite a few Aboriginals from the Catholic Mission at Bathurst Island (Nguiu) around the old St Mary's church, and a lot of young men from Bathurst Island worked for short periods as labourers for the army or the RAAF. I saw them at Mass on Sunday mornings. They wore service uniforms, even though they were not enlisted. They looked ever so smart. I had never seen anyone quite so black or shiny. They had obviously been polished.

After a few days of our football practice, two shy Aboriginal blokes appeared on the sideline. They stood watching us for a while, until I kicked the ball to one of them, and they joined us. And were they any good! I was from Melbourne, steeped in the traditions of Rules, fancied myself as a player, but this pair could run rings around us. Both barefooted. One, named Felix, sprang like a cat to mark the ball, and he would sail over the top of us every time. The other, Raphael, consistently hit you on the chest from fifty yards with torpedo-punt passes that never went above head height. They both had superb physiques, and, in fundamental terms, marking and kicking the ball, I'd never seen anyone like them.

'Who do you jokers play for?' I asked, in awe.

'We only play at the mission. Bathurst Island,' said Felix, his incredible white teeth flashing into a grin with his every statement.

'I used to play for the Services team, when I worked for the army during the war,' said Raphael, a bit more reserved, but pleasant.

The Aboriginals all went backwards and forwards to Bathurst Island every three months, and I had plenty of things on my mind other than football, so we didn't establish much in common. But they were friendly, and I was interested in them. I had never forgotten the time when, as a paper boy in Melbourne, I stood, enthralled, and listened to two New Zealand soldiers singing in Maori on a suburban tram. I forgot all about selling my papers, and marvelled at the two, a Maori and a Pakeha, both very drunk, but obviously so proud of who they were and where they came from. In meeting these two Aborig-

Like Beer, Just Passing Through

inal blokes I sensed that here might be the opportunity to one day develop a similar level of affinity about Australia. But not just yet.

Between the Workers' Club and the Oriental Cafe, next to Sun Cheong Loong's store, on the block now occupied by the RSL club in Cavenagh Street, was the NAWU (North Australian Workers' Union) Stadium. There were regular boxing nights featuring some good fighters like Billy Clarke, Tim Angeles, Dick Butler, Danny Holden and George Goldner and skilful kids like Benny Cubillo, the Butler boys, Johnny Mayo and Billy Roe. Boxing was very popular.

But the main activity at the stadium was basketball. I couldn't get enough of this new, challenging game. Our Works and Jerks team did reasonably well, although most of us were unskilled at the game, and played it more like football. Basketball attracted a huge following in Darwin, with women's matches often getting bigger crowds than the men. The women played netball, but it was called 'women's basketball'. The population of Darwin was only about 3000, but it was not uncommon to get 1000 people for the basketball nights each Sunday at the Stadium. The Razzle Gang used to watch the games and barrack enthusiastically as they drank to excess on the back verandah of the old RSL club, where Raintree Park is today. An Irishman named Mick Stinson walked up and down the court before the games started, offering to 'bet a pound' on his favourite teams. The smell of delicious food wafted over the court from the Oriental Cafe next door. Kids slept on blankets under the seats. Eddy Quong, the baker, gave everybody lots of cheek in a delightful mixture of Cantonese and pidgin English. We drank Fong Yuen Kee's lolly water and ate sartees, spiced meat skewered on wire, and *namas*, marinated raw fish. It wasn't surprising there was so much interest in the local competition, even allowing that there was no TV or other competitive entertainment, for the standard of netball played by the Darwin girls in those days was astounding. I know as one gets older the people of your own era seem to become more and more talented, but I like to think I am fairly objective in these judgements. As a general rule I acknowledge that today's athletes in all sports are better than they used to be, for all sorts of reasons, but I can't help feeling that Darwin girls of that time, like Jane Ahmat, Josie Perez, Rowena Stroude, Sadie Ludwig, Merle Cooper, Kathy Rynne, Jocelyn and Marian Wu and 'Deadly' Dallas Woods, were the equal of any of the international netball players I have recently seen. Fierce, talented, competitive. A joy to watch.

The women's games were hotly contested by four teams, Eagles, Kookaburras, Galahs and Marrenah, but the men's competition was a one–horse race, dominated by a team named Urgers. Urgers had two stars, Peter Macrides and Joey Sarib, who left the rest of us floundering in their wake. Peter was tall, unbeatable around the backboard at both ends of the court: Joe was only a little bloke, but a wizard of a ball-handler. As slippery as a butcher's dick, he weaved in and out of opponents, often scoring 40 points in a game. Joe was the captain of our first Northern Territory representative sporting team, which in 1954 participated in the Australian basketball championships in Brisbane.

To this day I think Joey Sarib is the best post-war all-round athlete the Northern Territory has produced, for he was not only a champion basketballer, he captained the Buffaloes and won the Nichols medal for best and fairest at Aussie Rules football, was a fine runner and jumper for his size, a dynamic tennis player. Joe still plays good golf. Next best after Urgers was the Parap team, with Cyril Ahmat, Alfie May, 'Sabbo' Briston, 'Froggy' and 'Bingo' Snape, and 'Kanga' Talbot as their stars. They later called their team Rusty Valley. Most of them lived in the old 118 (One One Eight as it was called) camp. The Darwin Chinese Recreation Club (DCRC) had a good side too. They were coached by Albert Chan, who became the NT's first coach. The rest of us were also-rans, but I loved basketball and, realising I did not have the star quality of players like Joey Sarib, I knuckled down to relentless practice to learn the fundamentals of the game.

After the basketball games there was usually a drink, and often a sing-song, for the two activities went hand-in-hand. We would 'get a case' and go to the wharf, or to the grandstand of

Like Beer, Just Passing Through

the Darwin Oval, or Mindil Beach, or Belsen. There were quite a few good musicians in Darwin, particularly among the people of Filipino–Aboriginal extraction, and invariably somebody produced a guitar. I came to learn all the old Darwin songs, most of which had their origins in the pearling industry of pre-war times. It was fascinating to discover that hardly anybody in Darwin knew the words of songs like 'Waltzing Matilda', and the only song which could be considered to be *the* Darwin song was *'Tanjin Pera'*

O Tanjin Pera sapi laro
Sapaya suka pulitaro . . . .

which has a rousing chorus.

Nona mani sapayan, punian
Nona mani sapayan, punian
Nona mani sapayan, punian
Rasa saya, sin saya, badimi.

The song probably derives from Indonesia or Malaysia. The songs I call 'the pearling lugger songs' were introduced to Darwin by the people from different parts of the Pacific who worked in the pearling industry at places like Broome, Darwin and Thursday Island. Those with catchy tunes became the 'work songs' and people felt free to introduce their own — sometimes meaningless — words, to the point that, today, nobody can establish any real meaning or origin of the songs, but the tunes are intact. There's a great field of study in these songs for an enterprising ethno-musicologist.

One day an ocean liner — I think it was the *Fairsea* — called into Darwin. There had been a cruise around the Pacific, and on board were Australians from the southern states. As Darwin meant they were now back in Australia the passengers lined the shiprails as the ship steamed towards the jetty. They were all calling 'Coo–ee'. Local Aboriginals asked, 'What does "Coo–ee" mean?' and I felt a bit stupid telling them that that was what Aboriginals were supposed to call out in the bush. And then the people on the ship started to sing 'Waltzing Matilda'. I was able to join in, but most locals had never heard it before. If the song had been *'Tanjin Pera'* it would have been different.

Various people at singalongs in Darwin had their 'party pieces'. As I was raised in a family where singing came naturally I sang some of the great American favourites of the day, songs like 'Mule Train', 'Ghost Riders in the Sky', 'High Noon' and 'Cool Water'. Jaffa Ahmat was always asked to sing his own composition, 'Old TI'. TI was the abbreviation for Thursday Island, in Torres Strait

> Why are you looking so sad tonight?
> Why are you looking so blue?
> I am dreaming of someone
> Far, far away,
> In a beautiful place called TI

Babe Damaso's special favourite was *'Manana'* and if pressed, or pissed, or both, Babe would also demonstrate the Charleston. Cyril Ahmat used to make up hilarious songs in pidgin English:

> Hey, I know you, Ted Hegan
> You the boy I'm look there
> Las'night longa Doctor Gully.
> Might be you me go there tonight
> Me two feller can catchim 'bout fish
> Lookim 'bout girl
> Drinkim 'bout winga
> Catchim 'bout crab
> Everything! Can't pinish him!
> What! Ted Hegan!
> You reckon, you no more like-a-that?
> You Christian boy?
> You not the Christian boy Ted Hegan
> That Stevie Abala, him the Christian boy
> Him talk the Father Henschke every Sunday
> You, Ted Hegan, you bloody pagan altogether.

Winga is the Tiwi word for 'salt water'. Any alcohol used to be called *winga* in Darwin, the rationalisation being that 'full blood', or 'unexempted' Aboriginals couldn't drink grog by law; and they couldn't drink salt water either. Once laws were repealed to allow Aboriginals to drink alcohol, *winga* was retained as the word for 'spirits' or 'hard stuff', and the new name for beer became *pwadjininga* — the Tiwi word for 'piss'.

Rusty Perez, Dolph Cubillo and Peter Cardona would lead us all in 'Goodbye to You, My Nona Mani', and invariably The Flying Chinaman had to sing 'The Donkey Serenade'.

The Flying Chinaman? Meet the one and only Chin Chui Hoong, better known as Ronny Chin. A tall handsome man, the son of Chin Loong (there's gold in them there teeth) Tang, his complete Anglicized name is Ronald Gordon Chin. This allows him to say to people, disarmingly, 'Despite my appearrance, I'm not Chinese. I'm really Scottish. I'm Rrronald Gorrrdon McChin.' Around Darwin he is called 'Ah Hoong Ah', Chinese style, or simply 'Hoonga' and he is one of Darwin's all-time greats. A fast, dynamic Aussie Rules footballer, he was nicknamed The Flying Chinaman — he says so himself: 'I was wery fast' — and many a tale is told about his prowess on the footy field. It is typical of the racial tolerance of Darwin people that nicknames like 'The Flying Chinaman' cause no raised eyebrows or unease from any quarter, no queries from the Human Rights Commission. Hoonga's singing is unique, joyous, full-frontal, loud, enthusiastic. And he never allows the tune to interfere with his own and everyone else's enjoyment of his performance. He also vowed and declared that he was a champion fisherman. We often took a couple of bottles of Rinegold wine and some 'green pea' (tins of peas) from his father's shop, went to the wharf, and slept there on the hot nights. Hoonga always took a cast-net and caught some bait, and we sat and yarned on the wharf as we waited, in vain, for him to catch 'the big one' he always promised us. Alas, I never saw him catch a fish, but others tell me he is a great fisherman, so who am I to demur? Maybe the fact that we were drinking plonk and probably making much too much noise had something to do with it?

Mostly the after-the-match parties were all–male affairs. There were ten men to every woman in Darwin, and it seemed like fifty to one. There were some young, transient, single white women in Darwin but they mostly lived in hostels like Marrenah House or Town Mess and had teams of suitors keeping them busy. The local Asian, white, or mixed-race girls were usually members of quite protective families, and they were probably 'warned off' about fellows like us, so we didn't see much of them. A pity, we all thought, because some of them were stunning lookers. If we went to The Vic, women who also worked at Works and Jerks often joined us in the beer garden, and could some of them drink! Maureen Blowes, Edna Morgan and Wendy Walker could drink most of us under the table, and the Murphy sisters, Carmel and Josephine, were, like us, avid learners. If we went to somebody's home there was some mixture of the sexes, but, because the Belsen Boys were a fairly rowdy bunch, we weren't invited to private parties too often. More often than not it was somewhere 'out on the flat' that we chose for our sessions. Heavy drinking has always been a feature of remote places in frontier Australia, where males outnumber females and alcohol is the great sexual sublimator.

I was never aware of any homosexuality in Darwin, despite hearing all the raucous shouts of 'Don't drop the soap' in the showers, but I wouldn't have known what to look for in any case. Occasionally you'd hear people say, 'Are you a Waratah or a pooftah?' as a shot at the local all-white Waratah football team. 'What's the difference?' was the required response. No difference. Everyone told me that one old bloke, Les, who lived at Belsen was 'a poof', but, again, I had no idea what that entailed! The old bloke seemed harmless enough. He tried to show us his collection of fairly dreadful photos one night, but we steered clear of him. He seemed particularly keen on The Flying Chinaman. Hoonga told him his name was Charlie Chan. The old bloke called Hoonga 'Smoothleg Charlie' because he had typically Chinese hairless legs. Apart from those couple of instances the old chap didn't worry us much, and we gently declined his regular invitations to 'share a bottle of wine', or rather, we'd refer him to the specific name of somebody. 'Try Peter Fogarty, Les. He's keen on wine.' We did see a bloke chase the old chap through the camp one night with a hockey stick, so I guess some sort of proposition was being rejected.

The majority of white people in Darwin were either transients or born elsewhere, and most of the permanent residents of the town were Asian or of mixed-Aboriginal descent. The latter tended, for understandable reasons at the time, to identify with the non-Aboriginal side of their inheritance, Filipino, Malay, Japanese, Indonesian, Chinese, European, whatever. Xavier Herbert's book *Capricornia* was being acted out in real life. In Darwin in 1950 the Eurabo Association was formed by a bloke named Yorky Peel, an Englishman with an Aboriginal wife, to promote better rights for people of mixed Aboriginal descent. It was quickly replaced by a very strong body called the AHPA (The Australian Halfcastes Progress Association) with the redoubtable Jack McGinness as its president.

The 'understandable reasons' which caused the formation of bodies like the AHPA were embodied in the law. The Aboriginals Ordinance classified people by race and decreed that 'Aboriginal natives of Australia' were subject to quite discriminatory rules that dominated their lives. A person deemed to be an Aboriginal within the meaning of the Ordinance was not allowed to live in town without the permission of the Chief Protector of Aboriginals. Aboriginals were not allowed to 'roam at large' between sunset and sunrise even if they had a permit to be in town. They could not vote, were not allowed to drink alcohol. 'Aboriginal' workers earned 'native' wages (maximum £2 per week, but generally lower) and even that money was paid to them at the discretion of the Director of Native Affairs. All persons of Aboriginal extraction were subject to this law, but those of mixed descent could apply for what was officially called 'an exemption'. The unofficial, derisive local term for this was 'the dog tag', and the system provoked considerable anger among many wonderful people I came to know. Steve Abala, Billy Muir and Dick Butler explained to me that they had been good enough to be in the Australian Army, but still had to apply for an exemption after the war. To this day I am appalled that the rest of us accepted the status quo. If we had really thought about the issues we should have taken to the streets on their behalf. It's fair to say there was a big distinction made locally as to who was an Aboriginal and who wasn't. Some very black people were quick

ANNO PRIMO

GEORGII V REGIS.

A.D. 1910.

****

No. 1024.

An Act to make Provision for the better Protection and Control of the Aboriginal Inhabitants of the Northern Territory, and for other purposes.

[*Assented to, December 7th, 1910.*]

BE it Enacted by the Governor of the State of South Australia, with the advice and cons
follows:

1. This Act may be cited as "'
Act, 1910."

Inter[p

2. In this Act, unless incons
matter—

"Aboriginal institution" me
reformatory, orphanage, t
tution for the benefit, ca
half-caste inhabitants of

"Chief Protector" means t
appointed under this Act

"Department" means the
Department:

"District" means a district

A—1024

Form 4.

Regulation 9 (2).

Nº 170

THE NORTHERN TERRITORY OF AUSTRALIA.

Aboriginals Ordinance 1918–1947.

Licence to Employ Aboriginals in a Country Distri[ct]

WHEREAS..

....has applied to me for a Licenc[e to] employ male and female aboriginals, and I am satisfied that he is a pro[per] person to be so licensed. Now, therefore in pursuance of the *Aborigi[nals] Ordinance* 1918–1947, I, the undersigned Protector, do hereby license

....

to employ...........................male and......................... female aboriginals in the Country District of................................. [*Name of District*] as specified in the Schedule on the back hereof.

This Licence shall remain in force until 30th June next succeed[ing] the date hereof, but may be cancelled at any time by a Protector by no[tice] in writing if he deem the licensee to be an unfit person to be so licens[ed] or if the licensee fails to comply with the Ordinance or the Regulation[s].

This licence is granted subject to the said Ordinance and Regulations.

Dated the...........................day of.........................19...

....
Protector.

Legislative instruments of quasi-colonialism

Fee : 10s.

to correct anybody who called them an Aboriginal. It was generally held that only 'full bloods' were Aboriginals. Because of the discriminatory legislation, most people of mixed race tended to identify with anything except Aboriginality. Today their children head up Aboriginal organisations.

I was a young whitefeller, and there were absolutely no restrictions on me. I was totally free, had a job, earned good money. I knew that I was still in Australia, but it was nothing like the Australia of my childhood. I was born in Melbourne, and lived there until I was fifteen. My parents were also born in Australia, but our allegiances were typically Irish and Catholic. In Melbourne anybody not just like us was looked at with some degree of cynicism, suspicion even. Yet in Darwin almost everybody was not like us, and I found the racial fruit salad delightful, from the privileged position of being a whitefeller. I later wrote:

> There's every race and colour
> That ever walked the earth
> But you cop no strife in Darwin
> If you want to prove your worth
> Just learn to hold your grog down
> Don't stack on a blue
> And you'll find that life in Darwin, mate,
> Is an endless barbecue

What a lucky young bloke I was. As fit as a mallee bull, twice as dangerous, and three times as ugly. I was in charge of my own destiny, and living Up North, in the greatest spot in the world.

2

Misspent Youth? What, Me?

As October approaches a young man's fancy turns to footy in Darwin. Let the rest of the country break out the blade of willow, or restring their racquets. Up North they pull on the boots.

Our Works and Housing football team was accepted into the Northern Territory Football League (NTFL) to provide competition — we hoped — for three old established teams, Buffaloes, Waratahs and Wanderers. I attended with Frank Whiteman and Bert Garrett as delegates to the meeting, and we were able to convince League president J W 'Fatty' Nichols that we would field a competitive team. We had talked with the army, navy and RAAF boys at the three services' bases, and attracted a lot of interest, particularly from the navy.

We knocked around with the navy lads, and what a bunch of dags they were. They refer to the Royal Australian Navy as 'Pussers'. Blokes who've been in the navy seem to have several things in common. They are invariably well-organised and tidy: I guess it comes from the training involved in living in restricted spaces on ships. Every one I've ever met says 'Yes, I'd do it again,' about their time as a sailor. And I've never heard anything quite like navy slang. Their conversations are sprinkled with their terms for the various ranks and jobs. They speak bewilderingly about 'jimmies', 'joss men', 'Number Ones', and 'kelicks'. Food is 'scran', 'jippers' is gravy and 'goffers' is soft drink. Being treated badly is called 'getting a green rub'. Sailors are at their best when they play mah jong, a favourite Pussers' game. They call it 'Slugbones'. The Chinese originators wouldn't understand their ancient game if they heard the Pussers' terminology, with 'trolley buses', 'shit ducks', 'bumholes', 'fingers' and 'snake eyes' embellished by some choice Australian adjectives. They invariably love a drink on a hot day, are greedy for women, and have a universal disrespect for authority, but in the nicest way.

As we got into footy training we met up with The Irish Chinaman. He was only 18, just back in Darwin after a period of schooling at the toffy St Peter's College in Adelaide. His name is Chin Pak Sin, and his Anglicised name is Wellington Patrick Chin, so we either called him The Irish Chinaman or, more affectionately, Nugget, as he was a stockily-built little joker. He was a good wicket-keeper, and a tough little footballer, so we signed him up, for the use of his dad's truck as much as for his sporting ability. His dad, Chin Sam, owned a red tiptruck, and this became the Works and Jerks footy club's mode of transport. After training we'd all go for a drink somewhere, never forgetting to 'get a case'. About thirty of us would pile on the back of the truck, but there was an ongoing problem. Every now and again, without warning, the tipper mechanism worked, and suddenly we'd be 'going up'. Usually we banged on the cabin roof, and Bertie Garrett, or whoever was driving, disengaged the tipper. But, just in case we ever were to be tipped off, we established the habit of sitting Frankie Burrell, Fatman or the Fat Chappy, as we called him, on the back of the truck. Our rationale was that if the beer fell off the back, Fatman would go off first and cushion the fall of the beer. Nice to have your priorities right. Before the footy season started we spent every weekend on the beach, swimming, organising various games and competitions, and of course, getting into the beer. At night we'd light a big bonfire, cook a feed, and sit around and sing and tell yarns until the grog ran out. If we had plenty of beer we camped on the beach. We didn't need blankets.

Frank Whiteman was very well-organised at getting food for these nights, usually steak and sausages and bread, but if ever we were short we pinched a few chooks from the fowlyard of a policeman named Tom Hollow, who lived at the police barracks next to Belsen. We derived great pleasure that Tom never caught us, although he had a fearsome reputation for catching (other) crooks, and 'doing deals' with SP bookies and informers around the town.

Our favourite pub was The Vic. It was run by the Lim boys, Arthur, Richard and Alec. Alec later became Lord Mayor of Darwin. They were champion fellows, and we got on famously with them, but their Dad, George Lim, wasn't too keen on us. Neither was the cashier, an old bloke named Sing. We called Sing 'The Inscrutable Oriental' so we wouldn't confuse him with Clarrie Moo, 'The Horizontal Oriental', who was always falling over at basketball. Old Sing sat behind the till at The Vic, eyes down, saying nothing. Old Confucian saying: first one to talk loses. If he thought we were a bit boisterous, he nodded to George Lim, who, in turn, told his sons, 'Tell those fellows to stop singing: they're disturbing the drinkers.' I was usually the culprit, as I tended then (and still today) to sing whether I need to or not. 'Sorry, Ted, but the old man says you have to shut up'. Many years later, when Richard had the Rapid Creek Hotel in Darwin, he paid me $1000 a night to sing the same songs!

I quickly worked out that if I was going to be a serious drinker I should always eat, often and sensibly, and I have never wavered from that habit. You see so many people who don't or won't eat when they drink. Eating was fairly easy at The Vic. There was usually an old Chinese cook around the pub making sartees (people today write it *satay* but in Darwin, where the meat was on wire rather than wooden skewers they were always called *sartees*) and spring rolls, or the Rendezvous Cafe next door, or, better still, a little hamburger and steak stall known as The Coolibah, on the vacant ground behind The Vic. The Coolibah was run by a colourful character named George Hopkins. Quite often we went there for a feed after the pub shut, and we had some good laughs with George as we polished off huge steaks smothered with eggs and onions. The Fatman had a big dog called Red Dog, and he always ordered two identical meals of steak and eggs, 'one for The Fat Chappy, one for The Red Puppy'. Red Dog became the mascot for the Works and Jerks boys. When the Fatman got full or disgraceful, or both, Red Dog shook his head and gave his master such a look.

If we had any money left after the pub and The Coolibah, we'd go and have a look at the pai kew games. They were run by either Nick or Mick Paspali, wealthy Greek-Australian brothers in Darwin. Nick eventually Anglicised his name to Paspaley, while Mick Greeked his to Paspalis. Nick owned a building called Roslyn Court, next to The Vic, and he operated a betting shop there on weekends, and ran a game of pai kew most nights. Betting and gambling were illegal, but there were three or four betting shops always open in Darwin, and the owners bribed the coppers to leave them alone. When the coppers had to stage a raid for appearances' sake, they gave the operators plenty of notice. A stooge was left in charge, with a small amount of money to be confiscated, minor fines were paid, and life went on much the same. But if Sergeants Jim Mannion or Tony Kelly were on duty, the coppers often staged a fair dinkum raid, and a couple of times we had to dive through the windows to escape. Hoonga's maternal grandmother, Granny Lum Loy, the oldest person in Darwin — she used to walk into town every day carrying the Chinese yoke, a bamboo pole balancing two baskets full of vegetables and fruit — told us of a raid on a gambling and opium den prewar in Darwin, when the coppers arrested so many Chinese men they ran out of handcuffs. They solved the problem by tying them in pairs by their pigtails, and then they marched them off to the copshop.

Pai kew is a great Chinese gambling game, played with dice and dominoes. A clerk runs the game and distributes the dominoes according to the roll of the dice, which determines who gets what dominoes. Each player gets four dominoes, and you make them up into different pairs and combinations, two 'in front' and two 'behind'. The person who has 'taken the bank' turns his dominoes over, and the clerk then shows and announces the combination of the dominoes of the other players. It's something like blackjack, in that you have to beat the banker. If you are equal, or perhaps stronger in front, but weaker behind, you 'go back' and retain your money.

Darwin has always been a big gambling town, and in those days the biggest gamblers were Greeks or Chinese. Nick Paspaley had his betting shop at Roslyn Court, Mick Paspalis was a couple of doors further down in Smith Street, next to Millers & Sandovers (Killers & Standovers we called them), and Chin Mook Sang, known as 'Mooky', was in Cavenagh Street. Quite often there were private games of cards or pai kew around the town, but we only ever went to Nick's or Mick's. The clerks were usually Cyril Ahmat, Maxie Sariago, Col Lathbury or Robert Chin. The clerks helped you make up your combinations if you didn't understand the game, and they dispersed all the money, charging one shilling *tong*, commission, on every pound won. You had two games as banker. You could 'take a bank' with only a pound, and then clean up the entire table if you happened to get good 'cards' as the dominoes were called. But if you lost, you merely forfeited your pound and the bank would move on. 'Hoo neck? (Who's next?)' Robert Chin would ask, and occasionally we took a bank. I never won or lost very much, and didn't develop the passion for gambling that some of my mates did, and I'm grateful. Every now and then somebody called *sart sai,* which meant that they would cover any bet as banker. At that point the big gamblers, who might be drinking beer or coffee, leaped into action around the table, and out came huge rolls of money. The scramble for seats was like Parliament House when 'division' bells are rung. In a *sart sai* game thousands of pounds often changed hands.

There was a lot of banter around the tables, and it was fascinating that the Chinese and Greeks used to swear constantly, but with good humour, at one another, but in a mixture of the other bloke's language and their own. *'Ho nhe Kinezzo kai-ai-ah'* (You Chinese bastard) Paul Radomi would mutter at Robert Chin, who would be highly likely to reply *'Skatar stamutra su, Fung Quee Doy-Ah'* (Shit in your face, you white devil). One of the big gamblers was Jacky Burns, who was also an SP bookmaker. He had been a prizefighter in his day, as his nose indicated. I often had 'a quid behind' Jack. That meant you were betting on his dominoes, and the big players usually didn't mind. As the banker was only liable for the amount of money in his bank, quite often the entire bank disappeared in paying out someone like Jack Burns, who might have £200 as his bet.

That meant that anybody 'behind' didn't get paid, as the banker's money had run out. But if this was going to happen Jack always put my bet 'in front' so I would get my pound if he won. It was good of him, but I guess a pound wasn't much value to him.

In July 1950 my first cousins Frank and Bill Brennan (my mum was Grace Brennan) came to Darwin as crew on the *Dulverton*. I hadn't seen them for a few years, and was a schoolboy in Melbourne the last time we met, when they came back from the war. They had both been boyhood heroes of mine, and they were to become great mates now that I was an adult. They had no sooner docked when our mutual first cousin Leo Brennan arrived in Darwin on HMAS *Australia*. Leo had been in Darwin during the war in the RAAF, and had transferred to the navy.

Frunner, as we called Frank, said, 'Ted, there's nothing else for it. We're in Darwin for a week. You'll just have to take a week off work, and we'll teach you to drink.'

A week off work was easy to organise. And what a good time we had. I guess one shouldn't be too enthusiastic about a week-long bender, but it was drinking with a difference. The four of us sat around and talked. We ate lots of sensible tucker, compliments of West Australian State Ships, owners. We had mobs of laughs, discussed serious subjects, family matters and family history, firmed up our friendship, and got into a bit of derring-do, like swimming to the wreck of the *Neptuna*, which had been blown up in the Japanese raids. We sat on the wreckage of the *Neptuna* for about five hours one night, taking it in turns to swim back to the *Dulverton* to get more cold beer as needed. At the end of the week Frunner told me that on his next trip to Darwin, in about six months, he would take me as a stowaway on the *Dulverton* for a trip to Perth. I readily agreed to the proposal: I held him in almost God-like status.

The 1950 football season started. The Works and Housing team, which eventually became today's Nightcliff Football Club, proudly ran out in our Richmond (Frank Whiteman and I were both Richmond supporters) colours, black with a gold sash. The

Tigers. We thought we were about to make history, but quickly learned that we were going to be cut to pieces by the other three teams. There were some great footballers in Darwin in those days. The Buffaloes — today called Darwin — had Steve Abala as skipper, and some champion players like Leo Pon, Joey Sarib, Ali and Cyril Ahmat, Frank Perez, Froggy and Bingo Snape, Sabbo Briston, The Flying Chinaman and Alfie May. Wanderers had Gilbert Clarke as skipper, Tommy Burrinjuck, Bob Wilson, Steve O'Donoghue, Ginger Moreen, and the amazing Brucie Pott. Waratahs had Dinny Ganley as skipper, Bob Daniels, Ted Gunderson, Bluey McKee, Col Stokes, Johnny Tardif and a very tough bloke named Murray Hatch.

Waratahs were known as the 'Silvertails', because they wouldn't include anybody who was not white. They were nearly all itinerants, bank johnnies and public servants. Buffaloes were local mixed-race or Asian Australians plus the odd white bloke. Wanderers was a mixture too, mixed-race Aboriginals, a few whites, and a few 'full-blood' Aboriginals. Only full-bloods were referred to as 'Aboriginals' or, more often, 'natives' in those sensitive days, when being an Aboriginal meant there was so much you weren't allowed to do.

The most interesting players in the competition, to me, were two Wanderers players, Bob Wilson and Brucie Pott, both full-bloods. Bob Wilson eventually became Robert Tudawali, the film actor who starred in *Jedda* and other films, and I stood him in my first game in Darwin. I was full back for Works, he was full forward for Wanderers. We shook hands at the start of the game, and I mumbled some pleasantry I thought this primitive chap might understand. To my surprise he said, 'Gooday Ted. Nice to meet you. I've seen you around town a few times,' in a beautifully modulated voice. And then he proceeded to give me a bath, kicked six goals, shook hands and said 'Enjoyed the game, Ted' at the end of the match, which Wanderers won by fifteen goals.

Part of the reason why he did so well against me was that I kept seeing the incredible Brucie Pott, wingman, soaring above packs, taking the most amazing marks, and then kicking the ball high to Bob Wilson, who was able to outmark me most times. I have seen all the great high-flyers of Aussie Rules football, Bob Pratt, Ron Todd, Keith Warburton, John Coleman, Alex Jesaulenko, Ted Kilmurray and today's climbers Gary Ablett and Tony Modra, but none of them was better than Brucie Pott. You literally felt the ground shake as he ran in from any angle to start climbing over the backs and heads of the other players, and there he was, standing on top of them, marking the ball. Then he hit the ground, but cat-like, it didn't matter how he fell, he never hurt himself. 'Pottsie' as he was known, was an incorrigible larrikin, the son of Mosek, the Wagaitj dancer described in 1951 by American choreographer Ted Shawn as 'the greatest dancer in the world'. Bruce had been reared by the Pott family of Darwin, and thus spoke good English, although he hadn't had much schooling. Nothing wrong with his football though.

It's hard to convince people just how isolated Darwin was in those days. Two ships a month, about three flights a week to either Adelaide or Brisbane — and those were DC3 aeroplanes which took 12 or 14 hours for the journey to those places. There was no television, no commercial radio, only the local ABC, which presented the local and national news, *The Country Hour*, the famous radio serial *Blue Hills*, the Saturday night symphony concert, and the Sunday night radio play on a land-line link, but that was the only contact with the outside world. You expected a day's delay organising an interstate telephone trunk call. Southern newspapers arrived several days old, but they were so expensive nobody bothered. There was just the once-weekly newspaper *The Northern Standard,* nicknamed locally *The Moscow Times.* It was run by the North Australian Workers' Union and was decidedly left-wing. My dad posted *The Sporting Globe* to me with his weekly letter, so I kept abreast of Melbourne sport. There was no fresh milk in Darwin. Everybody used powdered milk as a matter of course. Things like biscuits were a luxury, and quite often the shelves of shops were totally bare if a ship was late. Meat equalled beef and was as tough as old boots. Fresh fruit and vegetables were virtually unknown, although a few Chinese people grew lovely vegetables in the sterile Darwin soil which is leached, lateritic and devoid of trace elements. During the war the army established very productive gardens at places like Adelaide River, but after the war there was an attitude that everything had to be brought to Darwin.

The isolation added to the appeal of the place for me, and the little town of Darwin became the world. I knew everybody, and seemed to see a lot of them all, one way or another. It was quite normal for people to have 'open house' parties, where anybody at all could drop in. Mind you, there were social and racial divisions that affected things like that — I've mentioned the reservations about the Belsen Gang — but I was fairly lucky, in that I began to move in several different circles and was likely to be invited to a Chinese feast because of my friendship with The Flying Chinaman, to a function at the Catholic Palais because I was a Catholic, or to a party at Parap Camp (118) because of my sporting connections. About the only places not available to me were the Masonic Lodge, the Buffalo Lodge and the Darwin Club, which I considered to be a silvertail show, and wouldn't consider joining in any case.

There was no shopping centre, just a few multi-purpose shops like A E Jolly & Co in Knuckey Street, where Woolworths are today. A few of the Chinese shops had different sections. Lorna Lim & Sons, for example, had a milk bar because they were near Star Pictures. They also sold groceries and clothing, and George Lim himself was an expert tailor. Almost every bloke in Darwin had trousers 'tailor-made' by one of the Chinese tailors. I began a long association with Sue Wah Chin, The Irish Chinaman's family, where Eric, and later Ossie Chin were tailors. We had several pairs of long trousers and shorts made at the one time, and it was good to be able to incorporate your own ideas in the manufacture of your clothes. With long trousers I copied the style favoured by cousin Frank Brennan, what we called 'WA trousers', with twenty-two inch bell-bottoms, and a half belt of the same material as the trousers. I thought I was ever such a flash dresser.

There were some wonderful characters around Darwin. Jack Munsell, a 'punchy' ex-boxer, might offer to guess your weight for a schooner of beer. Tommy Flynn regularly amazed and astounded drinkers as he took huge bites out of a beer glass, and proceeded to chew up the glass. Tom O'Neill's boast was that he was the only man in town with a certificate to say he was sane; the fact that the said 'Certificate' was his discharge paper from the Callan Park Mental Hospital did not deter Tom from his constant reminders. Gerry Randall was a wild buffalo shooter from Mudginberry, and whenever he hit town you could expect Gerry to tip a bagful of baby crocodiles onto the bar at The Vic, or let a big python snake loose in the Star Pictures. Paul Becker and Carl Atkinson were two Errol Flynn types, always into something spectacular around the town, and always getting the pick of the new girls. They drove around Darwin in old Army jeeps bare-chested, and the women used to flip over them. Paul especially was a handsome bloke, and very popular with the fellows as well as the girls. He was always organising something exciting, fishing excursions, bush camping trips, crocodile hunting, you name it. Paul killed himself in a freakish accident. He and Carl were making fireworks one day, and the explosives blew up.

Gerry, Paul and Carl were about the only town blokes who had four-wheel drive vehicles — old Army jeeps — so most people were not able to go bush as much as they do nowadays. Today I meet people who've lived in Darwin only six months, and they know more about the surrounding bush and beaches than I ever knew. We were pretty much restricted to the town itself, all 23 blocks of it, and a few surrounding beaches and bush spots. I had no transport other than the occasional shared use of Hoonga's truck or Nugget's tipper, although occasionally we would pinch the 'departmental bicycle' which was always kept at the Works and Jerks office. In retrospect, I think it was good that we were stuck so much to the town itself, as I spent all my spare time getting to know people, to the point where I have a comprehensive knowledge of the old Darwin families whatever their background and origins.

Through the Catholic church I got to know Brother Ed Bennett, a friend to this day. He was a member of the Missionaries of the Sacred Heart order, a lay brother, the skipper of the Catholic mission's transport boat, a ketch called *Margaret Mary*.

He asked me if I'd like to do a trip to Bathurst Island with him, so once more I took a few days off work and had a tremendous trip, the first of many I would make to Nguiu, which is the name of the place where the Catholic mission was established. A lot of people find it hard to pronounce Aboriginal words starting with 'ng'. A way to learn is to say 'singalong' slowly, working out how you say it, stage by stage. Then gradually isolate 'ngalong' until you can say just that. So Nguiu is pronounced 'ng-we-you'. You can get it by practising 'sing-we-you' first.

I had a wonderful trip on the ship, for Felix, my footballing contact, had become a crew member of *The Margaret,* as the ketch was known. Felix promised to show me around and did just that. The Tiwi are friendly, ready-to-laugh people, and I began a lifetime connection on that trip. Always surrounded by a huge crowd of laughing kids, I strolled around the place, responding to the standard greeting which was 'Hello *mandani* (friend)'. Everybody was full of questions: 'Where you live?' 'What you name?' It didn't hurt when I joined in a game of football, and showed that at least I knew how to play. Again, I spotted the natural talent of those blokes at football, just waiting to be developed.

The first MSC missionary to the Northern Territory was a Frenchman, Father Francis Xavier Gsell, who went to Bathurst Island in 1911 to set up a mission station on the island. He eventually became known as 'The Bishop with 150 Wives', for he interceded in the Tiwi promised marriage system to buy young girls out of their promised marriages to old men who already had wives. Having agreed on a bride price Father Gsell then assumed the role of marriage broker and helped arrange marriages for the girls with younger men. He got away with it, and most Tiwi people today are all in favour of monogamy. Most other missionary intrusion of a similar kind was disastrous.

I met Father Cosgrove, the priest-in-charge at Nguiu. He was starting to get involved in a project which would become a lifetime obsession with him, recording many generations of the genealogies of the Aboriginals of Bathurst and Melville Islands, and helping them to establish a system of surnames based on their own families, rather than on some white-imposed system which unfortunately has become the norm with Aboriginal communities. The Tiwi don't get a permanent *tiniwui* (blackfellow) name until they are almost adults, and once they die that name may not be spoken again. So there was a need to go back a long way in their history to establish an ancestor whose name was long since out of use, and could be accepted as an ongoing surname even when people died. Most of the people at Nguiu had been converted to Catholicism, so they were given at Baptism the names of saints, often early Christian martyrs. Among the men were Pancratius, Boniface, Tarcisius, Saturninus and Marcellus. The women had names like Perpetua, Agatha, Mena, Mary Magdalene and Martha.

Thanks to Father Cosgrove, they took on new family names which were handed on patrilineally. So Felix became Felix Kantilla, Raphael was Raphael Apuatimi. It was much better than the demeaning system prevailing, particularly in Queensland, where Aboriginals had their father's first whitefeller name foisted on them as a surname by Government officials and missionaries. So you got stupid names like Mary Tom, Michael Frank and Sally Pat.

Nguiu was a very happy place, and it was a revelation to see the level of acceptance of the Catholic religion. I realised later that the Tiwi people love ritual, so the vestments, the statues, the cross as a symbol, the thuribles, monstrances, candles and incense would have helped to attract them to Christianity in the first instance. Their traditional singing style is very much like Gregorian, long repetitive narrative chants. Their rendition of the Catholic hymns is strident, powerful and in tune, while not all that melodic. Ten out of ten for enthusiasm though.

I saw my first ever crocodile, *yirikapai* as the Tiwi call them, as *Margaret Mary* sailed up Apsley Strait to another Catholic mission, Garden Point. The big croc just sat, disdainful, on a mudflat and watched us go past.

Garden Point, on Melville Island, is near Fort Dundas, the site of the first, ill-fated British settlement in North Australia in 1824. The Catholic Mission established at Garden Point (now known by its Tiwi name, Pirlangimpi) in the 1930s was to service the government policy of removing 'half-caste' children from their Aboriginal mothers, in order to bring them up to be 'like whites' and to ignore the 'unsatisfactory' Aboriginal side of their heritage. Today that policy is universally condemned, although it is interesting to talk to some of the people who were reared at Garden Point. They speak with nostalgia of the happy times they had on the mission. What happened in fact was that a new tribe was created. The Garden Point people are now a closely knit, intermarrying, cohesive group, fiercely loyal to one another. They took on the 'white man skills' taught by the missionaries, and tacked them on to the bush skills they acquired living in a place like Garden Point, in regular contact with the Tiwi people. Many of the 'Garden Point mob' — as they call themselves — had Tiwi mothers, and so retained their language and a certain amount of traditional knowledge. They were to become powerful people in Aboriginal society when all the stupid discriminatory laws were repealed, land rights were recognised, and they could decide their own lifestyles, affiliations and associations.

I played only half the season of football in 1950, and then Frunner came back to Darwin on the *Dulverton*. I left my job and blithely stowed away with him when the ship sailed out of Darwin, heading for Fremantle. It was as easy as just staying on the ship when it sailed. The crew were all aware that I was a stowaway, and I was simply told to keep out of the sight of officers, eat in the crew mess, and sleep in various vacant bunks. As the crew were all on shift work, eight hours on, sixteen hours off, there was always an empty bunk somewhere.

The Seamen's Union was incredibly powerful, and demanded and got the very best conditions for its members. The food on the coastal ships was excellent, wages were high. We berthed at Wyndham, Derby, Broome, Point Sampson and Port Hedland, and I was able to slip ashore at each place and have a look around. Broome was exciting, but the other places had nothing to offer except the bar of the pub at the end of the jetty. At Broome I had a few beers at the Governor Broome Hotel, a few more at The Conti, the local name for the Continental Hotel. I walked to Chinatown, had a good look around and stayed until very late, drinking at the Roebuck Bay Hotel. I met lots of people my mother would have warned me not to talk to, and one very dark chap took me to his home, where we had a couple of beers and a congenial meal as he showed me an impressive display of pearls and pearlshell. On the second day at Broome I went off to the Japanese cemetery where all the divers who died from the bends, the diver's paralysis, are buried. There are 1000 graves. The pearling industry, about which so much has been romanticised, took a great human toll. Many of the Japanese buried at Broome were young blokes, about my age, I noted sadly, as I read the records at the museum.

The seas were frightening coming into Fremantle, and I was seasick for a few hours, until I worked out that the best way to combat seasickness is to stay erect in the fresh air and continue to eat and drink. I have never been seasick since.

At Fremantle I met Frank's wife, Dot, and her family, and we teamed up with Frank's brother, my cousin Bill, who was on shore leave from his ship the *Duntroon,* which did the run from Fremantle to Melbourne. Bill told me he could stow me away to Melbourne on the *Duntroon* in a couple of months time if I wanted to visit my parents. In Perth I stayed with Frank and Bill's father, Mick Brennan, my mother's brother, and my Aunt Isobel at Shenton Park. I met cousins Bob and Cecil Brennan for the first time, and got reacquainted with cousin Len. The last time I had seen Len, in 1942, he was as skinny as a match: he had escaped in an open boat from Singapore when the Australian troops surrendered to the Japanese.

I had a great time for a few weeks, swimming at Scarborough, playing tennis with Bill, and drinking with the Brennan boys at their favourite waterhole, the P&O Hotel at Fremantle. Bill Brennan was a devastating darts player, and used to win lots of money and beers playing 301, start and finish on a double. I had never seen darts played at all, let alone competitively, but it was certainly popular in the West.

When I ran out of money I went to an employment agency and got a job at a place called Wagin, 200 kilometres south-east of Perth. I stayed at the Federal Hotel in Wagin and was introduced to the deadly job of wheat-lumping. Those were the days before bulk-handling, when the wheat was in 180 pound bags, which had to be picked up, carried on your back and stacked in the huge sheds near the railway yards. A lot of the carrying involved technique, and it became relatively easy eventually, but my knees buckled for the first few days.

After six long weeks on the wheat Bill wrote to tell me that I should come back to Perth if I wanted to travel to Melbourne with him. I hitched a ride on a truck — in fact, the driver was drunk and asked me if I could drive. I didn't have a licence, but I could drive a bit, so I drove his truck to Perth while he blissfully slept.

We left Fremantle on the *Duntroon* a few days later. I walked on board with Bill, said, 'Crew' to the security guard, and slipped into the same routine as on the *Dulverton*. It was very rough going across the Great Australian Bight, but I had a great voyage. I practised darts every day, and was fairly good by the time we hit Melbourne.

It was terrific to be back with my family, picking up the news, and seeing how much my nieces and nephews had grown. I decided to stay in Melbourne for a few weeks, and had a great surprise when I got a letter from Darwin from The Flying Chinaman, who announced that he was going to visit Melbourne. He suggested that we get together for 'a few drink' and I was all in favour. He was only there for a couple of days, but we had a good time together, drinking at Young & Jackson's and going to places like Luna Park. My family thought Hoonga was a great bloke. He was probably the first Chinese person any of them had ever spoken to.

Grace, my Mum, was a bit shocked when I came home smelling of beer, and demanded to know what had caused me to break my sacred vow about not drinking until I was twenty-five. She didn't perform too much, though, for I could hold it all right.

Meeting up with Ron Chin made me homesick for the first time in my life, and at that point I realised that Darwin was more home to me than Melbourne, so I took a job for a few weeks to save enough money to enable me to travel north again.

I went by train to Brisbane, for Hoonga had told me that Ron Bridgett was on leave there. I met up with Ron and stayed with him at his brother Joe's place at Kedron, until we went north to Townsville by train. We had a mighty time — 'mighty' being the adjective Queenslanders used at that time to describe anything pertaining to their state — in Brisbane, and fortunately we went to Eagle Farm races and won enough money to pay our train fares to Townsville. I had sent some money to a Townsville bank, so once we got there we would have enough to get to Darwin, we hoped.

While in Brisbane, and flushed with our win at the races, Ron Bridgett and I drank every day at the Grand Central Hotel, where he regaled the barmaids with the most outrageous lies, about how he was a cattle station owner, that I was his head stockman, and he was down south to buy some racehorses. To keep up his image, he insisted that we both go every day to have a shave at the nearby barber's shop, where he continued the bullshit.

Being shaved by a barber became one of the great loves of my life. It's sad that the practice is virtually discontinued nowadays, for there is nothing better than lying back in the chair, being lathered and then shaved with a cut-throat razor, as the barber talks away about this and that and anything at all really. Hot, then cold, then hot towels again, and you feel great. We always had a shampoo and a hair and face massage as well. It cost a fortune, but that's what I call luxury.

Bridgo and I travelled from Brisbane to Townsville, Townsville to Mt Isa by train. He got into a card game on the train, so when we hit Mt Isa we had the princely sum of four shillings between us. We hitched a ride with a semi-trailer, riding on the back, and travelled across the Barkly Highway to Tennant Creek. There we went back on the old sixpennorth of bread and butter diet as we waited two days for a lift. Bridgo was furious when I gave sixpence to the Salvation Army man who was collecting in Tennant Creek, for we had just spent a freezing night on a bench in front of the Tennant Creek Hotel.

'Quit moaning. Something will turn up,' I said.

'It had better, or I'll job you, you generous bastard,' he

retorted. The words were no sooner out of his mouth, than in rolled the Bond's coach from Alice Springs, heading to Darwin On board was Charlie O'Dwyer, our mate from Belsen, heading back from leave.

'Charlie, mate. Lend me a spin,' we said in unison.

With five pounds each borrowed from Charlie, we had a slap-up feed and a few beers at the Goldfields Hotel, paid our fares to Darwin and headed Up North again, back to God's country.

3
You'll Learn, Son

I arrived back with no money, no job and nowhere to stay. But this was Darwin, the friendly town, the 1950s, and the endless barbecue of my song was still on. Ron Bridgett was allocated a hut to himself at Belsen so I moved in with him. Everybody at the camp knew me, and either assumed I was legally in residence once more, or else didn't give a damn.

I got a job as a builder's labourer with John Stubbs & Company, who were the only people doing any building work in Darwin. They were on a cost-plus scheme of payment for some contract construction jobs, under supervision by Works and Jerks, and were paid 10 percent of the total cost of the operation as their fee. It was a strange and probably very lucrative way of doing things: the more inefficient, wasteful and long-winded the job, the higher the commission. They had built five blocks of flats in Wood Street, and when I joined them they were about to build the Nurses' Quarters at Myilly Point.

A bit flabby from ten weeks of soft living since wheat lumping, I arrived just in time for some big concrete pours. If the building operation was inefficient it didn't show on those first days. I never stopped running with barrow-loads of concrete. We mixed by hand, carted and poured 30 cubic metres of concrete a day. And I can vouch for the solid building: the Nurses' Quarters was one of the best survivors of Cyclone Tracy in 1974. It was a good way of getting fit again, as I was soon back into the sporting roundabout in Darwin.

I was a much better basketballer in my second season with

Works and Jerks. Life was pretty much the same, and I was on £10 a week with Stubbs & Co., and paying no board as a squatter at Belsen. Then my life changed.

Ron Smith had started going with a girl from the Works and Jerks office named Marie Pierssene. She was terrific-looking, and shortly after I got back I noticed her sister Rae, just back in Darwin after a long holiday. They were the two best-looking girls in Darwin by a mile. I saw Rae at a party one night. I was nervous about girls in general, but after a few agonising days working out tactical approaches I summoned up the courage to ask if I could take her to the pictures. Yes, I could.

Rae was playing netball for Marrenah, so I saw her at the basketball as well. We regularly went to the pictures — she had worked at the Star Theatre the previous year, although I had never seen her there — and she had permanent bookings in the front row upstairs at the open-air theatre. VIP stuff. I had never sat upstairs before. I used to sit downstairs in the cheap seats with the blackfellers.

Rae worked in the Records Section at Northern Territory Administration. I saw her at Admin when I applied for and got a job as a clerk in the Housing Section, keeping a record of all government tenancies, for the government owned every building in Darwin under the powers of the Darwin Town Acquisition Act, passed by the federal government when war with Japan was declared. Most civilians were evacuated in 1941, their houses acquired for military purposes. In the immediate post-war years a lot of old Darwinites tried to regain title to their homes, but nothing much had transpired by 1951 when I started in Housing Section. In many cases former owners were living in their old homes again but were unable to restore them or do anything pending the return of their title. Things were in a state of administrative chaos, and various Darwin Town Plans were formulated, to be inevitably rejected. Everybody had a fortnightly tenancy over the premises they occupied, and token rentals were charged. My job was great, in that I had to do regular checks on all units of accommodation, but not on any tedious basis, so I didn't get assaulted or anything like that. On the contrary, as my inspections were a minor part of the process of resettlement, I was welcomed in most cases, so there were lots of cups of tea and chats with old Darwin families, and I learned a lot about the place.

Rae's parents, Eunice and Bert Pierssene, had just finished building a new house in McMinn Street, Darwin, in 1941 when the Pacific war broke out. The family was evacuated to Sydney, although Bert stayed on in Darwin during the Japanese air raids, working for the PMG (Postmaster General's Department, forerunner of Australia Post, Telecom, Telstra). Their house was acquired and used by the army but flattened in the first raid, so after the war they were still trying to get compensation.

When the Pierssene family returned to Darwin in 1947 they were allocated another house in Wood Street, and I began to spend a lot of time there, and had some memorable talks with Rae's parents. They had both been in Darwin for many years before the war. Eunice had travelled to the Northern Territory in 1921, to be a companion to her cousin Ada who lived in a buffalo-shooting camp at Kapalga, on the East Alligator River at the edge of the Arnhem Land reserve, with her husband Hazel Gaden. Eunice went straight from suburban Sydney to this area, where the only access was by lugger once or twice a year. She told me hair-raising stories about life in the real bush, living compatibly with wild bush blackfellows. She gave me chapter-and-verse about the primitive camps, the cruel spine-shooting of the water buffalo who had been brought to Australia to be beasts of burden but instead had run wild and bred in their thousands in the swampy Arnhem Land plain country, the skinning, the salting of the hides. She and the Gadens lived for months on end in the bush, occasionally going 'down' to Darwin from the East Alligator River on the sturdy little luggers, loaded with salted buffalo hides. I listened to Eunice for hours. She was a great cook and I was a good listener. We got on well. She was a very quiet person, but liked to be asked questions about life in the buffalo camps, for she knew she had participated in a unique part of Northern Territory history. She was a true pioneer.

Eun met Bert Pierssene at Kapalga in the late 1920s, when he came from Broome to work with the Gadens as a buffalo-shooter. He had served in the Australian army in Palestine in World War 1. He was a crack shot, and when I met him he was still the champion of the Darwin Rifle Club.

Bert Pierssene was probably the handsomest man I have ever met, and he had the reputation of being the strongest man in the Territory and a formidable grass fighter. It was legend around Darwin that one of his more memorable feats of strength in pre-war Darwin was to tie a surcingle round a person's waist, and lift them above his head with one hand. He did this to the famous aviator Charles Kingsford Smith one night at The Vic and the surcingle broke. Poor Smithy went smashing against a cupboard, but suffered no long-term harm. Bert and I got on well together, which I guess was fortunate for me in all sorts of ways. I saw him in a couple of very short fights, and he was frighteningly tough. There was a cranky, blustering old bully named Jack 'Boorie' Hales who ran the Koolpinyah Iceworks for the Herbert Brothers in Smith Street. Bert and I went to get some ice one Christmas morning.

'There's no ice,' snarled old Boorie.

Bert picked him up by the shirtfront and slammed him over the top of the big moulds where we knew there were lots of blocks of ice.

'Listen, you bastard,' said Bert, in a soft but convincing voice, 'I could beat shit out of you in the old days, and I might just do it again if you don't produce a couple of blocks of ice, real fast.' He released his grip.

'How would a couple of free blocks suit you, Bert?' said the suddenly compliant Boorie. The locals, used to putting up with Boorie's filthy moods, enjoyed it immensely.

Through the 1951 sporting season I played cricket, basketball and footy for Works and Jerks. We won the cricket premiership, and I had a good season as something of an all-rounder. We did reasonably well in basketball, and a bit better in the football, although we finished fourth, or, to put it another way, last in the competition. Buffaloes and Waratahs were fierce rivals, and both had very good teams. The matches at the old Darwin Oval were memorable events. There was fiercely partisan barracking at the games. Dick Johnson and

Goorie Galora roared themselves hoarse on the sidelines as they urged on the Buffaloes — 'Come on you *Annaburoo*, fair between the big sticks.' *Annaburoo* is a local Aboriginal word for Buffalo. Big crowds, the occasional punch-up — usually between women, but no names, no packdrill, for some of them are respected grandmothers nowadays. Animosities were usually forgotten after the game, when players from the four teams had a drink together somehow or other. It was common practice to do a pub-crawl, a few beers at the Darwin Hotel, a few more at The Vic, then round to Cavenagh Street for a session at The Don. If one particular club had a social function members from other clubs were usually welcome. The Waratahs were more exclusive than the other three teams: whites only.

One Saturday night the Waratahs had a social and, although we hadn't been invited, we went along after the pubs shut. We were told we could come in, but it was going to cost £2 each. This was pretty steep, but there was nowhere else to go, so we paid up. There were about ten of us, mainly navy boys, all members of Works footy team. We got inside, were given one glass of beer each, and then told the evening was over: 'Sorry, gents, the beer's off.' We were furious at being conned like this, felt certain they had more beer, were simply going to get rid of us and keep drinking themselves. One of our boys, a sailor named Teddy de Campo, who was something of a madman, scouted around, and came back to us.

'The bastards have got a nine-gallon keg hidden in a drum of ice out the back,' he reported.

Three blokes were given the job of hijacking the keg, and the rest of us sauntered over to the supper table, where there were still trays full of meat pies. We smothered the pies with tomato sauce, and on 'Go' from Teddy de Campo we threw them at the Waratah club officials. She was on for young and old, pies splattered on starched white shirt fronts, and the most dreadful mess. When we ran out of pies we threw sausage rolls. A few punches were thrown before we saw our three keg-stealers giving us the 'mission accomplished' wave from the door, so we beat a quick retreat. The Waratah function was at the Belsen Recreation Hut, and the navy boys knew their way around the camp from many previous parties there. They had hidden the keg in the laundry block, so we waited quietly until the Waratah blokes who chased us had gone, then regrouped at the laundry.

A wooden keg of beer is not much good without a tap, but Teddy de Campo showed remarkable initiative. Being the youngest, and a Belsen resident to boot, I was told, 'Get over to the mess and get some pannikins, young Egan.' I got back just in time to see Teddy put a plug into one of the laundry troughs, grab an axe from the woodheap, and deliver one almighty blow in the side of the beer keg. The beer gushed into the trough, and we stood there scooping it out by the pannikin-full until we finished the 9 gallons, a reprehensible 40 litres. One of the Royal Australian Navy's finer moments. The Waratahs never forgave us.

Early in 1952 Bishop O'Loughlin, the Catholic Bishop of Darwin, asked me to call on him at the Presbytery. I wondered what I might have done wrong. Had Grace, my mum, written to ask him to tell me to get off the grog? No, he was all smiles and have-a-cup-of-tea. He told me he had been 'keeping his eye' on me, and I hoped he hadn't been watching the night we pinched the keg, for The Bishop's Palace, as it was called, was just across the road from Belsen. His Lordship wanted to talk to me about sport, and he asked me if I'd like to be involved in starting a football team, mainly to cater for Tiwi Aboriginals, and a basketball team to cater for young Catholic fellows around Darwin.

Let me rephrase that. Bishops don't 'ask' you anything, they *tell* you in their authoritative way what they want, and then wait for you to nod the head. I simply said I thought it was a good idea, and told him I felt a football team would do fairly well from my observations of the Tiwi players. We left it at that, and the bishop told me he'd get Father Aubrey Collins, a keen young priest who had just arrived in Darwin, to talk to me.

In the next season St Mary's fielded a team in both competitions. Getting into the basketball competition was easy, but entry into the Northern Territory Football League was a different matter altogether. For one thing, the entry of a fifth team would create a bye. But opposition stiffened when we announced to the League meeting that most of our players would be Aboriginals from Bathurst Island. There were a couple of old Darwin conservatives on the NTFL committee, with typically racist objections — 'We know these boongs . . . they won't turn up for the game . . . they smell . . . they won't wear boots, they'll take over the competition.' I was dark, and about to get a bit emotional when my fellow delegate, Sergeant Greg Ryall, took over the talking. Greg was very well-known in Darwin, a highly respected policeman of formidable size but he was gentleness itself as he steered us into the competition that night. Greg was the big Territory policeman who appeared in the world press when he applied a stranglehold on the Soviet agents holding Mrs Petrov at Darwin airport in 1954.

So began a wonderful experience for me. I started to coach the kids from the Catholic school at basketball, although I'd only been playing the game for three years myself. In terms of fundamentals I was a good coach, for in all sports I realised I would never be a champion, but boy-oh-boy, would I practise to get the basic skills in place! And I began to recruit and train a few young blokes around the town for the senior team. A local chap, Charlie See Kee, saw me one day, said he was an experienced coach, and asked if I wanted a hand. I told him that if he liked he could coach the senior team, as I really didn't know all that much about tactics or team plays, and felt that as I would be playing anyway it would be better if somebody else was coach. So Charlie started with us.

I had a great time coaching the kids, as it gave me the chance to practise more and more myself. It also gave me access to a few more old Darwin families, for among the boys I coached were Benny, Murray and Steve Cubillo, Gordon and Basil Roe, Primo and Martin Cardona, and Michael Ahmatt. Michael Ahmatt eventually played in three Australian Olympic basketball teams. I don't seek any credit for that. But I *was* his very first coach.

We got together quite a creditable senior basketball team, and finished up fifth out of twelve teams in the competition. Towards the end of the season I met a bloke drinking at The Vic. His name was Rimgaila Gasiunas. He was a Lithuanian migrant, and I had already heard of him through Ron Bridgett, who said Gasiunas was the greatest drinker ever to hit the town. A bloke named Tony Amoni had recently won a lot of money by drinking twelve large bottles of beer between 10 am and 6 pm at the Workers Club. 'Bluey' Gasiunas — as locals had dubbed him because of his red wavy hair — heard about Tony's feat and scoffed, saying he would do the same in two hours. He proceeded to do just that, so the hard-drinking Darwinites held him in great esteem.

'Ah, Ted Egan,' he said when we met. 'You play forward at basketball, but you should play guard.'

'Oh, yeah, who says so?'

'I do. I watched you play the other night.'

I invited him to have a throw of the basketball with me. Darwin had seen nothing like him He wasn't all that tall for a star basketball player, about six feet three inches, but his ball control was superb, and he could ping in what today are called 'three pointers' from almost any angle and distance. He showed me the fundamentals of playing guard, so I immediately swapped positions and was a much better player as a result. Naturally, I recruited Bluey for St Mary's, and he began to play with us. One great problem was that he would never train, and that irked a bit, and he would often turn up at a game straight from the pub, although I have never seen any one hold his grog like he could. While he was never as good as I knew he could be, for those reasons, he was a great player to have in the side because we were all learning so much from just watching him.

But one day I got a summons from Bishop O'Loughlin. Imagine my shock when he started on a great diatribe about 'this Gasiunas fellow' and how I must get rid of him from the team.

'Why, my Lord?' I asked, totally bewildered.

'Because he's living in concubinage,' he replied.

I had the most un-Catholic of reactions. You pompous, judgemental old bastard, I thought to myself. But didn't quite say it. I had never heard anyone use the word 'concubinage' before, and haven't since, but I knew from my school Latin that it had something to do with 'concubine' and therefore must mean 'living in sin'. Full of Christian charity, His Lordship told me it had 'come to his attention' that Blue was living with a woman — he named her, which I thought a bit unethical — and said this was hardly the type of man to be playing in a 'Catholic basketball team'. The Bishop had obviously not taken on board the Darwin dogma of 'No names, no packdrill'.

I amazed myself. 'My Lord, I'm not going to do anything about this. For one thing he's a really good player, and we're all learning a lot from him.' Somewhat tongue-in-cheek, I went on. 'Maybe we good Catholic boys might be a good influence on him.' And then I thought to myself, 'Better shut up, Ted. God will strike you dead.' I wondered what Grace would have said. 'Respect for the cloth, my boy. Always have respect for the cloth.' The Bishop contented himself with a curt 'Well, that will be all for the moment,' and I was left to find my way out. I was only nineteen, and it felt pretty good once I was out in the fresh air.

St Mary's basketball team improved a lot that year. Blue Gasiunas played on, but not all that well, although you could tell he was a champion. But he was also a monumental drinker. The important thing was that we, and others in the competition, learned so much about basketball from him.

I was enjoying my work at the Housing Section, and Rae and I were getting on fine. The Pierssenes lived in Wood Street, near Belsen. We both had pushbikes and used to go to the beach some Saturday afternoons, and the pictures a couple of times a week. Rae was born in Darwin, and all the old-timers knew her, so through her I got to know even more about Darwin and its history. Eunice, Rae's mother, was especially knowledgeable, and I came to realise that the best historians in many places are the little old women who live quietly and note carefully everything that happens. The blokes tend to get on the grog and strut around, instead of keeping tabs on things.

We used to often visit Rae's cousins, the Gadens, who had left the buffalo camps and now lived at Salonika in Darwin, near the old Vestey's Meatworks. At their house there was an endless stream of bushies who had 'come down' to Darwin from various cattle stations and buffalo camps. I got to know the Hagans, Tim Blackmore, the Yates Family, Clarry Wilkinson —

'the bandy-legged bugger from Brock's Creek', and the famous Yellow Charlie, doyen of buffalo shooters. There were endless card games at Gadens, and bushies camping in swags all over the verandah. I listened, open-mouthed, as they drank rum and talked of their amazing lives in Australia's last frontier. They talked of the days when they spine-shot from horseback hundreds of buffaloes in a day to cripple them, but keep them alive. Following them came large teams of Aboriginal men and women to put the poor creatures out of their misery, and then skin them, salt the hides and sell them to Australian and overseas markets for industrial belting. Buffaloes had been brought to Australia from Indonesia by the British in the 1820s and had later run wild, breeding into millions. The talk at Gadens was sometimes of skirmishes with wild blackfellows. The paradox was that relationships between the Aboriginals and the buffalo-shooting families like the Gadens had been remarkably good, and it was my hunch that the presence of white women in the Gaden camp made the difference. I had heard of brutal experiences in other camps where the Martini Henry and Lee Enfield taught English. Ada and Hazel Gaden had two good-looking daughters, Eileen and Hazel, and two sons, quiet Neil and gregarious Frank, living in Darwin at that time, and through Rae I struck up good friendships with all of them, and with their sister Madge, who lived in Sydney.

Frank Gaden used to say he was part-Chinese, and referred to himself as Frong Kee. He always told people not to be mean with money. 'Never go short,' he'd say. 'Be like me. Bookim up longa Charlie On.' Charlie On, like most of the Chinese storekeepers in Darwin, always allowed you to buy on credit. Frong Kee was generosity itself. One day he came back from the pub and stuffed $100 into the shirt pocket of his wide-eyed nephew Geoff McGill. 'Geoffrey, cut that out in sartees for the kids,' he said. He had style, Frong Kee.

October 1952 rolled round, time for football. I had a couple of trips to Bathurst Island to line up the Tiwi players for the coming season. The arrangement we made with Father Cosgrove was that the lesser players would come to Darwin to work for the army or the RAAF before Christmas, replaced by the better players for the second half of the season, when the finals were played. Three months was their usual term of employment in town. The Darwin season starts in October, and the Grand Final is at the end of March Our first team consisted of one Chinese — David Lee, three mixed-race blokes — Benny and Murray Cubillo and Gordon Roe, two whites — Johnny Vaughan and me, and the rest were Tiwi from Bathurst Island. We had a lot of trouble raising funds and we needed plenty, for the Tiwi had no money and the club was obviously going to have to pay for all the outfits. We ran gambling nights and raised quite a bit of money. Rae and a friend named Dot Mellifont organised local women to make green and gold shirts — green with a gold sash — which was the first St Mary's jerseys. With the prospect of changing the entire side half-way through the season, we set up the practice of collecting all the gear at the end of each game, except for shorts. Jerseys, sox and boots were all collected, and a few of us accepted the responsibility of washing the clothes and polishing and 'sprigging' the boots in readiness for each game. It was a lot of work.

The Saints had an inauspicious start. Although the Tiwi were fundamentally very skilful, with magnificent reflexes, they had no idea of team play or anything connected with roughness. Wearing boots was a decided handicap. But the biggest drawback was that they saw no sense whatsoever in playing football if it was raining. Darwin's footy season is in The Wet, when an average of 60 inches (1500 mm) of rain falls. At first all the other teams beat us easily, but I could see that we were getting better each week. We used to have regular pie nights where our coach, Jack Sweeny, an old East Perth player, talked about tactics. We all drank lolly-water — as soft drinks were called in Darwin. Aboriginals were not allowed by law to drink alcohol, so there was an agreement among us that when we were together as a team all players and officials abstained. We managed to get a short instructional film, and showed this over and over.

At about this point I met up with Aloysius Puantulura. He and his wife Mena stayed at the Catholic presbytery. They camped in a big shed. Mena worked at the convent and Aloysius was employed by the Customs Department. It was the practice for some of the government departments to have an old Aboriginal man as a sort of major domo, to greet visitors, take messages around to other departments, but mainly to be 'a wise presence'. Their wages were only £2 per week, so it didn't cost the government much. These grey eminences took their jobs very seriously. They were always immaculately dressed, in starched long white trousers and white shirts. They greeted visitors graciously, and took no nonsense from anybody. Aloysius was at customs, Tipperary was at the court house, Bismarck was at the police station, Johnny Driver was at government house. They were all Tiwis. Tiwi Aboriginals were held in high regard in Darwin, and I noticed that we were getting a good crowd of supporters at each football game. Not just Catholics, people from all walks of life who admired the new team and its potential.

I was appointed the first captain of St Mary's Football Club, though I was only twenty. I considered, then and now, that it was one of the greatest honours of my life.

After one of the first games Aloysius introduced himself to me: 'I'm happy you start the football' he said. 'I want you sit down with me. I'm not read and write, and I'm worry for my language, keep him proper way. I want you book him down. I teach you my language, my story, my songs. Then you can talk straight way all that young boy.' That started regular classes for me, two or three nights a week. I was still living at Belsen, so if I didn't go out with Rae I went over to talk to Aloysius, Mena, and two old Tiwi men, Cardo and July. It was the start of a lifetime friendship with Aloysius, which ended 40 years later when I sat alongside Mena at the funeral of Aloysius at Nguiu in 1993, my face painted by her in his totemic designs to indicate that I was a principal mourner for that great man.

For my language lessons Aloysius started off with a few little Gregorian-like chants, like:

Ngia, nginta, ngara, nyirra, ngawa, wuda
(I, you, he, she, we, they)

He was a comprehensive teacher and I quickly became functional in Tiwi. I began to incorporate bits of language into my instructions during the games, because I could see that the

Tiwi players did not think in English, but in their own language, which I began to think of as Australian. Tiwi is an explosive language, with the standard Aboriginal practice of doubling up to achieve greater effort. *Kali* means run, *kalikali* means 'run for your bloody life'; *pipwa* means chest, *pipwa pipwa* 'mark the wet ball on your chest or you'll be dropped from the team next week.' High morale has remained a feature of St Mary's teams to this day, largely due to the constant presence in the early days of respected old elders like Aloysius. All the time in my association with Aloysius I found myself thinking of the two New Zealanders on the tram in Melbourne.

Eventually we won a game, beating Wanderers, and we were thrilled to bits. We were on the road to becoming serious competitors. After the game I was confronted by Paul Hasluck, Minister for Territories, who was visiting Darwin.

'I was very interested in what I saw today,' Hasluck said.

'Thank you,' I replied. I knew who he was.

'Where did you learn their language?'

'Oh, an old chap is teaching me.'

'I'm very interested both in football and Aboriginal people. Would you like to work among them?'

'Too right I would.'

I told him I was already working for the Northern Territory Administration, and he instructed me to see him on Monday morning. After talking to him and Mr Frank Moy, the Director of Native Affairs, it was agreed that I should become a permanent public servant and apply for a position as Cadet Patrol Officer. Within six weeks I was transferred, and I felt ever so important when I saw my name in the *Government Gazette,* listed as a 'Protector of Aboriginals'. I sent a copy to my mum, and she did a lot of skiting about her son Up North.

My immediate boss at the Native Affairs Branch was a chap named Gordon Sweeney. He was very austere, a former Methodist missionary. I don't ever recall seeing him smile. Ever. But he was a straight shooter and had vast experience among Aboriginals in Arnhem Land. He gave me a lot of files and a few books to read, and started me on some routine jobs. One was to go to Channel Island Leprosarium every week to see the patients and help them with any problems they might have, apart from medical matters. I had to organise any funerals of Aboriginal people, and I worked in close co-operation there with an old Aboriginal bloke named Fred Waters. His blackfellow name was Nadpur, and there is now a Nadpur Street in Darwin to commemorate him. His knowledge of local Aboriginal people was encyclopaedic. He had been the leader of the first Aboriginal strike in Darwin in 1951, when a few hundred Aboriginals had a meeting at the NAWU Stadium and demanded better treatment and equal pay. It all came to nothing and Fred was brutally committed for six months to Haast Bluff in Central Australia, 1600 kilometres from his country. He was not at all bitter, though, and we became warm friends. I learned a lot from him about the immediate Darwin Aboriginal relationships. He would be interested in the present land claims around Darwin, for Fred was adamant that Frank Secretary, who we buried in 1953, was 'the very last of the real Larakia. Everyone else is mixed with something.'

Frank Secretary was an amazing man. He got his name because he worked at the *Northern Standard* office, where he used to help with the typesetting, even though he could not read or write: he simply recognised the symbols. Mirror image symbols, mind.

> Trouble has flared again on Groote Eylandt, where police and Welfare officers quelled a native revolt last month.

I found out about Frank Secretary from Don McKinnon, an old editor of the *Standard*, who lived next door to the Pierssenes when they moved to a house on the corner of Smith and Daly streets. I knew Don was one of the most famous men in Darwin, and I relished the chance to have a few good yarns with him. Don was one of the union leaders who went to gaol in Darwin pre-war for refusing to pay income tax, on the old grounds of no taxation without representation. In those days there was no federal parliamentary representative for the Territory. There was a strong union presence in Darwin, and the North Australian Workers Union set up the local newspaper. When the new paper, the *Northern Territory News,* started in 1952 Don McKinnon asked me to see Baylon Ryan, NAWU secretary. As a result I become the football writer for the *Standard* until it closed down in 1954. I used to get a shilling per inch for copy, which was good pay.

I issued the permits for Aboriginals to attend the pictures on Wednesday nights, the only time they were allowed in town 'between sunset and sunrise'. I thought it was unjust then, but now I realise the absolute inhumanity of it all. It's very easy to rationalise things and say, 'I'm only a small player in this big game, I can't change things,' but if somebody did it to me it would be different, wouldn't it? Attitudes are more enlightened now.

Another of my jobs was to attend Darwin Police Court every morning as 'Protector and next friend' for any Aboriginals charged. Usually they were in the court for minor offences like drinking liquor or being in a prohibited area; and almost invariably I entered a guilty plea on their behalf, and then sought the lightest possible punishment. The facts were usually cut-and-dried. If the charges were more serious, I had to arrange for a qualified lawyer, and brief him to appear on behalf of the defendant. I was involved in quite a few murder cases where one Aboriginal was charged with spearing another, almost invariably in disputes over women.

The special magistrate was Mr J W 'Fatty' Nichols, who knew all the old lags from many years experience on the bench in Darwin. He insisted that all Aboriginals speak in Pidgin — today it's called Kriol — even if they could speak English properly. He wasn't a top speaker of Pidgin — I eventually became much better at it than he was — but he was keen to demonstrate that his style represented the pre-war system, when blackfellows were 'kept in their place'. He loved to show off his ability in Pidgin as he delivered the standard warning to Aboriginals, which took the place of the oath. He would say:

> You savvy that bigfella trouble bin come up there longa [place name]. Orright you talk truefella for that business. No more talk way nother boy talk long you. You talk way you seeim long you roan eye. No more gammon, no more lie, talk truefella allatime. Orright? Now you sing out loudfella, allasame corroboree.

and proceedings would start. Some regular offenders came up with ingenious yarns as alibis or to establish their innocence. One old bloke named Green Ant Paddy was charged with stealing fowls from Chinese storekeeper, Charlie On. Tom Hollow, the arresting policeman (and . . . ahem . . . the one whose chooks we Belsen boys used to steal) gave evidence that, 'acting on information received', he watched as Paddy climbed Charlie On's fence and entered the fowlhouse. He told of eventually finding feathers and bones in Paddy's camp at the Railway Dam. Mr Nichols SM asked if Paddy wanted to cross-examine Constable Hollow. Green Ant Paddy, a veteran of courtroom procedure, told me he could handle this, so I sat down and listened to this exchange:

Paddy: Conchable, you bin seeim me there longa Charlie On chooky fowl house?

Tom Hollow: [to the Bench] Yes, Your Worship I saw the defendant at the site of the crime.

Paddy: You bin seeim me go inside?

Tom Hollow: Yes, Your Worship, I observed the defendant as he entered the premises.

Paddy: You bin hearim allabout chooky fowl sing out?

Tom Hollow: Yes, Your Worship, there was quite a commotion.

Paddy: Orright, Conchable, you bin seeim me sneak out back way?

Tom Hollow: Er . . . no, Your Worship, I did not see the defendant depart the premises.

Paddy: [to the Bench] Well, Mr Nichol, you can't convictim me. Me still there inside!

We all had a good laugh, and Fatty convicted Paddy, but with no penalty. It was always funny when the habitual offenders were charged with drinking liquor. Fatty invariably asked, 'Which way you bin catchim that grog?' and the standard reply was always 'Me bin findim long grass.' Which was usually true. They were not about to disclose the name of the supplier. The arrangement was that the supplier, quite often a taxi driver, purchased the liquor for them, and left the wine 'in the long grass' somewhere pre-arranged. If the supplier was caught, the penalty was six months' gaol, no magisterial option.

Until 1954 the Aboriginals Ordinance applied to Aboriginals of mixed-race, unless they had an exemption. Some of the penalties were mandatory and severe, and one section of the Ordinance decreed that a non-Aboriginal male found in the company of a female Aboriginal between sunset and sunrise was automatically sentenced to six months' imprisonment. One morning in the court a young white sailor was charged with being in the company of a local mixed-race girl, who was not exempted. I was there to represent the girl's interests. The sailor told Mr Nichols he knew nothing about the law, and Fatty accepted the story, but, of course, ignorance was no excuse. Fatty was a kindly man, and said to me, 'Mr Egan, I want you to contact naval headquarters. It seems to me that this young man's entire service career might be in jeopardy here. He's obviously going to be convicted, and I have no option but to give him six months at Fannie Bay. Perhaps he could be transferred from the region. Then I could adjourn the charge *sine die*.'

I rang Commander Arnold Green, who was an arrogant old bastard if ever there was one. He was Naval Officer in Charge, known locally and in the navy by his acronym 'Noic'. A A Milne is right: people do look like their dogs, and vice versa. Noic had two ugly bull terriers, and he walked them around Darwin on leashes. They were from the same litter, the arrogant porcine naval commander and his two slathering companions. I explained to Commander Green that I was ringing at the

ABORIGINALS.

No. 16 of 1911.

AN ORDINANCE
Relating to Aboriginals.

[Notified in *Gazette*, 8th January, 1912.]

BE it ordained by the Governor-General of the Commonwealth of Australia, with the advice of the Federal Executive Council, in pursuance of the powers conferred by the *Northern Territory Acceptance Act* 1910 and the *Northern Territory (Administration) Act* 1910, as follows:—

1. This Ordinance may be cited as the *Aboriginals Ordinance* 1911. <small>Short title.</small>

2.—(1.) This Ordinance shall be incorporated and read as one with the *Northern Territory Aboriginals Act* 1910 ^(a), an Act of the State of South Australia in force in the Northern Territory as a law of that Territory. <small>Incorporation.</small>

(2.) In this Ordinance the expression "the Act" has reference to the *Northern Territory Aboriginals Act* 1910 as incorporated with this Ordinance.

3.—(1.) Without limiting or affecting any other powers conferred upon him by the Act, the Chief Protector shall be entitled at any time to undertake the care, custody, or control of any aboriginal or half-caste if in his opinion it is necessary or desirable in the interests of the aboriginal or half-caste for him to do so. <small>General powers of custody and control of aboriginals vested in Chief Protector.</small>

(2.) The powers of the Chief Protector under this section and the two next succeeding sections may be exercised whether the aboriginal or half-caste is under a contract of employment or not.

(a) *Infra*, p. 465.

Legislative and bureaucratic instruments of Northern Territory 'care, custody, and control' direction of the Special Magistrate, Mr Nichols, told him the essential facts of the case against the young sailor, and put forward the magistrate's suggestion about a possible transfer. Noic listened to me, paused for a moment, and then roared in my ear, 'Egan, are you suggesting that if one of my men wishes to be transferred from this region he simply has to go and stuff a boong?' Crash! went the phone in my ear. The poor young sailor got six months in the slammer, and, I guess, was thereafter dishonourably discharged.

In 1953 I made the national ABC News — Darwin was always over-supplied with journalists looking for sensationalist stories — when I emotionally told the Court it was a 'national disgrace' that a Larakia man named Bob Secretary (son of Frank) could be charged with being in a prohibited place, the town area of Darwin, between sunset and sunrise. I explained that Bob was walking to work at the ironically named Larrakeyah army base at the time of his arrest, and I went on, passionately, 'If Your Worship pleases, Darwin belongs to the Larakia.' Fatty Nichols gave me a look which clearly said: 'You'll learn, son.' Fortunately, I never did.

Some old Aboriginal lags were not averse to doing deals with the coppers. Two policemen in particular, Sandy McNab and Tom Hollow, were always into devious set-ups, trying to trap Aboriginals and non-Aboriginals alike, and they were assisted by an equally tricky police tracker named Jack Makuljar. I naively assumed that Aboriginals always told the truth and were loyal to one another until I met Makuljar and saw him in action. Other Aboriginals said that Makuljar always slept with his spears under his swag. I guess he had made many enemies among his own people.

It was sad to visit the patients at Channel Island each week. Leprosy was introduced into the north of Australia in the late 1800s, and spread at an alarming rate, among Aboriginal people in particular. The leprosarium was staffed by dedicated nuns, particularly Mother Marion and Sister Eucharia. I became a good mate of both of them. Eucharia ran the kitchen, Marion was matron of the hospital. But my old sparring partner, Bishop O'Loughlin, was to give Mother Marion a big lesson in humility.

A week after she was awarded the Order of the British Empire for selfless nursing services to the patients at Channel Island Leprosarium he transferred her (as *Sister* Marion) to be teacher at the junior school at Bathurst Island. Can't have those nuns getting the accolades, can we? No, my Lord.

The level of disfigurement among many of the patients was shocking, but most of them were amazingly cheerful. Before my weekly visit to the leprosarium I used to go shopping in town for various patients and they were very grateful for this. I offered to write letters home for patients, and sat with them as they dictated their poignant messages to remote cattle stations and missions. I started taking photographs of the patients, sending them with the letters to their relatives back home, and asking if family photographs could be sent back. One of the most agonising consequences of contracting leprosy in those days was the removal to Channel Island forever. I addressed my letters to the station manager or the mission superintendent or the police officer in charge of the area the particular patient had come from. I got splendid co-operation from everyone concerned. I guess the response indicates an inescapable feeling of sadness that everyone has inherited since biblical times about the dreadful, wasting sickness. The gratitude of the patients for the photographs from home was overwhelming. Poor things, they didn't have much going for them in life after contracting leprosy.

4

St Mary Kamwari

Work in the Native Affairs Branch totally absorbed me, particularly as I was left to organise my own timetable and movements.

Gordon Sweeney, my former boss, had been put on a special project to compile a comprehensive census in anticipation of new legislation to replace the Aboriginals Ordinance. The legendary Bill Harney — who was always known by his Aboriginalised name Bilarni — had formerly been a Patrol Officer, and he spoke on my behalf to Frank Moy, the Director of Native Affairs. 'Send young Egan bush, Frank,' said Bilarni. 'He won't learn much in town.' Frank Moy agreed. I virtually went anywhere I nominated.

I had a memorable trip to Melville Island with Bilarni and others as we accompanied that great poser Charles Mountford on one of his so-called 'expeditions'. Mountford always called himself Monty — probably identifying in his mind with the great English general, Montgomery — but subordinates were expected to call him 'Leader'. He was a self-styled ethnologist, a master at scoring huge funding from organisations like National Geographic. He would then surround himself with real experts like Bilarni, and in this case two young American anthropologists. His tactic was to pick the various brains and claim the knowledge. He was an absolute fiend with Aboriginals, using up their compliant natures to exploit them mercilessly. 'Boy, come here,' he would order grown men. I know, he tried it on me too. I proved to be very insubordinate, but most of the Aboriginal blokes copped his rudeness. He comandeered weapons and artifacts without a please or thankyou, and certainly no cash payment. I do acknowledge that he was a magnificent photographer, but again, he never paid for any of his portraits, although he ordered people around shamefully in getting them.

I was encouraged to go to places in Arnhem Land, where I made routine 'inspections', and checked out the census records — the department always insisted that we do this, but there never seemed to be any point to it in my opinion. What did it ever achieve, other than to give vague indicators about how many people were in a particular area? We always seemed to be trying to do New Guinea type things in a country that was nothing like New Guinea. We wrote our reports in 'officialese' and never 'went' anywhere — we 'proceeded on patrol'. It was all a bit absurd when you come to think of it, but after the 1939–45 war the Northern Territory and the states with comparatively large Aboriginal populations had recruited former *kiaps* from Papua New Guinea to be the various directors of native affairs. They brought with them to Australia the colonial trappings and nomenclature, and it is ironic that Australia did not develop a *modus operandi* in respect of its own Aboriginal people in 150 years, but felt content to import a colonial system — a system based on 'control' — from a foreign territory acquired by default.

I travelled by boat with Leo Hickey or George 'Noondi' Haritos when they took supplies to the various mission stations along the Arnhem Land coast, and to the Cape Don lighthouse, where a small group of Aboriginals regularly congregated. I was never treated as anything special, but rather as one of the crew on those trips, and I learned a lot from the two famous Territory sailors. Both Leo and Noondi employed Aboriginal crew. There was lots of banter and skylarking, yet at the same time the Aboriginal crew was always required to display absolute efficiency or else they lost their prestigious jobs. For many years Bill Neidji, later to become internationally known as 'Kakadu Man', was Leo Hickey's principal crew member on the *Zena*. Bill, a huge, powerful man with a resonant Paul Robeson speaking voice, became a great mentor in my life. Like most

St Mary Kamwari

Aboriginals I encountered in those wonderfully formative years, he was always happy to give wise, considered answers to my questions. And I asked thousands.

Lee Brothers of Darwin used to run an old army landing barge to deliver supplies to a few coastal places, and return with cypress pine timber that was cut at their sawmill on Cobourg Peninsula. I travelled on the barge a few times and met up with Ankin and Ali Ahmatt who ran the sawmill. It was there I first tasted dugong, beautifully cooked by Mrs Ahmatt. They ran a very efficient operation, and enjoyed excellent relationships with the local Aboriginals.

I always took a football and basketball with me when I went bush, and I coached kids and adults at the various mission stations and government settlements. There were no set duties for a junior officer like me, but I always wrote a comprehensive report when I returned to Darwin, and these were usually well-received. In town, as well as playing my own sports, I coached the Bagot basketball team, which was immensely successful in the B Grade of the competition, and provided the first–ever opportunity for 'full blood' Aboriginals to participate in the Darwin competition.

I look back on the years 1953 and 1954 with mixed emotions of joy and sadness, for many things important to my life occurred. Rae and I were engaged in 1953 and got married in October of that year. It was a big show at Darwin's old St Mary's Church, and the reception was at the Palais. The famous priest and eye specialist, Father Frank Flynn performed the ceremony. Rae and I were both twenty one. I look back now and shudder as I realise how immature I was; and on reflection I know that I was much too young to marry, but I had insisted. We were in love and were to spend the next twenty years together and raise four fine children. Many people said they considered it the perfect marriage. But when I left the marriage in 1974 as part of a colossal mid-life crisis one of my reasons was that I felt totally unfulfilled, and knew that in this once-only lifetime I was going nowhere. The fact that at that time I finished up in hospital with a bleeding ulcer indicates the level of stress I went through. I'm not apportioning blame, and did not feel good about it then, or now, but I had to do what I did.

My language lessons with Aloysius and Mena went on until I left Belsen Camp to get married. My association was very beneficial. Not only did I become conversational in Tiwi, and exposed to Aloysius's wisdom and sense of fun, but he was always able to put a dance group together — with himself as star performer, of course — whenever there were important visitors to town. Quite often I was instructed to organise a corroboree for visiting groups of VIPs, ship's crews and the like. Aloysius had two favourite dances — *The Bombing of Darwin* and *The Wallaby Hunt*. The Tiwi are very innovative in their ceremonial life, and they compose *kulama* songs about different things that happen in the given year. A *kulama* is a hot, sacred yam, around which quite a lot of ceremonial activity is organised, including the composition of topical songs. It was logical for an important event in their lives like the bombing of Darwin by the Japanese in 1942 to be immortalised in song and dance. Aloysius had composed the song, and always danced the main role, a Japanese bomber flying in low over Nguiu. As he circled the mission station, other dancers re-enacted the established facts that, on 19 February 1942, the Aboriginals at Nguiu had reported the Japanese aircraft to Father McGrath, who got on the pedal radio and tried to alert Darwin, 45 miles away, of the impending attack. Because Father McGrath's warning went unheeded Darwin was totally vulnerable when the Japanese struck and the town, wharf area and airstrip were smashed to bits. Dancers took on the roles of spotters, wireless operators, anti-aircraft gunners, and Allied aircraft seeking to shoot down the destructive Aloysius. Eventually he succumbed, shot down in flames, only to rise again and join in a spirited duelling dance with the machine gunner. The dance finishes with a group of old women who dance into the ring as Lincoln bombers and they, in turn, are mercilessly shot down. Not very accurate history, the reference to the Lincoln bombers, but great theatre, and typical of the expansive Tiwi. It provides a role for the women, and it's a ton of fun.

St Mary Kamwari

When it was announced that the Queen would visit Australia in 1954, I was told to organise a group of 21 Aboriginals who would go to Toowoomba, Queensland, to meet the Queen and dance for her. Included in the group was Albert Namatjira, the famous painter, Ginger Moreen, who had served with distinction in the Royal Australian Navy, Aloysius Puantulura and five other Tiwi, six Arnhem Land dancers led by an imposing man named Bungawuy, six men from Central Australia led by the renowned camel man Nosepeg Jabaljari, and a big, impressive police tracker from Anthony's Lagoon, Dick Janajanakanu. The Tiwi were to dance *The Bombing of Darwin* and *The Wallaby Hunt*. The Arnhem Landers would dance and give a display of spear-throwing and the famous *makarrta* peace-making ritual. The Central desert men, all with *marabindi* bones through their noses, were to dance and display the techniques of hunting with boomerangs. Albert, Ginger and Dick would be formally presented to the Queen.

We spent about a month in Darwin with the group going through their routines, and it was agreed that I would accompany them to Toowoomba. At the last moment I was beautifully shafted by a more senior bloke in the department — no names, no packdrill — who convinced the director that I was much too young and immature for such an important job, so the usurper took my place. You get that sort of bastardry on the big contracts.

I went to the airport to farewell the group, who were flying out to Brisbane on the old TAA DC3, a 14-hour trip. Aloysius was very matter of fact about it all. A newspaper reporter asked him what was programmed. Aloysius said: 'You know that Queen? Well, him reckon him wantim that Wallaby Dance too much.' Dick, the police tracker, asked me: 'Ted, this aeroplane, him fly over Anthony Lagoon?' I said: 'Pretty close to it.' 'Good,' he rejoined, 'I'll drop a note for my wife.' To this day I conjure the mental picture of Dick, who couldn't write, his wife who couldn't read, and the Anthony's Lagoon cattle station, about 10,000 square miles in area. A DC3 flies over, and a little note flutters out, floats around on the breezes, and then lands safely in her hands. She doesn't have to read what's on the note. She simply looks up at the fast disappearing aircraft and says, 'It's from Dick. He's off to see the Queen.'

Bungawuy was tall for an Arnhem Land blackfellow, a six footer. One front tooth missing in an otherwise perfect set, which tells me something special. He was a total bushman who had dodged Christianity and all its ramifications, as he continued the old lifestyle around Ramingining, in central Arnhem Land. He was a superb dancer, and floated over the ground as he performed the age-old ritual dances as freshly as if they were invented yesterday. And spear throwing! Many Australians are ignorant of the fact that the woomera is one of the greatest inventions of this land. Forget the boomerang. The woomera created an extra arm, to enable primitive man to throw a spear twice as effectively as previously. Bungawuy could hit a kangaroo, on the hop, from 100 metres, every time he threw a spear. One day, at Bagot Reserve, as we prepared the group to meet the Queen, Bungawuy hit a banana palm (about 20 cm thick) three times out of five throws from a measured 80 metres. He demonstrated that a moving target was easier to hit than a stationary one. In the *makarrta,* where the human target has to dodge the thrown spears, there is a chance if you stand still, watch the thrown projectile, and then move. But, said Bungawuy, 'Suppose you run away, I kill you more easy.'

The world-renowned painter Albert Namatjira was very quiet, very dignified. He stayed with Rae and me for a couple of weeks while the group prepared to meet the Queen. Among other things I had to take Albert and Ginger to George Lim, tailor and publican, to get two suits made to measure. The government paid, so George charged plenty, but did a great job. I did not become a close friend of Albert Namatjira, for he was very reserved, but I had long talks with him and could sense the sadness in the man. The bewilderment of being famous and fawned over in one aspect of the white man's world, in that he painted great and valuable pictures and thereby made a lot of money, but was totally rejected when seeking recognition as an equal human being, seemed at the heart of it. Because of his 'ability to handle his own affairs' he was already exempted from the Aboriginals Ordinance, but he had been told very clearly that he was not allowed to buy a block of land in Alice Springs. That was the ultimate irony, for the town is built on his own tribal Arrernte land. He was also warned that if he, a person allowed by law to buy and drink alcohol, was to supply liquor to his relatives he might expect the full wrath of the law.

That was bound to happen, and it eventually came to pass in 1958 that the police nabbed him sharing a bottle of wine with his sons. He was sentenced to six months imprisonment for 'supplying liquor to persons who were wards within the meaning of The Welfare Ordinance'. The wily Paul Hasluck, Minister for Territories, stepped in. Realising the political dynamite of incarcerating in the Alice Springs Gaol a world famous artist for sharing a bottle of wine with his sons, Hasluck quickly had the Haast Bluff Reserve gazetted as a prison within the meaning of The Prisons Ordinance, and Albert was sent there, away from the prying press, on the understanding that he was free to move anywhere within the Reserve, but was not locked up at any time. On appeal, his sentence was reduced to three months. He served eight weeks committal with remission for good behaviour. It was a more humane resolution of a stupid situation, but it all proved too much for Albert Namatjira to handle. His health began to deteriorate, his morale slumped, he stopped painting. He was released from Haast Bluff in May 1959, but died after a heart attack on 8 August 1959. The last couple of years of the famous artist's life represents one of Australia's most tragic stories when you think it through. I was moved to write a song about Namatjira:

> Sitting in the dirt
> The trial is finally done.
> I'll spend six months in gaol
> For sharing with my son.
>
> When I was young I walked this land
> With wise old men who said,
> 'When we change you to a man,
> If you don't share, you're dead.'

I endured the great ordeal
Promised to obey the rules
Vital desert laws that teach
Better than the white man's schools.

Learn to paint the white man's way
Told that I must know my place.
They wanted me to meet their Queen,
Tokenism for my race.

Then they split me from my own
With tricky white man's laws
Waited for me, then they pounced,
Clang the closing prison doors.

So I sit here in the dust
Thinking how I know this land
But legends from the ancient past
Flow no more from painter's hand

Sit and think my age-old thoughts
A fading memory
Take me to your prison now
Leave me with my dignity.

When they returned to Darwin Aloysius had the makings of a new dance and *kulama* song, but not about the Queen. He had visited Sydney and seen Luna Park! Nobody could transmit the thrills of the Big Dipper like that wonderful Tiwi man as his eyes rolled, and he convulsed with laughter. He was a one—man fireworks show, rattling off bursts of his own emotions, and the reactions of the other dancers as they were introduced to this white man's madness.

I helped to organise a few athletics meetings in Darwin, and again Aboriginals were encouraged to compete. Previously they had been not disbarred, just simply not considered as participants.

On one of those days we had a javelin throwing event, and a Tiwi bloke named Bill Larrakeyah broke the Australian javelin record with his first ever throw of a javelin. It wasn't world—

shattering, for the Australian record was only about 60 metres and Bill threw about 64 metres, but I started on a campaign to convince the Director of Native Affairs, Reg McCaffery, that the department should sponsor Bill at the next Australian championships in Sydney. Bill spent a month with Rae and me in Darwin, to accustom him to living in a house, and then he went off to Sydney. He came third in the Australian championships, but threw only about 60 metres. It became a talking-point around Darwin that when Bill Larrakeyah returned from Sydney he had a present for Rae and me: a boomerang he bought at Kings Cross. We didn't follow up javelin throwing as a sport for potential Aboriginal champions, although the Tiwi were particularly suited to the sport, as they, unlike all other Aboriginal groups in the Territory, do not use a woomera to throw their spears. Rather, they throw their ironwood spears (*tungi*) javelin style. But the javelin was much different in terms of weight distribution, and the Tiwi and other Aboriginals had to abandon their old style if they wished to throw javelin effectively. There were, however, a great number of Arnhem Land blokes who, using a woomera, could throw a spear 50 metres further than today's world javelin record. In 1976 I was the organiser of the Australian Aboriginal and Torres Strait contingent that visited New Zealand for the South Pacific Festival. At the Rotorua rugby stadium an Aboriginal named Djaylama brought the house down when he grabbed a spear, hooked it into his woomera, danced 20 metres behind one set of goalposts, and threw the spear, which went over the first crossbar, the length of the rugby field, and over the other crossbar. When the crowd stopped clapping he threw another spear over the grandstand.

In the 1953 basketball season St Mary's came second, and in the 1953–4 football season we came third, a sign of things to come. Early in 1954 the Darwin Basketball Association acquired some land on the corner of Daly Street and the Esplanade, and we put down a concrete slab which became the new Darwin Stadium. We ran a series of hugely successful exhibition games, with The Vic hotel team pitted against the Workers Club. The Vic teams were usually successful, and we had some monumental parties at Quong's Bakery after each game. I and all the other Darwin players were getting great benefit from Bluey Gasiunas, still playing for St Mary's despite the bishop's reservations. It was a big thrill for me when St Mary's won the basketball premiership for the 1954 season, with me as captain. There were 2000 people at the Grand Final, when St Mary's played Urgers. It was the first time I had ever seen Gasiunas play sober, and he turned it on. He scored 30 points and was absolutely unstoppable. After the game that night Gasiunas, Billy Roe and I were three St Mary's players chosen to represent the Northern Territory in the Australian championships in Brisbane that same year.

Welly Chin (The Irish Chinaman), Joey Sarib, Ron Bridgett and I were given the seemingly impossible task of raising £1,500 to send the team away. I guess it would be like raising $50,000 today. We decided that the only way to do it was via pai kew, so we went to our mate Greg Ryall, the Station Sergeant of Police, Darwin, and asked him if the coppers would 'turn a blind eye' if we ran some picnics at Rapid Creek beach. Greg gave us the nod, so we spread the word around Darwin that we would run five Sunday picnics where we would supply free beer and tucker for anybody who turned up, and guaranteed that the game would not be raided.

Not unexpectedly, hundreds took up our offer. We had trucks running non-stop, bringing endless supplies of beer, lolly water, ice, chickens, steak, sausages, salads and bread. It was all absolutely free, so we were taking a considerable risk, spending hundreds of pounds each day on food and drinks, but we raised the £1,500 easily, just by charging one shilling *tong* (5 per cent commission) on each pound won at the tables. As well as pai kew we had crown and anchor, heads and tails dice, and two-up, but the big money was on the pai kew table. The big gamblers, Jackie Byrnes, Paul Radomi, Doug James, Scotia McGowan, Charlie On, Mick Paspalis, Nick Paspaley, Chin Mook Sang, Chin Sam, Tiger Lyons, Leo Fortiades and Lester Quong used to arrive at the picnics with gladstone bags full of ten pound notes.

Resplendent in our green and gold uniforms, we went to Brisbane as the first-ever Northern Territory (Darwin actually, as my mates from places like Alice Springs are quick to remind me) representative team. Our team consisted of Joe Sarib (captain), Ray Yee, Don Bonson, Johnny Mayo, Terry Lewfatt, Ted Egan, Billy Roe, Rim (Bluey) Gasiunas, Jacko Angeles, Phil McLaughlin, George Sarib and Cedric Chin. The Irish Chinaman was our manager, Albert Chan our coach, and they did a fine job. We won only one game, beating Tasmania, but we almost beat Queensland, and we were all pleased with our performance. Victoria and South Australia were in a class of their own, and only Gasiunas of the NT team rated comparison with their players. But Johnny Mayo, Don Bonson and Cedric Chin came back immensely improved as a result of the interstate competition.

A highlight of 1954 was the birth of Greg Egan, on 1 October, and what a delightful bloke he was on arrival, and is to this day. Rae and I were allocated a fairly awful, white-ant ridden flat on the corner of Peel Street and the Esplanade, one of four of what were called 'Seaspray Flats', and we lived there for the next couple of years.

It was obvious at the start of the 1954–5 season that St Mary's would be a considerable power in Darwin football. We had overcome our problems about playing in the rain: we'd become the best 'wet weather' footballers. Gone were the days when Aboriginal footballers folded under pressure: players like Urban Tipiloura had the crowds gasping as he knocked down anybody between him and the ball. In my opinion, no team ever fielded in Darwin, or Australia for that matter, could name five better players than our stars of that year, Raphael Apuatimi, Bill Roe, Edmund Johnson, Dermott Tipungwuti and Saturninus Kantilla: they were champions. We had done the sums and we had our best Tiwi footballers available for the latter half of the season, January to March. So, after comfortably easing ourselves into the Grand Final against Buffaloes, we proceeded to win the premiership by five goals. Our supporters had backed us for big money to win the premiership, which was never in doubt. Best on the ground was our Nichols Medallist (NTFL Best and Fairest) Bill Roe. Later in 1955 I accompanied Bill to Perth, where he began an illustrious career with East Perth, the highlight being his best-on-the ground in their Grand Final win of 1956. That's how good our players of those days were. Raphael Apuatimi used to regularly thrash players who came to Darwin from the south with big reputations. One of these was a bloke named Don Glass, a champion forward from South Fremantle. Raphael absolutely trounced Glass each time they were opposed, but Don had kicked 100 goals for South Fremantle the year before he came to Darwin, and went back there from Darwin and kicked 100 goals in his first season. We used to call Raphael 'Uncle' for he was always saying that he was too old. 'You should have seen me when I was a young bloke. Then I'm proper champion.' What a man. And modesty itself. His son, Luke Apuatimi would also be a champion for St Mary's in later years. On the day of our first premiership a bloke named Johnny O'Callaghan, a good footballer who played for Waratahs, came to congratulate me. He said: 'I don't know what you've started here, Ted, but it all looks a bit awesome to me.' How right he would be proved.

Not many football teams have celebrated victory with soft drink, but St Mary's did that night in March 1955. As our Aboriginal players were not allowed, by law, to drink alcohol, we all returned to the Palais and sat down to a meal of curry and rice, washed down by Mandarin Crush, Cherry Cheer and other soft drinks supplied by Albert Fong, one of our patrons. After we had taken the Tiwi players back to the Army and the RAAF bases, where they lived, I took our large body of supporters, who were allowed to drink, firstly to Dot and Mick Mellifont's place where we drank all the grog we could lay our hands on. Then, at 2 am, we bought two cases of beer at Pancho's sly grog joint in Daly Street and went to the Buffaloes 'wake' at the old Steam Laundry in McMinn Street. There, in true Darwin spirit, we were welcomed as victors and we in turn commiserated with the losers, who were — we assured ourselves as we tearfully sang *'Tanjin Pera'*, 'Old TI' and 'Shuffle Off You Buffaloes' — our very good mates. Eight hours earlier, we'd have slaughtered one another, given the chance.

Our first premiership was immortalised in a *kulama* song by an old Tiwi bloke named Ali Uraputway. He did it in the format of the *ABC Radio News*. In those days the local ABC station was 5DR, and a well-known newsreader was Kevin Chapman.

> Port Darwin Port Darwin 5DR
> *Aungwara news ingani*
> Here is today's news
> Read by Kevin Chapman
> *Parlingari arnungka tunuwui*
> *Pootball play Pordawinup*
> A long time ago none of our people
> Played football in Darwin
> *Waiya nguwa ingardi kukunari ingani*
> *Taikwapi tunuwui kukunari ingani*
> *Ngeningatingauila kukunari ingani*
> But now there are plenty of us playing
> A big mob of us is playing today
> We are all there, all of us, playing today
> *Garden Oval ingani St Mary wangunuwara*
> *Buffalo yetti pudi* [five: literally, one hand] *goal*
> Today St Mary's beat the Buffaloes by five goals
> *Raphael Apuatimi ngara maratingali nganingati Superman*
> Raphael Apuatimi he can fly like a Superman
> *Ted Egan ngara angeraya taikwapi*
> *Maratingali! Kalikali muruka! Wamuta-ini! Anawunau!*
> *Kari pakateringa wamuta-ini pipwa! Pipwala! Puttim goal!*
> Ted Egan told all the players
> Fly high! Run fast! Mark the ball! Kick it!
> If it rains mark the ball on your chest! On the chest! Kick goals!
> *Joe Saturninus ingardi bumbuni keringara goal anawunau*
> Joe Saturninus is too good, he kicked six goals
> *St Mary kamwari! Kriu! Yiruka! Purim!*
> St Mary's are just too good! Straight up! They did it!
> *Ngara pangkina yiloti*
> They'll be on top forever
> *Tapinamini nguwa taikwapi kerawala! Paupau Yoi yoi mangkarana!*
> Tonight all of us will sing! Clap the buttocks! Dance hard!

The Tiwi clap two ways: normal clapping, both hands together; or slapping their buttocks, *paupau*. Talk about sound echoing sense. Bill Armbrust, well-known Darwin poet, wrote this piece for the *Northern Standard* in 1955:

It was back in 'Fifty Two'
When the game was just a cub
They formed an institution
Called St Mary's Football Club

They were mostly wiry natives
From the Bathurst Island side
The fleetest–footed runners
Ever wrapped in hide

Perhaps they learned their tactics
Chasing possums in the scrub
But they're brilliant are the members
Of St Mary's Football Club.

They played the final Saturday
As everybody knows
So we went to see St Mary's
Play the mighty Buffaloes

Though the Buffs showed little science
They'd a mighty lot of dash
And were all over St Mary's
Like a Darwin sandfly rash

That was for the first half only
Then the Saints began to go
Led by Joe Saturninus
And a goal from Billy Roe

Then a brilliant mark by Egan
Made the Buffs look rather ill
You'd have thought that old Jack Sweeny
Was there, and coaching still.

Well, anyway, the game was good
From at least my point of view

St Mary Kamwari

For I had a tummy full of beer
And I'd backed St Mary's too.

My advice to all you other teams
Who hope to win next year
Is to train on yams and bandicoots
And stay away from beer

It's good to look back with pride on those days in the early 1950s. St Mary's has since become one of the most famous football clubs in Australia. They have won 22 premierships since inception, and from 1993 to 1997 won more than 50 games straight, an Australian record for a senior football team. St Mary's won 11 premierships in 13 years under coach John Taylor. They have provided many players to interstate clubs, the best of these being Maurice, Sibby and Manny Rioli, Michael Long, Bill Roe, David Kantilla, Benny Vigona, Ronny Burns, Scott Chisholm and Basil Campbell. But I'm always fascinated to contemplate how other players would have fared if given the same chance. Players like Stanislaus Mungatopi, Raphael Apuatimi, Dermott Tipungwuti, Edmund Johnson, Walter Kerinaua, Hyacinth Tungutalum, Terry Joseph and Brian Long did not have the same opportunities to show their class, but they were every bit as good as the players who did go interstate.

I had an interesting experience late in 1955. We had just signed up Neil Davies, selected in the all-Australian team after the interstate Aussie Rules Carnival of 1954, to play football for St Mary's, and we had a barbecue one night on the Fannie Bay Beach, just below the cliffs in front of Fannie Bay Gaol. During the fairly boisterous night somebody recalled that a former mate of ours, whose nickname was Moose Jaw, was languishing in the cells, and would probably love a cold beer. It was agreed that Neil and I should take him one. Wearing only shorts, and both bare-footed, we each grabbed a cold long-necked bottle of beer, and headed for the gaol. It was disarmingly easy. Through a wire fence, over a galvanised iron fence, up into the empty guard's tower, and drop to the ground inside the gaol! But we had no idea what to do next or where Moose Jaw might be found, so we just looked at one another stupidly holding our bottles of beer. Suddenly a guard appeared, with a spotlight and shone it on us. I don't know who got the bigger fright. The guard left the light and ran inside.

'I'm off,' I said to Neil.

'I'm with you,' he replied and we ran to retrace our tracks .

As we dashed a shot rang out. We increased our speed. Suddenly, I was flat on my back. A single strand of barbed wire, about neck height, had ripped open my chin and knocked me near senseless. I quickly got to my feet, and actually beat Neil, who was mighty fast, back to the barbecue. We swore everybody there to secrecy, and quietly resumed the barbecue. I didn't feel any pain from the lacerated chin until the next day, and still have a scar.

The incident made headlines in the *Northern Territory News* and there were calls for an official inquiry into the general question of security at the gaol. Marie, Rae's sister, was working for the Prisons Branch, and had to keep a very straight face on our behalf during the next few days. She'd been at the barbecue. But the strangest thing about the whole affair is that, over the years, I have listened to at least ten different blokes, at different parties, tell of the night when they broke into the Fannie Bay Gaol with Ted Egan. It gets a bit disconcerting when they turn to me and say, 'Isn't that right, Ted?' I usually smile conspiratorially, and content myself with saying, 'Those were the days.'

5
Who's Protecting Who?

The canoe wobbled precariously as Harry turned to me, and whispered, '*Maradila*. Big one.' I sat immediately behind him, trembling with fear and excitement. I grabbed the .303 rifle hard, to stop my hand from shaking too much, and looked along the white pencil of light created by the spotlight. A bright red spot, 100 metres away, in the mangroves. So this was how it happened.

I had no idea what I was supposed to do, if anything, for nobody had given any instructions. There were three of us in the frail wooden dugout canoe, Jacky Nabulaya paddling expertly at the stern, shaking every drop of water from his paddle as he silently steered us down the Liverpool River, me sitting in the middle as useless as tits on a bull, and standing in the bow Harry Mulumbuk, totally relaxed. With a secure push he fitted the harpoon head into the shaft. He handed me the spotlight, stood — how in the hell can he have such balance? — on the narrow sides of the wobbly dugout canoe, and indicated that I should shine the light through his legs to keep the red spot in sight. It was no easy task, given my shaking hands, and the fact that I was still trying to clutch the rifle, and at the same time place between my feet the butcher's knife I had been told that day to make 'properly sharp'.

Closer. Not a sound, except the the roar of my breathing, and the tide gently curbing the canoe's progress as we slid through the darkness. The absolute darkness, the black velvet darkness, stabbed by the searing shaft of light shimmering on the water and still pinpointing the now brilliant red spot. Fifteen metres. Ten. And then I saw it. Christ! Did he say a big one? No sooner did the thought register than Harry threw the harpoon. *Smack!* It hit the big crocodile in the neck, the steel head came out of the shaft, embedded in the soft yellow skin, and it was on. The croc took off, and so did we, in opposite directions. Harry jumped down into the canoe, and began playing out the rope. Nabulaya paddled feverishly, backwards, trying to keep the rope in front of the canoe. I was frantically waving the spotlight here, there, anywhere, with no idea what was about to happen. Shine the light. 'Torchim,' shouted Harry. Up into the mangrove trees, forward, backward, up, down. Absolutely petrified. Three inches of freeboard. Oh my God. Where did it go?

'Give me that,' Harry commanded. I passed him the light. He held it in one hand, and at the same time began to gently take up the slack of the harpoon rope. Nabulaya paddled backwards, backwards, lots of splashing now. No need for quiet. The wet rope began to curl into the canoe. Hand over hand, Harry pulled in the slack, gently, firmly, evenly, no sharp tugs. And then I saw it, coming to the surface, the harpoon still imbedded. The huge crocodile struggled, but only slightly, probably totally confused at its own lack of progress and the inhibiting pain in the neck. Harry gently played it alongside the canoe. It's longer than us!

'Orright, you twofella argument now,' Harry said to me.

I looked bewildered.

'Killim. Rifle.' His eyes rolled. Another dumb white man, he was probably thinking. Then he began to laugh, as only Mulumbuk could laugh, a husky, evocative rumble that was the trademark of a man whose addiction to tobacco-smoking was a legend in Arnhem Land. He had spotted my hands, the rifle tensely clutched in my left, the butcher's knife in my right.

'You want to jump out? Killim like a Tarzan?' Harry asked, and Nabulaya roared with laughter.

I got a bit miffed, dropped the knife, rammed a bullet up the spout of the .303 and prepared to demonstrate what a crack shot I was, a good spit away from a still target, the croc's head the size of a dinner plate. It was all too brutal, too easy. *Bang!* The blood-stained water. Then the two veteran Aboriginal hunters, masters in the bush, did what blackfellows do so easily. They passed all credit to me.

'Oh, good shot.' This from Mulumbuk.

'You gottim, boss. Too smart,' said Nabulaya. He knew most white men liked to be called 'boss'.

For days afterwards, as they recounted the story time after time for anyone who wanted to hear it — and everybody did — they made me look more and more intrepid, and played down their own part. I began to believe it myself. 'Oh, boss him bin spottim that biggest *maradila*. Him bin torch him, torch him, and then him bin killim, pinish, one shot, right in the head. Too smart altogether we boss.' Harry, who had travelled throughout the Top End, and could speak a smattering of all the languages, would then talk to me in Tiwi, a phrase or two that he knew I understood. When I responded fluently he would say, 'Him very smart man this Ted Egan. Him talk just like blackfeller. Him savvy everything.' The others would seem impressed and then Harry would say, disarmingly, 'You got any *ngarali,* boss?' The only time he ever called me 'boss' was when tobacco was needed. What a con artist. But what a beaut bloke. Harry was what most Australians idealise as the 'typical Aussie'. Most white Australians don't realise how much we have picked up from the locals in terms of 'she'll be right' attitudes, banana-skin humour, and a preparedness to put up with annoying foibles in others. All of this is governed by an intrinsic laziness, or, if you want to dress it up in fancy language, a pragmatism derived from the knowledge that we are living in a harsh, uncompromising but strangely beautiful continent, a land which must always be our mother rather than our mistress. A land to be loved, not tamed.

There had been talk since the 1930s of the need to establish a trading station in the middle of the Arnhem Land coast line, somewhere near the big tidal rivers, the Liverpool and the Blyth. The decision was precipitated by the arrival in Darwin one day in 1951 of a big group of naked blackfellows who set up camp on the outskirts of town. They came from central Arnhem Land, from a region that had no contact with the various mission stations already established by the Methodist and Anglican churches. They had resisted efforts to relocate them at Anglican Oenpelli on the west, and Methodist Milingimbi in the Crocodile Islands to the east. They said they thought Darwin might be better, as they did not want to become Christians. 'Him no good, that mission station. Too much one man, one wife business, too many Jesus altogether.'

My boss, Ted Evans and I were sent in 1955 to the Liverpool River to check out illegal landing of Japanese crews who manned the Australian-owned pearling luggers operating out of Darwin. The Japanese had been given permission to call at the various mission stations to get water and stores, for it was felt that they would be 'under control' at those places. They had been specifically instructed not to land anywhere else. For decades there had been unhealthy contacts between lugger crews and local Aboriginals, with all sorts of sordid exploitation relating to sexual access to women. We had been told that it was common for Japanese, during the 1955 pearling season, to land at Entrance Island, in the mouth of the Liverpool River, that there was a supply of drums of fuel on the beach, and that the Japanese used to get fresh water at a natural spring called Maningrida on the mainland at the mouth of the Liverpool. Ted and I went out with HMAS *Emu* to the Liverpool River, were dropped on the beach at Entrance Island, where, sure enough, there were twenty drums of diesoline. The *Emu* sailed off to do some survey work. The Royal Australian Navy was still using the original charts of Matthew Flinders, 150 years after the navigator charted the coastline.

A few local Aboriginals spotted us on the beach from the mainland, and came across to the island by canoe. We spent an idyllic week with them, catching fish, swimming, yarning and waiting for the Japanese. Sure enough, in they came, three luggers, cockiness itself, with the blackfellows greeting them individually 'Gooday Aki. Gooday Kenji.' The Japanese skipper was Aki Kumamoto, a brazen bastard. His arrogance was appalling, given that it was only ten years since the war, and Darwin harbour was still bristling with the wrecks of ships sunk during the 1942 Japanese bombing. 'This first time we come this place,' said Kumamotu, and tried to ply us with gifts of a couple of bottles of beer, baroque pearls, and tinned peaches. Ted Evans was aloof officialdom itself as he proceeded to read his version of the Riot Act to them. Ted said, imperiously, but with a 'don't you dare laugh' wink at me first, 'I hereby order you to sail directly to Darwin where charges will be laid against you in Her Majesty's Court.' So there.

As a result of our successful prosecution of those Japanese and their Darwin shipowner bosses in 1955, the decision was taken in 1957 to set up a 'trading post' at Maningrida. Again, very New Guinea. I had been promoted to Patrol Officer, following my successful completion of the Patrol Officer's Course at the Australian School of Pacific Administration at Mosman, Sydney, in 1956. I was instructed to travel by sea with three other white people to set up the post. I would stay in the region for a few months, do a census (of course) of the region, and leave my three white companions to establish and run the small but important station in central Arnhem Land for quite a few hundred Aboriginal people.

We sailed from Darwin in May 1957 on Pete Pedersen's boat *Temora*. My companions were Dave and Ingrid Drysdale, a middle-aged couple with a lot of experience in the north — they had once been missionaries — and a young fellow, about my age, named Trevor Milikins. Trevor was a great bloke, a good bushman who'd have a go at anything. He was a ton of laughs with blackfellows, and he had a lot of contact, from Darwin, with the Arnhem Land Aboriginals. We took from Darwin about twenty blokes very happy to get a free trip home, and they promised to be the workforce in setting up the station.

I had a little dinghy, and at high tide we unloaded the supplies on the beach, set up two tents, one for the Drysdales and one for Trevor and me, and so Maningrida, now a township, started. The *Temora* sailed away, and we were totally isolated. Yet I have never felt so secure. We had adequate white man tucker, and the services of some very smart people to augment our food supplies through their knowledge of the coast and the local waters and bushland.

We worked hard, but it was immense fun. Talk about good

to be alive. And I was being paid! Work, did they call it? Dave Drysdale was a great enthusiast, to the point where Ingrid, Trevor and I had to institute a rule whereby Dave was not allowed to talk until 10 am each day, for he used to drive us mad with his plans. He was a tireless worker nonetheless, and he quickly had a garden and a bakehouse going. He was an excellent baker. Ingrid Drysdale was an absolute saint. I never once heard her complain about anyone, or anything. She was not a trained nurse, but was experienced at nursing and first aid, and quickly won the trust of the women, children, and old people who were thrilled to receive medical treatment for their various ailments and infirmities.

I quickly did a few trips into the bush — sorry, I 'proceeded on patrol' 20 to 30 miles in every direction — and met up with many small groups of Aboriginals. A few of them either knew me or my patrol assistant, Tommy Fry, and there was general enthusiasm at the news that the station had started at Maningrida. I said it was imperative that they stay in their country, rather than come to live at Maningrida, for we did not want to start up the equivalent of a mission station. Missionaries liked to have all the Aboriginals living on the station so that they could (hopefully) become Christians.

I put across the government policy, as I understood it. 'We wantim youfella stay long bush. Suppose you gottim anything sell, alligator skin, mat, basket, bark painting, anything, alright you bringim there long Maningrida. Sellim. Then you can buyim something, anything, tin-a-meat, calico, tobacco, trouser shirt, dress. But no more camp there. More better camp here, roan place. This one you country.' Alas, only a couple of years later, I was appalled when told that 'the permanent population' of Maningrida was over 1000. But that's another story.

On the second morning there was a big 'Yackai' from the Aboriginals camped with us. A young bloke we called Toby, ran to Trevor and me.

'Naked blackfellers! Look!'

Along the beach were about twenty men, totally naked, carrying their spears, but standing, as is the custom, in the open where they could be seen, just out of spear range. Johnny

Naliba, a local Gunavidji leader, said: 'They're bush blackfellers from Mamadba side. I'll tellim come look you.' He waved, talked to them on the fingers, and they slowly walked in to our camp. There was a lot of talk, and everybody was amicable. Johnny said to me: 'They'll stay here couple of days and then they want you to look their country'. 'Fine,' I replied.

Ingrid Drysdale was modesty itself, and she quietly got a roll of red calico, our principal trade item. She tore off one metre square lengths of the material, and handed the pieces of cloth to Johnny, indicating that the naked blokes might like to make *nargas,* or 'cockrags' as we called them, to cover the crown jewels. The calico was handed around to their great delight. As one, they tied the red material around their heads! Ingrid's face was the same colour as their new sweatbands.

In the bush camps I located quite a few people suffering from leprosy. Poor things, they used to try to run away when they saw me coming. 'Policeman! Policeman!' they shouted, for they knew that in the past any lepers located were captured and taken to Channel Island, never to return to their country. We sought to allay their pathetic fears, and told them that we would bring 'the Missus' out to have a look at them, and we would probably start a little 'bush hospital' for them at Maningrida: they could get some treatment but still remain with their people. Eventually, Ingrid Drysdale did set up a little hospital at what came to be called 'Hospital Beach' at Maningrida, and she and her offsider 'Doctor Jimmy' spent countless hours dressing the wounds of the lepers, making them as comfortable as possible. Nowadays, the hospital at Maningrida is called the Ingrid Drysdale Hospital, and let's hope that any activists who criticise the exploitative role of white people in Aboriginal affairs are reminded to contemplate the selfless years of unstinting service of people like the Drysdales.

I struck up a good relationship with the leaders of the various clans in the Liverpool-Blyth River area. The principal languages were Gunavidji, Nakara and Burera. The immediate Maningrida area was Gunavidji country. The country to the east, covering the vast swampy plains called Anamayera, belonged to the Nakara, and the different Burera groups were located further east, on both sides of the Blyth River, up to about Cape Stewart. My prime contacts were with Johnny Naliba and Jockey Bundubundu, two brothers who became spokesmen for the Gunavidji, Jacky Nabulaya for the Nakara, and Harry Mulumbuk and Barney Jajapun for the Burera. They weren't anything like chiefs, but they spoke with considerable authority for their people, and they were all supportive of our new station.

I travelled around the region extensively. Arnhem Land is tough country. Dry inhospitable ranges of ragged hills inland, endless swamps, full of leeches and crocodiles, run down to the coast. The beaches are beautiful but featureless, with casuarina trees here and there to provide minimal shade. No cliffs, no caves, totally exposed to the unremitting winds that threw sand into our food and eyes. A few small creeks run down to the coast, but thay get very brackish near the sea. Inland, there are also great dry expanses, where the only fresh water is in rancid soaks. I often had to pull away a dead wallaby before getting an unpalatable drink from a baler shell. Close your eyes and think it's Foster's.

We sought to encourage men in the different places to hunt crocodiles, for there was excellent money to be made from the sale of skins. The going price was 8 shillings an inch, measured at the widest part of the belly of the skin. After my first experience with Mulumbuk and Nabulaya, I became quite proficient, and soon Harry was happy to be No. 2 and I was in the bow doing the harpooning and shooting. That way he could smoke in comfort. Most times we didn't use a bullet but killed the crocodile with an axe. I don't feel all that good about the hunting we did in those days, but it was a commercial exercise, and it was something the Aboriginals had always done, as they ate crocodile meat. I noted, though, that they didn't eat it if there was any possibility of getting other meat, but once, for a week on the Blyth River, we only had crocodile meat to eat. Nowadays, I laugh when I see crocodile served as gourmet tucker in restaurants. I find it tasteless and boring, as I did then, when I had to live on it.

Our harpoon heads were simple, made from three 3-inch nails, bound together with string, spliced into the end of a long rope — we used 'blackfellow rope' made from bark — and fitted into the hollowed end of a long wooden spear shaft. When the harpoon struck the target the stick fell away, and was recovered later. When we skinned the crocs each day we salted the hides and offered the meat to anybody who wanted it. I soon had about ten teams organised, and when I went back to Darwin a few months later I took thousands of pounds worth of skins, sold them, and sent out specific orders of food, tobacco and clothing to the shooters and their families. It all worked very well, very easily, for there were plenty of crocs, and no desire on the part of the hunters to eliminate them.

We had some great times together, croc hunting. I always preferred to be with Mulumbuk, as he was a consummate bushman, and one could learn something from him every five minutes. There were a few tricky experiences, a laugh in retrospect, but not so funny when they happened. One night we were travelling along a creek with very steep muddy banks. We were shining the torch as we went along and suddenly, 10 metres above us, sitting on the mudflat, was a good sized croc, over 3 metres. No need to harpoon it. I lined up the spotlight over the rifle's sights and shot the croc through the head. A convulsive twitch, and it was dead.

'I'll get it,' I said. I grabbed a rope, and hopped out of the canoe, up to the armpits in oozy, black mud. Absolutely immobile. I began to struggle to get free, and cursed myself for being so stupid as to jump. If I had just eased myself onto the mud and sort of skated over it, I'd have been all right. No, too impulsive. But a couple of minutes, I'll be OK. I'll just . . .

The croc got up, very undead, and instinctively headed for the safety of the water. Straight towards me. I turned to my companions, reliant on their bushcraft, their hunting skills in a crisis.

'Get the bastard,' I roared. Who was the 'Protector of Aboriginals' now?

Mulumbuk was standing in the bow of the canoe, taking this great opportunity to have a piss. Frank Maylgura, Kapula as we called him, was scratching his balls in the stern.

'Kapula,' I shouted.

I'll never forget the next five seconds. Frank, also known as Left Hand for obvious reasons, reached into the canoe, grabbed a spear, and in the same motion let it fly, in the darkness, straight at the croc. The spear hit the croc, went through its neck and impaled it in the mud. Frank slid gently out of the canoe with an axe in his hand, and put the croc out of its misery with one whack.

'Finish now,' he said quietly. Harry tried to contain his infectious chuckle, but it exploded into an echoing guffaw. Ah, the crazy *balanda*.

On another night we were in Gajarama Creek. We had decided to call it a night. We already had four crocs, all pulled into the canoe with us, so we had a thumb's length of freeboard as we paddled out of the creek on the outgoing tide. We used to go up the creek with the swirling powerful tide, and come back with it when it turned. Otherwise paddling was impossible. And illogical. Blackfellows only do things the right way. The sensible way. There, right in the middle water was a huge croc, perhaps 5 metres long. What do you do? It's about thirty quids' worth of skin, half a year's wages for our hunters. In the middle water they are easy to harpoon. Straight up to it. Clunk! The harpoon is in. All I have to do is play it on the rope and then shoot it. Easy. But it was a huge, powerful beast, and it headed straight for the security of the mangroves on the bank. It was new moon, 2 am, and we only had a small torch as our spotlight. The croc went down among the labyrinth of mangrove roots and swam around frantically. There I was, pulling on the rope, and a mangrove tree was shaking to tell us that the rope was entwined around its submerged roots. And somewhere else, swimming fairly freely on the other end of the rope, was a 5 metre croc. Stalemate.

'I'll cut the rope,' I said. I was now quite experienced, and knew we had no show of freeing the rope and getting the croc.

'No. I'll fixim,' says Mulumbuk. He grabbed the butcher's knife, stuck it between his teeth, stood up, and slipped over the side of the canoe. He disappeared under the water before I could do anything other than gasp with shock. I shone the torch around in the darkness. The rope was still taut, the mangrove tree was still shaking. Down below, there was a rope entwined around the mangrove roots. Somewhere else down there, on the business end of the harpoon rope, was a very angry crocodile, and a bloke named Mulumbuk, whose obvious plan was to swim to the mangrove tree, cut the root of the tree, and free the rope. But where was he? Where was the croc? I shone the light on the tree, but suddenly there was a thump behind me. Bang! Against the side of the canoe. I almost died of fright. It's the croc! No, it's not. It's Mulumbuk!

'I forgot my tobacco,' he said.

He handed me his tobacco tin, took a deep breath and dived under the water again. In ten more seconds he surfaced again. A grin. The tree stopped shaking. He'd cut the root. The croc was swimming, totally free again, the harpoon still in its neck.

'I gottim,' said Mulumbuk. He hopped back into the canoe. We slowly pulled the croc to the surface, shot it and towed it to a place we called The Landing, a clearance in the mangroves where we used to camp. We hauled the five crocs on to the beach, lit a big fire to confuse the mosquitoes, and prepared to camp for the night. We would skin the crocs at daylight.

'*Ngarali, lei.* You got my tobacco?' Harry asked me.

'Oh, yeah.' I reached into my pocket and gave him the tin. He opened it. The tin contained three cigarette butts, just enough tobacco for one smoke of his beloved long pipe, the Macassan *larua*. He unpicked the butts, rolled the tobacco in the palm of his hand, stuffed it in his pipe, picked up a coal from the fire, and dropped it on top of the tobacco to light it. His cheeks almost clashed as he sucked a long draw of the pipe, then swallowed the smoke as was the fashion. After a long pause, he let go a monumental blast of smoke. On and on he blew, like a factory chimney stack.

'Good one, *ngarali,* ' he said. 'Strong tobacco. Make me strong.' Who was I to disagree?

Dave, Trevor and Ingrid set up a functional station at Maningrida. We had taken a radio from Darwin but it never worked, so I decided to walk to Milingimbi Mission, about 150 kilometres east of Maningrida, to send a message that when the

Temora came out next we needed a new radio. It was an intriguing walk, Tommy Fry, Jacky Nabulaya and me, along the coastline, swimming across tidal rivers at the estuaries. That *was* hairy, for there were plenty of crocs. To shorten the swim we waited for the lowest tide. So often people think blackfellows are just sitting around. It's often for a good reason. I noticed that the blackfellows always threw one of their dogs into the water and made it swim across in the lead. You clever feller properly, I thought to myself. On the mainland opposite Milingimbi Island we met up with a group who offered to lend us their canoe to travel over to the island. We sailed 20 kilometres using my canvas swag campsheet as a sail, and I was intrigued at how steady the canoes were under sail, compared to the precarious wobbling that occurred when inept people like me propelled them with paddles.

Milingimbi was set up by the Methodist missionaries in the 1920s in the Crocodile Islands group, to conform to their policy that, as they were called Methodist *Overseas* Missions, they should not be on the mainland. All a bit silly, when you think about it, but they ran quite good stations, and, in my opinion, were the best missionaries in the north, for they did not interfere too much with traditional custom. They stressed to their staff the need to learn local languages, and not to be in too big a hurry to impose Christianity. Reverend Edgar Wells made me very welcome at Milingimbi, and I spent a pleasant week meeting local people, discussing various issues with blacks and whites, and coaching the local football team. I met up with Bungawuy, who had led the Arnhem Land group to meet the Queen, and was introduced to a very impressive bloke named Baraltja. He had been an invaluable ally to the great linguist Beulah Lowe in her work of translating the Bible into Gupapuyngu, which is the *lingua franca* of Arnhem Land. I had heard so much about Beulah Lowe and was thrilled to meet her, with Baraltja. Baraltja and I got on famously, and we exchanged letters for years thereafter. His first letter to me was funny. He was a very fluent speaker and writer of his own language, Gupapuyngu, several other Arnhem Land languages, and

English. He obviously wanted to do a good job on his first letter, and must have asked somebody what 'Ted' was short for. I got this letter that started, 'Dear Hardwood . . . '

On the walk back to Maningrida, I stayed for two weeks with Mulumbuk at a place called Gaupangu, on the western side of the Blyth River, right at the mouth. We went out after crocs most nights, and during the day we sat around and talked about anything at all really. Harry Mulumbuk had been with the army in Darwin during the war, so he knew a lot about the outside world, and offered shrewd opinions and observations. It was disarming talking to Harry, for he was in the process of decorating his father's skeleton before its final placement in the log coffin. The Burera bury their dead, then exhume the skeleton to check all the various pieces as they reassemble it to make sure no bones are missing. That might spell mischief or magic afoot. Harry had to sing various songs as he painted intricate designs on his father's skull and bones. At the same time we might be talking about some aspect of the war, or I'd be describing the big cities to him, or he'd be telling me of various fights and skirmishes between coastal Aboriginals and various visitors, Macassans, Malays, Japanese. Scientists disagree about how long visitors have sailed along the Arnhem Land coast, but the tamarind trees at Milingimbi, obviously deliberately introduced — for they are systematically planted — have been verified as over 500 years old. There are tamarind trees all along the coastline, a sure sign of Macassan trading camps set up when those intrepid sailors from Sulawesi came in their *prahus* to spend The Wet season getting trepang, pearls and sandalwood before going back home on the south-easterlies of The Dry.

One day Harry finished painting and singing, popped all the bones into the beautifully decorated log coffin, and said: 'Now we can forget that old bugger.' That night they had the final *bunggul* for the dead man, and some other relatives took the coffin away. I was told that they would do a tour whereby everybody could pay their respects. It went without saying that the father of Harry Mulumbuk must have been one helluva bloke.

I eventually travelled back to Darwin on HMAS

Cootamundra, which was on patrol covering the activities of the pearling fleet. Rae was just about due to have our second child. It was unfair on women in situations like that, where the blokes had fascinating jobs that took them away for long periods into the bush, while the women had to look after the home and kids in town. The department promised that soon I would be given bush postings where the family could accompany me.

That didn't happen for a couple of months, for shortly after the birth of Margaret Egan, a fat, happy, healthy girl who then and always evoked my absolute love and affection, I was sent on my own to the Katherine region for two months, to relieve a bloke named Allan Pitts as Acting Superintendent of Beswick Creek, these days called Barunga. That was fairly humdrum stuff, for it was made patently clear that I was to make no changes to what was a very smoothly-run place, so I didn't. Aboriginals don't like change: in fact they have an inbuilt resistance to it, the result of countless centuries where they developed a lifestyle compatible with this harsh land of ours, rather than seek to 'take on' the country, as those who demand 'progress' would have us do.

As I had free time I accepted an invitation to visit Mainoru cattle station, owned by the legendary Jack McKay, and his sister, Mrs Dodd, who ran a wonderful school at the station. They knew that I was an old mate of their brother Sandy, one of the Razzle Gang at Belsen.

On the way to Mainoru I met up with the famous Tiny Swanson, who was camped on the Flying Fox Creek, doing a bit of prospecting. I had heard all the stories about Tiny, who was reputed to be the strongest man in the Northern Territory. I had my doubts about that, for I had seen Bert Pierssene in action. The usual claim to strength was and is to this day that so-and-so can lift a 44 gallon drum full of fuel single-handed. Certainly Bert Pierssene could load a 44 gallon drum from the ground onto a truck single-handed. And so could Tiny, who was happy to demonstrate. He was certainly the biggest man in the Territory, weighing in at 32 stone (200 plus kilograms). By contrast his little Aboriginal wife, Nelly would have weighed no more than 40 kilograms. Tiny was a quiet, simple, pleasant man who got on well with the Aboriginals and had spent most of his life in the district. Like Jack McKay himself Tiny had come to Maranboy, 80 kilometres south-east of Katherine, just after World War 1, when there was a gold and tin strike. I had a cup of tea and a yarn with Tiny and travelled on. I never met him again, and the last thing I heard of him was when he died in Darwin Hospital ten years later, having faded away to a mere 27 stone (170 kilograms). They had to lower his coffin into the grave with a crane.

Jack McKay was renowned as the drinker who used to measure bogs in the bush by the number of bottles of rum he drank in the process of digging his truck out. He spoke of spirited five bottlers, seven bottlers and one awful experience, a twenty-seven bottler, when he was bogged for a month, up to the truck's tray, at a black soil flat called Tandangal. Jack renamed the place Damn Tangle. 'Mind you,' he said to me, 'You won't find that turnout of mine in the *Guinness Book of Records*, because it was not a genuine twenty-seven bottler. You see, I left my shovel behind in the previous bog and in the Damn Tangle affair I had to use a frying pan to dig my way out.' A reasonable feat though, Jack. A reasonable feat.

I took young three-year-old Greg Egan to Mainoru. Jack had a pet cow, which used to hang around the homestead. She was a quiet old thing, so Jack placed Greg on the cow's back and said, 'Come on Gregory, I'll show you around the station.' He led the cow to Mrs Dodd's schoolroom. 'Say hello to Gregory Egan, children,' says Jack. 'Good morning, Gregory,' the Aboriginal kids chanted. 'And this is the dining room, Gregory,' says Jack as the tour continued. 'This is Mum's bedroom. Good morning mother, this is Gregory Egan.' Eighty–year–old Mrs McKay didn't turn a hair. When the tour ended, Jack lifted the wide-eyed three-year-old from the cow's back. 'Well, Gregory, you're the only boy that's ever ridden a cow through Mainoru.' Greg has never forgotten it.

Relationships between whites and blacks at Mainoru were down-to-earth, real, superb. No other way to describe it. Nobody was patronised. Everybody treated the house, its contents, its food supply as their own, and nobody abused the system. Mrs

Dodd was a wonderful teacher, as was her other brother Sandy. Sandy taught for many years at Top End schools, and many of today's Aboriginal leaders were students who benefitted from Sandy's skill. Mrs Dodd was featured in the wonderful documentary film *I, the Aboriginal,* which covered the life story of Phillip Roberts (Waipuldanya or Watjarr Watjarr to use his more correct names). Phillip was a dear mate of mine. He built up a considerable reputation as a health worker among his own people — Doctor Phillip they used to call him. He and I subsequently worked together for the Office of Aboriginal Affairs.

The Mainoru homestead was built overlooking a chain of crystal clear billabongs, and Jack McKay used to delight in catching a saratoga or a barramundi in these waterholes, and having a regular swim. He had lived among the blacks all his life, and was totally uninhibited with them. They used to swim naked. So did Jack. He had balls like Paroo mailbags, and his crown jewels were a constant subject of discussion among the Aboriginal women, who talked about such things with absolute candour. I had a laugh one day. There was this really old woman, about ninety I reckon. She was sitting under a tree.

'What's wrong with you, darling?' called Jack.

'Oh, I'm bery sick, old man. Bery sick,' she replied.

'Get out. Nothing wrong with you,' says Jack. 'All you need is a good fuck. I'll be down tonight'.

I thought the old lady would die laughing.

'Oh, you naughty boy, Jack. You naughty boy,' she giggled. He'd made her day.

6

The Great Loo Debates

Rae nudged me in the ribs. 'This bloke's lost,' she said.

Sure enough, Sid, the sheepish pilot, turned to me and asked, 'Would you recognise the Roper River if you saw it?'

'Not a chance,' I replied. 'Never been there. But it's got to be a big river. Why not fly a bit further east, and then we'll eventually hit the coast? We can follow that down to the islands at the mouth of the Macarthur, and then go back in to Borroloola. Have you got enough fuel?'

'I hope so,' said sad Sid.

'I bloody well hope so too,' retorted Rae.

I looked down on the featureless ragged expanse of Arnhem Land. We were about two hours out of Darwin, flying over what is called the 'escarpment country,' forbidding rocky gorges that stretch for hundreds of miles in every direction. Not a good place to crash, I mused. I suddenly began to panic. Not too bad for me to die, but Rae and my two beautiful kids. My God, what have I taken them into?

'Give me the map,' I snapped at Sid.

I had been posted to Borroloola, on the Macarthur River, in the Gulf region south-west of Darwin. There was a ration depot there and it was my role as resident Native Affairs Officer — don't titles give you that puffed-up feeling of importance? — to live in the manager's house, generally be an imposing presence, issue licences to employ Aboriginals, operate the Flying Doctor radio, report weather observations, distribute rations once a week to pensioners and (wait for it) 'pregnant and lactating women', run a cash store for other residents of the area (mostly Aboriginals, but occasionally some white customers), and generally maintain and be responsible for the government assets in the region. The wife of the Native Affairs man was expected (no pay of course) to provide medical care to anybody needing it, and do hundreds of other unexpected jobs that came up in such busy but isolated places in those days. It was November 1957 and Rae and I were travelling to our first bush posting together.

We flew out of Darwin with Sid in a De Havilland Rapide, a twin–engine biplane that had lots of patched, but nonetheless disconcerting holes in its canvas skin. How Sid ever got a pilot's licence beat me, but eventually, as Rae and I established where we were from the map, we saw what must be the little settlement of Borroloola, and landed. (It was in fact about five landings, but the strip was long enough to cater for Sid's bumpy drop from the heavens.) Greg Egan was three, Margaret a brand new baby having her first blissful ride in an aeroplane.

It was stinking hot, the 'suicide season', all prickly heat and humidity, just before the rains make the summer tolerable. Once it rains The Wet is the best time of the year in the Top End. Frogs start to sing, plants gulp in the welcome water and the countryside changes from burnt brown to emerald green. It hadn't started to rain yet, but it did the very next day. We would live in the old police house, built in the 1890s and, as it turned out, riddled with snakes of every description. The office, radio room and weather observatory were in the old police station, and the cells, complete with huge ringbolts in the floor, were the storehouse. There was a Sidney Williams Hut 'at ground' at Borroloola, and in the first couple of weeks I got some of the very skilled Aboriginal blokes at 'The Loo' to help me erect that — or rather, I helped them. Thereafter we had a 20 × 6 metre store building — very flash.

It was my first experience with 'station blacks', and it was to be a wonderful exposure to the white and black people involved in a feudal lifestyle that has gone forever. Most people who have had no experience in the bush would cheer that the 'exploitation' of Aboriginals on cattle stations is over. But it is one of the Territory paradoxes that many Aboriginals remember the 'station time' as a period when life had some meaning for them. I don't know how Aboriginals classified whites into categories in those days — it would be interesting to find out. But Territory whites classified Aboriginals as town blacks, mission blacks, station blacks and bush blacks. Or 'myalls' as bush blacks were often called if they still lived off the land as so many did in places like Arnhem Land. Station blacks were generally held by whites to be 'better' than the rest, in that they had been 'knocked into shape' which is an appropriate but awesome euphemism when you think how harshly Aboriginals who lived in country favoured by pastoralists had been treated in earlier days — shot, poisoned, belted into submission. Yet they in most cases got on well with the whites, learned many skills, and made an unacknowledged but magnificent contribution to the cattle industry of the north. They also managed to retain an astonishing sense of humour. Even when talking about monsters like the dreaded Wason Byers, a brute renowned as a flogger and shooter, who once whipped some Aboriginal women and made them sit on a scorching tin roof for days, they would have a chuckle and say, 'Oh goodness, he cheeky old bugger that Wason,' rather than dwell on his cruelty or seek to take it out on other whites.

Borroloola was 'good blackfellow country' with abundant water, bush tucker and plenty of seasonal work on nearby cattle stations for anybody who wanted it. Because it was so isolated, particularly in The Wet, in those days before bitumen roads, it was the practice for the big stations on the Barkly Tableland to send trucks to Borroloola in March to collect employees, men and women, for the cattle season. Thus during the dry months, April to November, the big runs were mustered, branding and drafting accomplished, and store cattle were walked in mobs of 1500 to the Queensland railtowns. When we arrived, in November, the trucks had just brought all the workers back from the stations to Borroloola, so everybody was 'sitting down' and getting ready for Christmas. There was 'mobs' of money, the store was full, and there was plenty of bush tucker to enable the Aboriginals the therapeutic opportunity to retain their old hunting and gathering skills, which were still proudly functional and evident. Most of the roads were already 'out' for the next four months, so we were in a world apart.

And what a different world it was. The Aboriginals, about 400 peak population, lived on the south side of the Macarthur River, and had an idyllic camp of bush timber buildings with paperbark walls and either bark or corrugated iron roofs. Christmas time was understandably ceremony time, and every night saw a corroboree, either 'playabout', where everybody, including the whites, came along and had a great time, or 'business' where it might be part of the preparations for initiation of the kids or an ongoing (for many years it seemed) *Maraian* increase ritual. It was something of a cultural crossroads at Borroloola, where the didgeridoo met the boomerang. Despite what many people assert today, the didgeridoo did not exist south of Arnhem Land traditionally, and musical accompaniment to songs was done in non-didgeridoo places with clapping of hands, or sticks, or two *kylie* boomerangs. At Borroloola they had introduced the *yirdaki,* the didgeridoo, for playabout corroborees, but you could tell the difference when the fair dinkum stuff started and the *kylies* appeared. Serious business.

Most of the Aboriginals stayed south of the river, for there was no school or work going on at the time. We had four regular helpers around the police station, and I have seldom seen such wide-ranging competence. Musso Harvey and Barney Ross were incredibly smart men as mechanics, carpenters, you name it. Their wives, Roddy and Kathleen respectively, made great bread, and they sewed and cooked at a level that would leave most people gasping in envy. As Musso said one day, 'We've all had some hard bosses on the stations. We had to learn to be good, or out came the hobble chains.' The University of Hard Knocks indeed.

It was a fairly leisurely life for me at The Loo, which is what Borroloola has been called since it became a meeting place for blacks and whites in the Gulf Region in the 1880s. After completing my very easy chores like running the radio 'skeds' and doing the weather report, I had time for conversations with the many characters of all races and backgrounds who lived in the area, especially during sitdown time over Christmas. It was a hard life for Rae, with two small kids, and a dysfunctional old house where you were likely to encounter a snake whenever you opened a door or a cupboard or a drawer. The ones that eyeballed you as they slithered out of drawers petrified me. My only consolation was that the blackfellows were even more terrified of snakes than I was. It was a constant, unnerving worry in respect of the kids.

All the time the endless, debilitating, stifling heat. The temperature and humidity remained at the same steamy, sticky levels all night. Tilley lamps were all right at night, but they made things even hotter. We had to sleep under mosquito nets, hotter again. Sweat all night. We had no electricity, so there were no fans. Air-conditioning was not heard of in the Territory until 1960, when the Hot and Cold Bar was opened at the Darwin Hotel. One old kerosene fridge enabled us to cool water a bit, and Rae even managed to make ice cream. I make few claims to expertise, but I am an absolute wizard on Tilley lamps and kerosene fridges, so I have no worries about a job for my retirement years. Bound to be plenty of work. Old lamps for new. The water bags dripped away on the verandah, and did as good a job as the kero fridge.

The people at Borroloola, black and white, were so accommodating and kind it became easy to forget the hardship and isolation. Laughter was pervasive, because everybody was well-fed, fairly healthy, and there appeared to be enough money to see the Aboriginals through The Wet. No blacks received social services or pensions in those days; rations and clothing were distributed to eligible people as a substitute. Most of the whites were poor pensioners, with simple tastes. So blacks sat around, talked, ate, hunted a bit and laughed a lot. Whites sat around, talked, ate less, laughed less and drank grog if they had any. It's a real sitdown place, The Loo. A different turnout altogether, as old bushies say.

Aboriginals were not allowed by law to drink alcohol until 1964, and those at Borroloola seemed not to be interested in alcohol anyway, unlike many of the old lags in Darwin that I knew. Even when they were allowed to drink in later years blokes like Musso elected not to. In fact, the vast majority of Aboriginal people do not drink alcohol, but because those who do are so purposeful about getting drunk, and so obvious in doing so, there is a common assumption among many whites that all blacks are hopeless alcoholics.

Musso and I went fishing a few times, usually with a white bloke named Jack Bailey, 'The Silver Fox' as he was known. Jack had a boat with an inboard diesel motor, so we used to tow a canoe as well which was better to use, as Musso did not need fishing lines. He was deadly with a spear, even at night.

He suggested one night that I take my .303 rifle, and a spotlight, as he said there was a huge croc which had taken to following canoes as they crossed the river. We had a feed on a little island in the Macarthur, about 5 kilometres east of Borroloola, and were just about to resume fishing when I said I would test the spotlight. It was just dark. I switched on the light, swung it along the river, and there, 500 metres away, was the telltale red eye of a crocodile.

'Let's have a look at him,' I said, and began to put the gear into the canoe. Harpoon, rope, rifle, spotlight and an axe. It was only a very small canoe, about 3 metres long, with about 10 cm of freeboard, so Jack said he would stay behind. Musso said he would harpoon, and I squatted behind him, holding the light and the rifle. Another Aboriginal bloke, named Paddy, hopped in the stern to do the paddling. I noted he was not a very good handler of the canoe, not as good as I was used to anyway. We got closer and closer to the red light, and it looked like a medium-sized croc to me. Twenty metres away. Ten. And suddenly the croc turned its head and there were two lights! You could ride a bike between them! It was a monster, and we were at the point of no return. It was on the edge of the water: if it elected to come into the deeper water it would tip us over for sure. Musso was frantically signalling to Paddy to steer for the croc's tail, so that when the croc was harpooned we would be out of its wake. But Paddy didn't seem to understand. I heard Musso's sharp intake of breath as he threw the harpoon, straight into the croc's neck. It jumped and took off into deep water. That was OK until the slack on the harpoon rope was gone. Then we took off on the ride of our lives as the croc surged up the river, towing us at a speed nobody has ever achieved in a dugout canoe before or since. Paddy knew what to do now.

'Cut the fuckin rope,' he roared.

'No way,' I said. The mercenary white man was doing the sums on the skin.

'He might eatim wefellers,' Paddy lamented. Then the rope went slack. The croc had dived, and could be anywhere. Underneath us? Behind us? He just might eatim wefellers, Paddy. Musso gave me the rope, manoeuvred himself over the top of me, and took Paddy's place at the stern. Musso began to paddle backward, as Paddy should have done. The rope was now in front of us. At least we knew where the croc was. And then, lemming-like, it came straight out of the water like a dolphin at Marineland, body exposed to the tail, huge head presented as an unmissable target, and I shot it. And I don't feel good about it now. I don't.

It turned out that Paddy wasn't a coastal blackfellow. He had worked on stations all his life, and had never seen a crocodile before. It was a good one to start with! It took the four of us, all expert skinners, two hours to skin the croc, as it was too big to take anywhere, and you have to get the carcass out of the water and skin it quickly, otherwise the scales on the skin deteriorate and buyers refer to the skin as 'a floater'. Jack Bailey had a tape in his toolbox. The croc was 19 feet 3 inches long and almost 8 feet around the girth. We took an 80 inch skin from it — that's the measurement across the belly. You leave the hard flutes along the backbone when you take a belly skin. Inside the croc's gut we found bullock hooves, the bones of devoured dogs and a live snake about a metre long! As well as the normal pile of stones which crocs seem to swallow for digestive purposes. I could climb between the crocodile's jaws without touching a tooth. Might not be able to now!

It all caused quite a stir at The Loo the next morning. Jack had towed the skinned carcass behind the boat, and everybody came down to have a look and offer expert opinion.

'Jesus, it's a big bastard,' said Willy Shadforth's wide-eyed three-year-old son. Albert Morcom, an old pensioner who was the local correspondent for the *Northern Territory News*, dubbed it 'The Bullock-Eating Bugbear of Bing Bong'. The bullocks it had been eating at the rate of about one per week were from Bing Bong Station. Albert wrote an article for the *News* which was apparently syndicated around the world, so for the next six months I received letters asking for photos and data. We sold the salted skin in Darwin for £40, probably the equivalent of $1000 today. His £10 share was a month's wages for Musso in those days.

Albert Morcom had been a great athlete in his time, and the locals at The Loo called him 'The Towers Flash' for he had won the Towers Hundred in Charters Towers, in its day a footrace as famous as the Stawell Gift. Albert ran a little store at The Rocky, a little creek just below the Borroloola airstrip, on the north bank of the Macarthur. He was a member of a group of blokes that over the years came to be known as the Borroloola Hermits.

I met the Hermits in my first week at The Loo. A bloke said to me, 'Will you be at the church service on Sunday?' To steal a line from my song 'I'd been around a bit', and I knew he wasn't talking about a church service, but a drinking session.

'My oath,' I replied. 'Count me in. Where is it?'

'At Albert Morcom's camp. Under the mango trees. 10 am.'

I strolled down on the Sunday morning, and there they were, the Borroloola Hermits. About ten white blokes, middle-aged to old, sitting around on a ring of army stretcher beds.

'Sit down son,' said one of them. 'Like a drink?' He passed me a bottle of metho. What in the hell have I got into? 'Oh, no thanks,' I spluttered, thinking they're a mob of derelicts and I'd stay a couple of minutes and slip away. I passed the bottle to the bloke next to me and he took a ruminative sip. 'It's all we've got, unfortunately. We usually have Bollinger,' he said. Before I could leave they launched into the Great Debate.

I can't recall the topic that first Sunday, but it was heady stuff, and rest assured that every Sunday thereafter I was at the Debate. I was delighted to find that most of the Hermits had exotic sobriquets like The Whispering Baritone, The Reluctant Saddler, The White Stallion, The Mad Fiddler, The Calvert Lair, plus of course The Towers Flash and The Silver Fox. Some didn't have nicknames, notably Andy Anderson, Jack Keighran, Jack Mulholland — who was simply called 'Mull' — and the one and only, the best character I have ever met in my life, Roger Jose, with the surname rhyming with 'close'. I wrote a song about him which begins:

> Roger Jose lived terrible close
> To a place called Borroloola

They had some fairly erudite debates and arguments whose titles I do recall. 'Karl Marx: Right or Wrong?' was a fiery turnout, for their respective political beliefs were hung out to dry. More esoteric, and yet still lively, was 'Should Henry James be taken seriously?' and a reflective, serene sort of show revolved around the topic 'Is there a future in Buddhism?' The highlight for me was the day they debated 'Gray versus Browning' and Roger led the Gray team. He felt that Gray had no superior as a poet, and he held us enthralled as he discussed the relative merits of the two great English bards.

Scholarship of this order had come easily but slowly to these old Borroloola hands, who had once counted in their membership the smooth-talking activist and pacifist Michael Sawtell, and my mate, the illustrious white–blackfellow, Bilarni. Bill had lived in the Gulf before he enlisted in 1914. He returned to The Loo after *Harney's War*, title of a book he wrote, and was a trepanger and poddy–dodger for about 20 years. He and Horace Foster set up Seven Emus Station with cattle they had pinched. When I was at The Loo Willy Shadforth owned Seven Emus. Willy had to sell some of his country to keep the bank managers away, so thereafter the station was known as Three–and–a–Half Emus. At around the turn of the century a huge library was established at Borroloola. Local folklore has it a police constable was so perturbed when posted to such a remote station he wrote to the Carnegie Institute in the United States asking for some form of assistance to bring a bit of culture to the bush. Locals believe the Carnegie people sent 3000 leather-bound classics to The Loo. Peter Forrest, my historian mate, is not so sure that

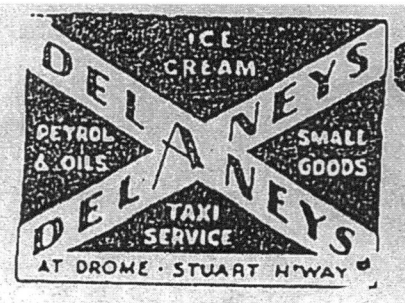

They just don't make headlines like these any more . . .

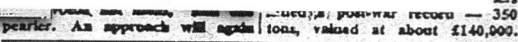

N TERRITORY News

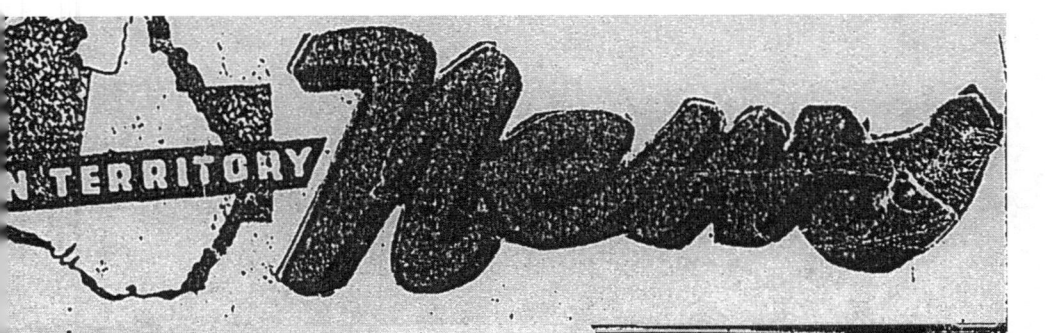

NUARY 16, 1958.

Glue in Triple Kill

'JAPAN WILL RUIN US'
NT Pearlers Call for Ban

A "stop the Japanese" move is being instituted by some Darwin pearlers who say the industry faces ruin if the Japanese fleet is allowed to continue operating here.

Mr George Haritos of Haritos Brothers said today that the beds in waters off the Territory had "fished out" by the Japanese.

Apart from that, with the world market glutted now, of survival of the country's own pearlers, as opposed to those... said Mr Haritos. ("Lost Reef"...

Mr Rafferty... directors and producer of Aus... lian Television Enterprises, wh... organised a recent expedition the Peterman Ranges with cel... bruted American commentato... Lowell Thomas.

Late last week Northern Te... ritory police served...

Watersiders Back on Job

Waterside workers returned to work this morning "under protest."

A spokesman for the men said that a complaint could be lodged with the proper authority that the local ASIA representative, Mr O'Toole, had condoned a breach of the award by the employer.

Mr O'Toole said this morning that the watersiders had seen reason and he was pleased they had returned to work as they were legally required to, under the terms of the port order when instructed by the employer.

The dispute concerns fork lift operators.

A new method has been intro...

The watersiders section by... had under a recent ruling by Mr Justice Ashburner applicable should be made to the court be... fore past practices are changed by direct action. "This was not... a case," said the spokesman.

On Thursday the work... carried an instruction that all fork lift drivers should report to the fork lift shed at 8 a.m... The drivers did this under protest, a representative said to...

...yra (Sally) Bowman, 46, ber daughter Wendy, 14, both of Glen Helen Station, and Thomas Wheland, 22, of Unley Road, Unley Park — an Adelaide suburb. Their bodies were found near the deserted Sundown Station...

LAST MON... WAS COO...

Darwin had a mild... with an average... temperature of 89.5... two and a half degre... normal, the chief of the... logical Branch, Mr... morning described...

Bullock-Eating Bugbear of Bing Bong Believed Dead

BORROLOOLA. — The bullock-eating crocodile of Bing Bong station is dead.

At least, Borroloola residents... hope he is.

The beef-loving monster was "star turn" in one of the worst years for crocodiles along the McArthur River.

He had plagued Mr Jim Mac... shall of Bing Bong for five weeks, eating one of Jim's prize beasts regularly, once a week.

After eluding an anti-crocodile campaign which loaded lines baited with whole wallaby carcases, and poisoned baits, the monster was shot a few days ago by Welfare Officer Ted Egan.

19 FEET LONG

This crocodile — which is believed to be the cattle eater — was 19 feet two inches long and old-timer Albert Morcom says it is one of the biggest ever killed...

...the McArthur River. The skin, pecked from the car... was measured 64 inches at the belly.

Mr Egan shot it at the five... mile. He was with a hunting and spear-fishing expedition including storekeeper Jack Bailey, told na... tives Mussolini, Simon and Paddy.

They were shooting from Mr Bailey's motor boat which was towing an aboriginal dug-out canoe.

The dead croc was too big for the canoe and had to be tied to the motor boat and hauled in. Shooters have declared war on saurians which infest the river this year and have been sighted in the heart of Borroloola settlement.

The bugbear of Borroloola — ...

...will probably... be committed to the Supreme Court for trial.

A few days before Christmas, Robinson and his party returned from an expedition to Winter's Glen in the Peterman Ranges.

(now deceased) — used to raid Bing Bong regularly.

Mr Marshall has contracted to supply beef to the Welfare Branch at Borroloola.

The cattle for this are kept in a paddock and killed when needed.

Once a week for five weeks the crocodile used to lie in wait and take bullocks as they came to drink at Rocky Creek.

When lines were set for him, with whole wallabies as bait, the crocodile ate the wallabies and evaded the hooks.

Saurians also have worried aborigines by showing signs of a desire to change their menu.

At least twice crocodiles have followed dug-outs loaded with natives across the river.

...with us assured us that it was the skeleton of a man of the same build as Lasseter. Unfortunately we forgot to get the Coroner's permission to disinter."

"GREAT ROMANCER"

In Adelaide this week Lasse...

N.T. POLITICAL CHANGES SOON?

Possible changes the year in the Northern Territory's political set-up were forecast by the Territory's Canberra MHR, Mr Nelson.

In his New Year message — issued a week late because of flood hold-ups — Mr Nelson said he hoped the political advances which the Territory had sought for so long would receive "worthwhile attention" in 1958.

He hoped the vital problems of housing and high cost-of-living also would be solved.

Mr Nelson added that the NT still needed secondary industries to balance its economy and en... sure full employment. Lack of secondary industries was hampering progress, he warned.

...from Bowman's Glen Helen station west of Alice Springs to Adelaide.

Police said a man, a woman and a child were in the Zephyr car.

it happened that way, but nonetheless a huge library was once in existence at The Loo, housed in the gaol. So the best prospect of enhancing one's education was to do the odd stretch in the slammer. All the old Borroloola lads had been in gaol for supplying liquor to Aboriginals, living with Aboriginal women, pinching cattle and horses, you name it. Over the years they had read, stolen, borrowed, memorised and swapped the books: I came on the scene 50 years later when the only remnants of the library were a few old ant-eaten covers.

Roger Jose could quote great bursts of Homer's *Odyssey* in English translation, or Vergil's *Aeneid* in Latin. He knew Shakespeare inside out and back to front, and constantly chucked you excerpts from the *Rubaiyat of Omar Khayam*. He could debate most subjects with erudition, and, if he had no specific knowledge he would fix a fierce gaze on you as he asked endless questions. Arthur Calwell, the Labor leader, was not a very good politician but he was a great scholar of Chinese history and the Mandarin language. When he visited The Loo Arthur was delighted to find in Roger a man whose scholarship matched his own in that field of study.

Mind you, Roger Jose *was* eccentric. I'll grant that. He had developed some fairly interesting beliefs on the basis of his reading, but was always prepared to put these into action. He had a thing about clothing. He said to me one day:

'Look at these stupid Australians. They take their clothes off when it's hot. They should be like the Arabs and cover up. If you want to keep a water pipe cool you cover it, don't you?' Roger on the hottest of days would wear a couple of those old flannel undershirts your grandfather wore, an army greatcoat, a scarf around his neck, and a striped pillow case over his head to make what he called a *burnous*. He had a slit cut for vision. There was a little well, behind the police station, where he liked to draw some water, and he was an Archibald Prizewinner as he went across the airstrip to his tank, carrying two buckets of water on a Chinaman's pole yoke.

Yes, his tank. That was where he lived. With a supporting theory of course. He said:

'If you live in cyclonic regions like this, you should have a round home. Then, if a cyclone blows your house away, you can roll along in it.' To prove his point he built an architectural gem, a functional split-level home. The ground floor was a 10,000 gallon rainwater tank, upturned. Wired to the top as a mezzanine he had a 5000 gallon tank, where he slept on summer nights to catch the breeze. And 'out the back' he had a 1000 gallon tank, which was of course the dunny, but you wouldn't get Roger using crude words like dunny. It was the 'Amenities Block'.

His most radical theory related to the use of strychnine as a heart stimulant. When told that Roger took the poison in occasional small doses I did not believe my informant, but one day I had the opportunity to check it out. Andy Anderson had three sons from their Aboriginal mother, and originally they were named Lenin, Trotsky and Stalin. Oh, the Hermits bestowed fancy names on the blackfellows as well as themselves. Pompey, Nero, Cicero, Virgil. It was apt that most names matched the personality. Eventually Trotsky Anderson came to be called Hector. One day Hector and I rode out to the Six Mile Plain on horseback to shoot a bullock as a killer. Hector climbed a tree, I walked the cattle quietly underneath the tree, and he shot this unsuspecting bullock. We 'overlanded' the carcass, that is, we butchered it on the ground, using leaves as a blanket to keep the meat clean. We took the meat back to the Loo in packbags, and distributed it among the old age pensioners. I saved some fresh and some salted beef for old Roger, for I was intrigued by him, and took every opportunity to have a yarn.

Next morning I strolled across the airstrip to Roger's tank, two muslin bags full of beef as my conversation piece. Imagine my surprise. There was the old chap, deep in conversation with himself. I waited for a break in proceedings, then strolled in.

'Good morning, Roger. I brought you some beef.'

Roger elected to respond in the toffiest English. 'Oh, thank you young man,' he said. 'I often sit here craving one of the master's oxen, but more often than not I have to be content with slaughtering yet another poor unfortunate marsupial.'

He put the beef in his Coolgardie Safe, and invited me to sit for a while. I was in like Flynn.

'I noticed you talking to yourself as I came across. Do you often do that, Roger?'

'I do, as a matter of fact. Ever since I developed my superiority complex. I find it's nice to talk to somebody intelligent every now and again.' Cop that young feller. No, blow it, I thought. Ask him, Ted.

'Roger, is it true that you take strychnine?'

'Oh, yes my boy. For the ticker. Been taking it for years. The Aztecs used to take poison in small doses as a heart stimulant. Good enough for them, good enough for me.' I still didn't quite believe it.

'Could I watch you do it?'

'Of course. I take it every Tuesday morning. About 9 am usually. You're welcome to watch.'

The following Tuesday, at the tank, there was Roger, with a little bottle of strychnine and a spoon. But he took me well away from his camp, out on the airstrip in fact.

'Where are we going?' I asked.

'Out onto the strip. You can't run the risk of hitting your head on a tree when you take this stuff,' he replied. He ordered me to 'stand back'. I felt like the person who calls 'Contact' and then swings the propellor. He opened the bottle, poured and swallowed a teaspoonful of strychnine, shook his head a couple of times, hung on to the backs of his legs in a squat for a moment, and then came over to me. He took my hand, and put it on his heart. *Ptoom. Ptoom. Ptoom.*

'Get a load of that, son.' For once in my life I was speechless.

I drank metho once. Just the once, with Roger of course. When a truck came to pick up some workers for Brunette Downs Station they had to stop on the other side of the dreaded Six Mile, a swampy black soil plain so treacherous it would bog a duck. We ferried the workers out to the truck in The Reluctant Saddler's Buick, which was pretty good in the bogs. On the last trip we burnt out the clutch, and had to abandon the Buick and walk back, through the black mud, to The Loo. Every step raised your bootsoles an inch, so it was walk, shake the mud, walk, shake for the whole six miles. Roger and I had accompanied The Saddler, whose real name was Tommy Lee, on the last trip so we shared the walk together. Tom cursed all the way and when we got back to Roger's tank Tom demanded a drink. Roger pulled out three pannikins, a bottle of metho, and a tin of Sal Vital. He poured us a nip each, added a vigorous spoonful of the fizzy powder, and handed the pannikins to us. He gave us an appropriate quote for the occasion from *The Rubaiyat:*

> Come, fill the Cup, and in the Fire of Spring
> The Winter Garment of Repentance fling:
> The Bird of Time has but a little way
> To fly — and Lo! The Bird is on the Wing.

'Bagman's Champagne, boys. Let the bubbles assail your nostrils.'

'Mud in your eye, Roger,' grunted Tom . No finesse at all, Tom.

'A little in yours, too, Tom,' rejoined Roger. Gregarious man.

'Cheers,' I said, not very originally, and threw down the effervescent fiery liquid. It didn't taste all that bad, but I suppose it was Roger's dynamic company that made the experience memorable. I certainly didn't take on metho–drinking as a habit.

If Roger and the others had money they preferred rum. Old Soldier was their brand. I used to send their telegrams to Elder Smith, Alice Springs, by radio. This sort of thing:

PLEASE SEND SPUDS ONIONS TOBACCO SIX OLD SOLDIER
ROGER JOSE

A bit different from the telegrams sent to and from the Aboriginal Inland Missionaries around the Territory, who always used some sort of theological base. Something like:

HAPPY BIRTHDAY CORINTHIANS 1:4 HOPE MOTHER WELL
SEE YOU SOON EPHESIANS 6 REJOICING EXAM RESULTS
MARK 1:10

The radio operators at the Overseas Telecommunications (OTC) base in Darwin used to chortle as I relayed those telegrams. Got that Ephesians right now, have we Ted? God bless you, my son. The local missionary at The Loo, Charlie Main, was called The White Stallion. The nickname derived from the fact that a female missionary once caught him in the act of seducing an Aboriginal girl, and threw a dish of flour over him. I wonder if she gave him a verse of the Bible to contemplate? Exodus 12:20 perhaps?

Christmas at The Loo was a mighty show. Everybody turned out. We killed a couple of bullocks. Musso drove the government Land Rover down to the coast and brought back a dugong and a turtle. All the women had new dresses. They cooked up a blowout meal and then we had the sports — races, tug of war, high jumps and spear throwing. All dressed in their station gear, fancy shirts, ten-gallon hats, gabardine trousers and R M Williams boots, the local Aboriginal blokes could still throw spears. The target was a 50 pound bag of government flour set on a 44 gallon drum at 50 yards. The star performer was a giant of a bloke named Splinter. We barred him after he had hit the target three times straight: the prize each time was the bag itself, and we couldn't waste too much of the taxpayer's money, could we?

I had a dozen bottles of beer for Christmas, and had made them as cold as possible. After the sports were over, and the Aboriginals had all gone back to the south side of the river, I invited a few of the Hermits for a beer. Jack Lane and Tommy Lee accepted enthusiastically, and in fact not only drank more than their share, they conveniently left their hats behind so they could come back the next morning with an excuse for 'a phlegm cutter'. The Borroloola calling card. Roger declined my offer of a beer. He said, 'No thanks, Ted. Beer is strictly for Bank Johnnies. But if you had a cold metho I'd join you.'

I said that Roger didn't have a nickname. Well, not among the Hermits. But one day I heard a bloke from out-of-town refer to Roger as 'The Old Death Adder', with all the connotations of him being like a poisonous snake. How dare you, you uncultured mug, I thought to myself. It prompted me to write my first-ever song–in the old man's defence. What did Thomas Moore say? I care not who makes the laws of my country, as long as I write the songs? Something like that. The song is called 'Roger was No Death Adder'.

The Great Loo Debates

Roger Jose lived terrible close
To a place called Borroloola
Folks called Roger an old Death Adder
But don't let that fact foolya.
A Death Adder is a lazy snake
He'll sit and never a move he'll make
Until he bites you for a drink
Then he'll move a lot faster than you'd think.

Roger was only a little bloke
And he carted all his water on a Chinaman's yoke
Around his shoulders his hair hung loose
'Neath a pillowcase which made a good *burnous*.
He wore a heavy coat on the hottest day
Said that was the way to keep the sun away
On his feet were strips of wallaby skin
Chasing wallabies kept old Roger thin.

And Roger liked to drink a little metho with his dinner
A spoonful of strychnine was certainly a winner
A rum and a johnny cake served for his tea
And he said Borroloola is the place for me.

He lived in an upturned rainwater tank
A house that would roll was as safe as a bank
In a cyclone, willy-willy, Cockeye Bob
A house that would roll was just the job.
He went to gaol a couple of times
But you'd hardly call the reasons crimes
Shared with a black man a bottle of drink
And did six months in the local clink.

On another occasion he got in strife
Just for living with his Aboriginal wife.
Didn't worry Roger, happy was he
Came back to Borroloola when he was free.
And Roger liked to drink a little metho with his dinner
A spoonful of strychnine was certainly a winner
A rum and a johnny cake served for his tea
And he said Borroloola is the place for me.

In another place, another age
Roger would have been treated like a sage
Plato and Socrates, out at The Loo
Would probably be called Death Adders too.
Roger liked astrology, history, anthropology
Poetry, politics and theology
Geography, philosophy, he'd read all of these
And liked to sit and argue underneath the shady trees.

He had a long grey beard and a glittering eye
But Roger never, ever worked for a boss
A long grey beard and a glittering eye
But he wouldn't have shot the albatross.
And Roger liked to drink a little metho with his dinner
A spoonful of strychnine was certainly a winner
A rum and a johnny cake served for his tea
And he said Borroloola is the place for me.

A telegram arrived, from Head Office, Darwin:

SENDING YOU GROOTE EYLANDT INDEFINITE PERIOD STOP LETTER
FOLLOWS
DENATAFF

When the letter came on the mail plane a fortnight later, it was a detailed five pager, personalised by my mate and boss in Darwin, Ted Evans. Ted said there had been quite a few disputes at Groote Eylandt Mission in the Gulf of Carpentaria. A couple of Anglican missionaries had been assaulted, and one wounded slightly with a knife. I was to go there to try to sort things out. Ted said he felt I might expect to be there about three months. He asked if Rae would be prepared to stay on at Borroloola, especially to do the medical work. He would send a young, single patrol officer, Colin Macleod, to take my place.

It was a big sacrifice for Rae to make, but she accepted the responsibility readily. On call anytime for matters minor or major, there was always the possibility of some event cropping up. Totally isolated, with two small kids of her own, untrained in nursing, it was a heavy burden. Conditions were impossible, the work unglamorous, little appreciated and unpaid. Women today would simply and rightly not do it under those circumstances. Rae, like lots of other bush women, the wives of policemen, station owners and managers, missionaries and Native Affairs blokes, did the really hard strokes that kept the whole show going. The blokes had the adventures, travel and fascinating experiences that provide the background for books like this. But the women bore the kids, tended the sick, and coped with the brunt of the hardship. Wives in the bush, good on you.

Sid and his De Havilland Rapide came to The Loo to collect me for the short flight to Groote Eylandt. Just as I was about to get on the aeroplane old Roger came running across the flat. But not to say goodbye. It was vintage Roger, and absolute Socrates.

'Ted, at Groote Eylandt, would you see what you can find out about the *inugwamba?*' I had to strain to hear him over the impatient slap, slap, slap of the propellors.

'The what?' I shouted.

'The *inugwamba*. See what you can find out about it for me.'

'What is it?'

'That's what I want you to find out.'

You bloody well know about the *inugwamba,* whatever it is. You're just gingering me, you old bastard, I thought, as the plane taxied for take-off, and I looked to see Roger standing with Rae and the kids, Barney, Musso, Roddy and Kathleen.

It would be two years before I got back to tell Roger about the *inugwamba,* but I'm glad he set me the task.

7
Bullocky's Joy and Jesus

'What does *inugwamba* mean?' I asked Nangwarra Wurrabadalamba, a Groote Eylandt bloke who had been quick to welcome and befriend me.

'Why do you ask?' he answered. Everybody called him Nango, a merciful shortening of his name: it rhymed with 'mango'. He was tall, loose-limbed, handsome, blue-black, and that rare commodity, a smiling Groote Eylandt Aboriginal.

'Old Roger Jose at Borroloola told me to find out about the *inugwamba*. What is it?'

Nango laughed, a throaty, knowing chuckle. 'Old Roger, eh? He'd know a bit about the *inugwamba*, I reckon.'

I was getting exasperated. Nango spotted that. 'In the old days here on Groote Eylandt all women had to carry a big stringybark blanket which was folded like a V. It was called *inugwamba*. Whenever they were in the sight of anybody they were not allowed to talk to or be seen by, they had to squat behind the *inugwamba* until the person had gone.'

'When did women stop carrying the *inugwamba*?' I asked, intrigued.

'Only a few years ago, when the missionaries built the dormitories for the young girls. They are locked in at night now, so there's no need for the *inugwamba*. We have new rules,' said Nango, with not the slightest trace of venom in his voice. The very concept of venom seemed alien to him. He would become a great friend and ally.

When I arrived at Groote Eylandt my accomodation was a

very large empty timber house, with a huge verandah all around. Banks of wooden louvres were the only walls, so it was a 'see through' house, designed to capture the faintest zephyr. I quickly realised that my every move was scrutinised by about thirty teenagers, nubile, mostly very pretty girls who did everything in the manner of a flight of parrots. They were called 'the dormitory girls'. They all wore the same patterned dresses, different colours on alternate days: wash one, wear one. One green dress, one red dress. On green days they were a squadron of budgerigars, on red days they were rosellas. They moved as one, shrieking, volatile, joyous in the strangest of ways. They would approach me as one body, and they called me 'Mistegan', for all white men had to be addressed as 'Mister' it seemed. From the body of the group, although I could never isolate the individual inquirer, there came an endless stream of questions. 'What you name?' Ted Egan. 'What you father name?' Joe Egan. 'What you mother name?' Grace Egan. 'You got anything wife Mistegan?' Yes. 'How many wife you got it?' Just one. 'What you wife name Mistegan?' Rae. 'She smoke cigarette?' No. 'You drink rum, Mistegan?' Yes. As the questioning went on, they would edge closer, as a body. Gradually, they would touch. Disarming, intimidating stuff, especially when one day one of the girls grabbed my bicep and said, '*Munda*, Mistegan.'

'What does *munda* mean?'

'Strong one. You strong one. *Munda.*'

Several of them had a quick squeeze. Then, with a shriek, they were gone. It was fascinating. There was not the slightest chance of making any individual contact with them, either verbally or physically. The minute I sought to catch the eye, or ask a question of an individual, like, 'What's your name?' she would disintegrate completely, and the group would be likely to fly away. It slowly dawned on me that, in the old days, they would have hidden behind the *inugwamba*.

To this day, when I go back to Groote Eylandt, I am likely to be addressed by some old women, the teenage girls of 1957, as 'O Mariana'. 'You know any song, Mistegan?' they asked when I first knew them. Yes. 'You teach us singing.' Groote Eylandt people don't beat about the bush when they want something. Requests are made in the form of demands, commands expressed in blunt imperatives. 'You teach us singing.'

I taught the girls a few songs, mainly what they called 'island songs', songs I had learned in Darwin that arrived in Australia via the pearling industry. *'O Mariana'* derives from, I think, the Trobriand Islands, but nobody really knows: the 'work songs' of the pearling luggers came from anywhere in the world, and each person singing the songs felt free to add his or her own words. In Torres Strait there is a song to the tune of 'D'ye ken John Peel' which locals insist is a centuries-old traditional song. True, but whose tradition? There is in the north of Australia a hotch-potch of terrific songs with meaningless but vaguely familiar words like this:

O mariana eh eh
O mariana oh oh
O mariana eta wa ineh
Alawa lumi eh

I taught the Groote girls this song and a few others. Their eyes narrowed as they concentrated, committing the words to memory, but never going to give me the chance to check them out, because an individual might be 'shamed' in the process. There's no *inugwamba* to hide behind. When I said, 'Your turn,' they would do just that. As one they turned their backs on me, and repeated the song, word perfect.

One of the girls was mentally disadvantaged, as they say nowadays, not the full quid, as we would say then. I realised that I had to be on my guard about her, as she was obviously not in charge of her own behaviour. I'll give her the false name of Diana, although they all used only their long, usually jawbreaking Aboriginal names in those days. Almost all women's names on Groote Eylandt start with D. Almost all men's names start with N. The other dormitory girls tended to leave Diana to her own devices. I had a vision of finding her in my bed or something like that. Groote Eylandt men have an awesome reputation for explosive violence, and I didn't relish the prospect of one of her relatives impaling me with his *lama,* a shovel-nosed spear. I had no lustful thoughts about her, or any of the girls really. It wasn't that they weren't attractive. Quite the contrary. I could probably have procured one or several of them sexually had I wanted to, but it would have been, yes, I'll use the word, sinful. Worse than that it would have been exploitative, and although I have lots of faults, I am not an exploiter.

But Diana was hell-bent for exploitation. One day I walked on to my verandah only to be confronted by her, leaping out of one of the 44 gallon drums that were around the place as rubbish tins, absolutely starkers

'I'm naked, Mistegan,' she shouted, gleefully.

'So you are,' I replied. 'What you need is a good old-fashioned *inugwamba.*'

Groote Eylandt, named thus by the Dutch explorer Tasman as a 'great island' to honour the memory of the religious reformer Gerhard Groote, was extremely isolated in those days, before Gemco, a subsidiary of BHP, began to mine manganese there in 1964. The supply ship *Cora* came from Brisbane once every three months. There was a gravel airstrip, but no established mail service. Occasionally a charter aeroplane landed. There were two settlements on the island, Angurugu and Umbakumba. Angurugu, pronounced Ung [as in hung] Oo Roo Goo, is on the river of the same name, on the south-west side of the island, inland a few kilometres. Umbakumba, pronounced as it looks is on the north-east corner, on the sea but sheltered by a magnificent lagoon. Angurugu was a Christian mission station, run by the Church Missionary Society (CMS), an evangelical branch of the Anglican Church. Umbakumba was run as a 'private' settlement by a wonderful bloke named Fred Gray. I had met him in 1953 when I sailed around from Darwin with Leo Hickey, and Fred Gray was to have a huge influence on my life for the next forty years.

As Ted Evans' letter explained, there had been several assaults on missionaries at Groote Eylandt by Aboriginal men, and one of the female missionaries had been slightly wounded with a knife. My task was to work out the cause of the dissent and provide remedies: we did not seek to usurp the role of the police, although we often worked with them. Reverend Rix

Warren, the superintendent of the mission, told me that the argument was over the question of polygyny, that branch of polygamy where men have more than one wife.

In 1917 an institution for 'half caste' children — the so-called 'illegitimate' children born on the mainland of white men and Aboriginal mothers — was established on Groote Eylandt. The Anglican missionaries did some trading with Groote Eylandt men, who bartered things like turtle shells and pearls for tobacco — remember that for centuries the Groote Eylandt people had traded with Macassans in similar fashion: the Groote Eylandt word for tobacco is *tambakwo* — but there was no attempt to convert the islanders to Christianity. The concentration was on rearing the mixed-race girls and boys for eventual life in the white man's world, the girls to be domestics and the boys to be stockmen or menial labourers. The definite policy of that period was to leave the 'full bloods' to their own devices, but to train the mixed-race people to become 'like whites'. Fuck them white, as it was crudely put among many white men. A major flaw in the policy was that there was no consideration of the mixed-race boys. It was assumed that the girls would elect to marry white men, and have paler-skinned children, but who were the boys supposed to marry? Once 'exempted' from the discriminatory Aboriginals Ordinance it was an offence for mixed-race people to mix with 'full-blood' Aboriginals. It was a common belief that as a Caucasian race the Australian Aboriginals would eventually disappear through miscegenation. It was an accepted fact that the 'fullbloods' were a dying, doomed race. Leave them alone wherever possible. In other parts of the Australian frontier, where bullets and poison cleared the land, Hitler and his gang would have looked liked bumbling amateurs. In the north it was more subtle, but nonetheless planned genocide.

In the 1930s missionaries saw 'full-blood' Aboriginal women on the island for the first time — for 15 years they were concealed behind the *inugwamba*. When the mixed-race children were taken from the island, as part of a policy change when people like Professor Elkin began to propose a new policy of also 'assimilating' the 'full-bloods', the missionaries began to concentrate on proselytising the native Groote Eylandt people. CMS declared at the outset that it was sinful for a man to have more than one wife. The missionaries built dormitories, and through the influence of flour, tea, sugar, treacle and tobacco — 'Bullocky's Joy and Jesus' as I referred to it later in a song — persuaded the locals that it was a good idea for the girls to be housed there. They received religious and secular instruction, and were locked away at night from marauding males.

None of the missionaries did any research, or sought to understand the traditional marriage patterns of the Anindilyagwa people. Part of the history of Groote Eylandt was that brother often killed brother, for they were genetically (consanguineously, as the anthropologists would say) 'in line' to marry the same women. Thereby the most powerful brother accumulated a lot of wives. If you believe that power equals quality, the most powerful genes in the male line were being passed on. That system had gone unopposed for centuries. And here were the missionaries seeking to dismantle it just because God told them they were right. The CMS motto was 'Allowed of God to be put in trust with the gospel.' Later they changed it to 'The best of all is [that] God is with us.' There's arrogance for you.

At the outset CMS received outrageous support. The old men with lots of wives were paid so that their daughters could be taken into the dormitories. There was no attempt to dismantle any of the old marriages, so the lives of older people were virtually unchanged. The younger men, who normally had to wait until middle-age for a wife or fight their way into the marriage arena, were promised by the missionaries that, when the girls were of marriageable age, they could state their claims. Wouldn't a Christian marriage be lovely, with the choir singing, and God's blessing on the gathering here assembled?

Thus, a generation of younger men received wives long before they would have in the old 'pagan' days. But inevitably the time came when some of the same younger men began to say, 'An important chap like me should now have my second, third, perhaps fourth wife.' Oh, no, say the missionaries, remember

God's law. Oh, no, Mr Missionary, we make the laws around here, mate. Whack!

Enter Ted Egan. I had absolutely no idea of what I might do or hope to achieve, so I remembered my mum's good advice: 'Wherever you go in life, Ted, keep sweet with the cook and be a good listener.' I asked if I could attach myself to any work gangs, or whatever, to fit in quietly, and allow locals to look me over as I sought to understand the place and the people. I sent a telegram to Ted Evans asking him to send me a couple of footballs and basketballs. I knew sport broke down barriers. I worked with the timber cutters, where my better-than-average ability with an axe helped me fit in easily. Groote Eylandt men were solid workers, used to the no-nonsense style of some of the early missionaries, who had done commendable physical work setting up a sawmill and constructing some attractive timber buildings from the local cypress pine and stringybark trees.

The men were suspicious when I said I preferred 'Ted' rather than 'Mister'. I was appalled that most CMS male missionaries insisted on being called 'Mister,' but that all Aboriginal men, regardless of age, were called 'Good Boy'. I am not kidding. 'Good morning, Good Boy,' an acne-ridden 25–year–old white storeman, fresh out of Pennant Hills Sunday School, would say to a bearded old warrior. 'Good morning, Mr So-and-So,' was the required response. No wonder Groote Eylandt people didn't smile much or laugh easily. A traditional system that called for the *inugwamba* and for brother to kill brother was bad enough, but evangelical missionaries on top of all of that! I hasten to add that some of the missionaries, especially the women, were excellent in all their dealings with the locals. But some of the white blokes could only have been there as some means of a better slot in the next life, for they were no great assets in this one.

The Anindilyagwa were nothing like any other Aboriginals I had met. But I spotted that the English words 'fair go' had been incorporated into their language. It came out like 'pairgo' and they obviously judged a situation by whether they thought a fair go had been achieved or not. Usually the latter. Keep that in mind, Ted, and don't forget the advice the wise Bilarni gave you years ago as he told you of experiences he, Roger Jose and Horace Foster had among the Groote people.

'The Macassans from Sulawesi got on very well with the Groote Eylandt blackfellows,' said old Bill, 'and when they were barred from coming to Australia in 1907 because of the White Australia policy they warned the locals to be very wary in any dealings they had with the *balanda* (the Macassan word for 'Hollanders', now the Arnhem Land Aboriginal word for whitefellers generally). That's why they are so guarded in their dealings with white people. Once they come to trust you, it's all right, but they don't trust easily.'

We cut and carted cypress pine logs for a couple of weeks, and I was starting to work out who were the authority figures. Four of the blokes in the timber gang had been charged with assaulting missionaries. It must all have evolved from great frustration, for the genial Nango was one of the assailants. That surprised me, but because he was an easy talker — rare, I can tell you — I got my first insights into the explosive situation that had developed. Two of the men charged with assault had been sent to Darwin for three months imprisonment. They had just returned, and gave their fellow timber cutters glowing accounts of a wonderful place called Fannie Bay Gaol: you get 'pairgo' there. I know the place, paid a visit there once, I told them with tongue-in-cheek. Nango had been fined £10, an enormous amount when top wages at Groote Eylandt in those days was five shillings per week. He had three months to pay, and time was nearly up.

Rix Warren asked me if I'd take the timbercutters to a spot on Wallaby Creek, 15 kilometres from the mission on the bush track to Umbakuma. When the heavy rains fell Wallaby Creek was uncrossable, and Rix Warren asked me if a bridge over the creek was a possibility. I was no bridgebuilder, but Groote Eylandt is heavily timbered with fine straight stringybark trees, and I felt confident that, using the considerable skills of the timber gang, we would be able to make something resembling a strong bridge over the creek. It would provide a good opportunity to camp out bush for about a week with the blokes, many of whom I then knew to be members of powerful families. We took a tractor and trailer, tucker and tools, to Wallaby Creek, and set up a camp. The crossing is about 20 kilometres from the sea, but, to our amazement, when we arrived there was a 4 metre saltwater crocodile sitting on the bank.

I have never seen anybody move faster. Nango, off the tractor in a flash, raced down to the water's edge. The croc took off, Nango flying after it. He stopped to pick up a bloody great rock, caught up with the crocodile, and smashed its skull. We walked over and there was Nango, sitting on the croc's back, as nonchalant as you like.

'The skin will pay for my fine,' he chortled. And he had some change.

That put us all in the mood to talk about the assaults that had brought on the police action, so each night I asked a few leading questions, and in the intimate atmosphere of the campfire they began to tell me how they were simply claiming girls promised them under the old system.

'Do the missionaries have any idea of these promises?'

It was obvious that there had never been any dialogue. The missionaries assumed that God's law would prevail. The men told me that every single girl on the island had a promise; and in some cases men were negotiating to marry unborn girls.

We made a very sturdy bridge crossing over Wallaby Creek, and a week later returned to the mission. I told Rix Warren of the discussions. He refused to believe that such a comprehensive promise system was in place. I said I would seek to provide him with chapter and verse.

I decided to visit Umbakumba. There were only two motor vehicles on Groote Eylandt at that time, the tractor at Angurugu, and a Land Rover at Umbakumba. I suggested to Rix that I take a few blokes with the tractor and trailer, and upgrade the road. Thus I could travel across the island and talk with Fred Gray: the marriage promises had implications for Umbakumba too.

It was February 1958, and the rains had started in earnest. Wallaby Creek was running a banker but we crossed over our new bridge and headed north-east. It's about 35 kilometres from Angurugu to Umbakumba. We 'corduroyed' a few other lesser creek crossings, providing a causeway made from logs wired together.

It was 3 pm, and we were within about 10 kilometres of Umbakumba. Travelling along a two–wheel track through stringybark trees, dead straight, dense, and towering all around us. An eerie stillness developed, and the light dulled to a macabre green. The sun had abandoned us. In minutes a cyclone careered on to the island. There had been ominous quiet for days, the build-up. It came through like a devastating, mile-wide chainsaw, terrifying lightning followed by bursting booms of thunder, a sweep of erratic howling flattening winds, and rain that stung like gravel thrown in your face. Trees snapped off at the base, crashing around us with not the slightest notice. The dreaded eye of the cyclone. What do you do? Run? Where to? Stand and wait, hoping a tree will not fall on you? Crash! Thump! There goes another one! And another, right behind you! Look out! There's no shelter, none, the rain blinding you and the wind threatening to blow you off your feet. I have never been so frightened. What if it was night time? I remember saying that, trying to pretend I wasn't scared shitless. We decided the best thing to do was stand as close as possible to the butts of the biggest trees, in the hope that they would survive or we would be in the best position to avoid being crushed if they blew over.

The terror lasted for the longest hour of my life. Then the wind subsided, and the rain started in earnest. It was freezing cold. If anybody told you it could be so cold on Groote Eylandt in February you'd laugh them to scorn. But it was.

There I witnessed one of the greatest bits of bushcraft I've ever seen. Nango always carried a tomahawk in his belt: it was a worry to me that many Groote Eylandt men did the same. In no time he debarked a couple of big stringybark trees and made a crude shelter. We huddled under it, five half-drowned rats. In the bucketing rain Nango went to a live cypress pine tree, cut a flitch out of the side of the tree, and brought it back under the shelter. With his tomahawk he began to split the flitch of wood into pieces the thickness of a safety match. On the back of the trailer, in his little swag, he had some firesticks. He now proceeded to twirl the sticks at blinding pace, and made fire for us, under the shelter, with the rain still pelting down.

'Ted, we call the cypress pine tree *yimendungwa*,' he explained. Even now his voice was soft yet authoratitive. 'It's like a kerosene tree.'

'I believe you,' I said, very impressed, and soon, much warmer. When the rain stopped a monumental task confronted us. The entire track was covered with fallen trees, and we were in the middle of the island. The only way out was to clear the road to Umbakumba, and eventually clear the return trip to Angurugu. It took two days to cut and drag our way to Umbakumba, where we got some tucker from Fred Gray. It took us another week to get back to Angurugu. Our bridge over Wallaby Creek had survived the cyclone. In fact, it lasted for the next ten years. Bloody good bridge.

At Umbakumba I had a long talk with Fred Gray. He, too, was surprised to hear of the intricate promise system in place, threatening to jeopardise the lives of any whites who sought to interfere. Although Fred ran the best whiteman's place I have seen for Aboriginals, he did not have or claim any great level of knowledge of their laws and practices. His policy was one of non-interference, although he had been caught up with procedural practices of CMS, and had also instituted a dormitory system. In his case though, it was more like boarding school, where both boys and girls lived in what today are called hostels, in order that they could be trained in hygiene and work practices, and attend school. There was not the same element of compulsion as was evident at Angurugu. Nonetheless, just prior to my arrival on the island, Fred himself had been threatened with a knife at Angurugu when he sought to intervene after one of the women missionaries had been knifed.

Umbakumba had been established in 1937 as a flying boat base for Qantas. The lagoon at Umbakumba was deemed one of the better spots for landing Catalina flying boats when it took four days to fly from Sydney to London. Fred, who had worked as a trepanger in north-east Arnhem Land since 1932, was asked by the government to set up a base on the other side of the lagoon from the flying boat headquarters in order to 'control' the Aboriginals. It was a unique situation in Australia, for all the centres for Aboriginals had previously been run either by Christian missions or the government. The notion of a privately run place was anathema to bodies like CMS, and they had tried to take over from Gray from Day One, in order to have total religious influence and control over the entire island. It was a stroke of luck for me that, in our discussions at Umbakumba, the name of Fred Rose came up. Fred Rose was stationed at Umbakumba in the late 1930s as a weather observer. Fred Gray gave me a look at the work Rose had done as an amateur anthropologist, unique work that subsequently helped him become one of the world's most renowned anthropology lecturers, even though his communist beliefs took him to East Germany for initial recognition. Rose established that Groote Eylandt Aboriginals were unique in terms of avoidance practices: certainly they have the most strictly enforced and most restrictive rules I have ever encountered in my lengthy experience. Most Aboriginal societies have restrictions on who you can talk to or look at. My judgement is that normally you can have straightforward dealings with about 80 per cent of the population, but there are often rules to be observed about the other 20 per cent. Can't talk to them, can't look at them, often required to fight them, generally to be avoided. At Groote Eylandt it works inversely: 20 per cent with you, 80 per cent represent possible trouble. Hence the *inugwamba*, and the generally unsmiling nature of the Groote Eylandt people. Life is a tough business. I compared them with the Tiwi who have few restrictions, and could see why one group was so outgoing, the other so introspective.

In the awareness of the many restrictions on personal dealings, Rose had the ingenious idea of photographing every person at Umbakumba. He compiled a journal, with each individual having a double page entry. He then went to every other person and basically said, 'Tell me about this person' as he showed them each individual photograph. People were totally uninhibited, apparently, about referring to a photograph of a person that they would normally never look at, have dealings with, or even discuss with their own people. Through hundreds of hours of cross reference, Rose traced and charted the intricate, delicate relationship system that prevailed among the 200 people who lived at Umbakumba. If only the missionaries and Fred Gray had taken the trouble to study this research. It was a system unlikely to be dismembered just by announcing that some white man's God thought they were a sinful bunch, no matter how much Bullocky's Joy and Jesus was handed out.

I was not in a position to seek to repeat Rose's research, but it gave me a basic idea: have a series of public meetings, with both men and women, at Angurugu and Umbakumba, and seek to establish just who was promised to whom. The Aboriginals welcomed my intention to have the meetings, but a few missionaries got a bit uppity about this intruder from Native Affairs 'prying into our work'. But by and large I got good support. There was a census book in those days, irreverently referred to as 'the stud book', compiled when new legislation was introduced in 1954 and the 'race' elements of discriminatory legislation were replaced by declarations that 'persons unable without assistance to manage their own affairs' stood 'in need of care and assistance'. What happened was that most 'part-Aboriginals' were thereby exempted from the new legislation, The Welfare Ordinance 1954. With a few exceptions — notably the famous painter Albert Namatjira — around 17,000 Aboriginals of 'the full descent' were named and declared to be 'wards' within the meaning of the new legislation. There had been a blanket declaration that all people on Groote Eylandt 'stood in need of care and assistance' so the census records for the island were accurate.

At my meetings with men and women, established as compatible to one another simply through being together in one place, I went through, time after time, each name of the 700 or so Aboriginals on the island, 400 at Angurugu, 200 at Umbakumba, 100 living in bush camps. Tell me about this person. Who is he or she promised to? What payments have been made? Who organised the promise? Gradually, over three or four weeks, I established a very comprehensive rundown on practically every resident of Groote Eylandt. The promises were not restricted to Groote Eylandt, for there were relationships and contacts on the mainland which added up to a very complex system. I checked it, re-checked it, cross-checked it, to the point where there was uniform agreement that I had an accurate knowledge of the marriage promises.

A letter from Darwin told me Fred Gray had agreed to leave Groote Eylandt, and that CMS would take over Umbakumba. The takeover would be on a date late in April 1958, and I was to be there as the government representative, for the government had agreed to pay Gray compensation for the work he had done and the assets CMS would inherit. Fred drove to Angurugu to talk with me, and I could see he was fairly bitter about things, but too much of a gentleman to rant and rave about being the victim of some utter bastardry. So much for Christian practices. The local missionaries were all on quite good terms with Fred, for he was a practising Anglican among other things, but the superiors of CMS in Sydney were a very tricky bunch in my opinion. They had long been jealous of the fact that Gray ran a much better show than they did.

The Umbakumba Aboriginals were not asked for their opinion about which whitefellows would henceforth dominate their lives by their mere presence on Aboriginal land. But then, it wasn't considered to be Aboriginal land any more. It was Crown land, government land, leased to CMS. No one told the blackfellows though.

As the takeover at Umbakumba was a month away, and I wanted to consolidate my thinking about the marriage system, I made a suggestion to both the missionaries and the Aboriginal leaders. One of the big issues raised with me by Aboriginals was the need to get more money, and the opportunity to buy things they felt they needed from the white man's world. They yearned for access to the wondrous place they believed Darwin to be. I had been writing to Ted Evans each week to let him know what I was doing, and we had between us organised that groups of Groote Eylandt men would henceforth be engaged for periods of three months in Darwin, working for the army, the RAAF, and now even the RAN, in the same way as the Tiwi were employed. It wasn't possible for me to organise anything meaningful for women, other than to encourage them to produce and sell to the very limited market in Darwin such things as mats, baskets and shell jewellery which Fred Gray had taught them to make. CMS used to buy those things in any case. But I knew from my experiences at Maningrida that crocodile skins were very valuable — didn't Nango agree? So I suggested to the men that a party of us go to the mainland, to areas where they had authority and rights of access, and shoot crocs for a few weeks, until I was required to be at Umbakumba. Thereby they should be able to make some relatively spectacular money. I could also see value for me to spend valuable time with these blokes who were obviously going to be the instigators if there was any trouble over the intrusion of the whites into the marriage system.

It was agreed that 20 men would take me to the Blue Mud Bay area. They had traditional rights to hunt there, and they knew that the Walker and Koolatong Rivers had plenty of crocs. They assured me we could live absolutely off the land and sea. It was a bit of a punt, but I agreed that the only white man things we would take were three 50-pound drums of flour, tobacco, two huge bags of salt, my .303 rifle, butchers' knives and steels, and ammunition.

We left Groote Eylandt in five canoes, all under sail. They unfurled sails in the same style as the Macassans who had introduced the *libaliba,* the dugout canoe, and it was immediately obvious they were superb seamen. One of the craft was huge by dugout canoe standards, and could seat 20 if necessary. They called it 'the steamer'. We sailed all through the first night. I could sense them throwing off the influence of white-man-style living, as though discarding old clothes. Most of them did just that, too. Shirts disappeared, shorts were replaced by cockrags, each one suddenly had a knife in the belt. They were transformed, no other word for it. How dare we stuff them up. That message was pounded into my head with every demonstration of the lifestyle they had known so intimately for so long. Suddenly I was the outsider, the inept one. I knew that our intrusion into their lives was criminal, no matter how well-intentioned. Not only were they alert, laughing, happy; they were good.

It was a joyous month, the most fascinating of my life. I learned something every five minutes. They concentrated, they laughed, joked. They were in charge, uninhibited, complete hunters. I just wish that every person in Australia, or the world for that matter, could share that month. Then you wouldn't hear any nonsense about 'useless blackfellows'. Every night we got our self-imposed target of five crocodiles, and then camped on safe beaches, the wind in the casuarinas blending with the timeless songs the old blokes sang for the young men. I'd never heard any traditional singing at Groote Eylandt, unlike most other places in Arnhem Land, where it is par-for-the-course that you are lulled to sleep each night by the soothing singing, the click of sticks, and the drone of the *yirdaki*, the real name for the didgeridoo.

We ate every type of succulent fish they speared with breathless ease. We cooked johnny cakes in the coals. We gorged ourselves on turtle eggs. We captured five huge green turtles, two sitting, unsuspecting, on a beach, and three we caught by harpooning them in the open sea and then pulling them, still alive, into 'the steamer'. We took them, poor helpless creatures, upside down, back to Groote. But the big thrill was dugong hunting at night. An unforgettable experience.

A dugong is a herbiverous, dolphin-sized, meaty sea mammal, sometimes called a 'sea cow'. It lives in shallow sheltered seas like those of the Gulf of Carpentaria, and grazes on sea grass. Because the dugong suckles its young it is the creature from which the mermaid myths developed. It is a much sought-after source of protein food by the coastal tribes of north Australia, although in present times some Aboriginal groups have forsaken their rights to hunt them in the interests of conservation. The dugong has tiny eyes, so is not good at seeing predators like hunters, but it is possessed of acute hearing, and is a very fast swimmer: hence, it is very difficult to catch.

We set off on a moonless night, in a medium-sized canoe, and paddled to where the men reckoned they would get a dugong. We sat in the canoe, motionless, nobody making the least noise, for about an hour. The only sound was the gentle splash of the little waves on the side of the canoe. Then we heard it. *Wheeeew,* the sound of the blowing waterspout that tells the hunter the location of the prey. Gently, our two paddlers, one in the bow, one in the stern, guided us towards the location of the noise. Five of us. I'm sitting in the middle of the canoe, supernumerary, fascinated. They paddled deep, then shook every drop of water gently off the paddle before it entered the water again. Eerie, absolute silence, ghost propulsion in pitch blackness. At the front of the canoe, our harpoon man, Samson, a magnificent specimen with appropriate biblical nickname, eased himself into a standing position, poised with the long harpoon pole, the cruel head wedged into the top of the shaft. His toes gripped the two thin sides of the canoe like steel fingers. The balance! We changed to paddling in a large circle, waiting. *Phoooo!* There it was. Close. Our circle tightened. Suddenly the dugong surfaced, as though stretching itself, ready for the next blow. Our paddlers were galvanised. Six quick strokes and we were at the dugong's tail. Then I almost yelled, shocked, surprised: Samson had launched himself into the air, a great long horizontal dive that took him directly above the dugong, and he drove the harpoon into the creature's neck as it performed its last tragic blow.

The dugong took off, pulling us at a billowing pace in its wake, the harpoon our capstan. Samson was somewhere back there, in the water, forgotten. The entire length of rope had run out as the dugong took off, and Samson let go. The bow paddler grabbed the rope and took up the frantic slack. All in a darkness that was absolute. The wet rope fell in coils at my feet, and I felt I was a member of the team as I wound it into a neat coil. A frantic minute, and the slack was gone. The impaled dugong flubbered to the surface, a huge, gleaming helpless mass, its tail flopping but not in control any more. I watched with a sickening feeling as the man with the rope grabbed the dugong by the tail, hugged it, and was slowly killing it by drowning the poor thing. It took an eternity. Samson called to signal his whereabouts, and we paddled slowly to retrieve him, the dead dugong tied to the side of the canoe.

They caught three other dugong on other nights, but I couldn't bear to accompany them, due to the cruelty of the drowning. We salted the meat to take it back to Groote, but I didn't eat any. I had tasted dugong, and it is very good meat, but I was now left with very mixed feelings. Anybody who wants to hunt dugong should be offered free tins of bully beef as an alternative. But I confess it was exciting.

We sailed back to Groote Eylandt, and a large crowd walked to the beach to view the turtles, the crocodile skins, and to divvy up the dugong meat and piles of fish we caught on the return trip. The turtles were carted on the trailer back to Angurugu and released in a big billabong section of the river to keep them alive until they were ready to be killed and eaten. When that time came, the little kids were all sent into the river to dive for and locate the turtles. Then, amid much laughter, the kids swam the turtles to the bank, and the preparations for the feast began. A big fire was lit, the turtle's throat cut, the guts stuffed with hot stones and the beast was cooked slowly in the coals.

A few days later, I went to Umbakumba to be present at the sad handover from Fred Gray to CMS. The Umbakumba Aboriginals were bewilderment itself as an important chapter in their lives ended, and the future must have looked dull by comparison. The feature of Fred Gray's time at Umbakumba was that every Aboriginal had an important role in the running of the place. Umbakumba was the only Aboriginal institution in Australia that was self-sufficient, with gardens, fishing, cattle, turkeys, fowls and goats feeding the people, and meagre earnings coming in through the sale in America of bark paintings, shell jewellery and artifacts: Fred Gray was fifty years ahead of the rest of Australia in that respect. He was paid a miserable £12,000 for the entire assets of Umbakumba, all the buildings, a fine launch and the new Land Rover. Nothing, it seemed, to compensate him for the selfless 20 years he had put in there, doing a better job than any other whitefeller I had seen among Aboriginal people. He went through the handover with great dignity, helped considerably by the fact that the incoming CMS superintendent, Keith Hart, was a fine man with a proper appreciation of the work Fred had done.

Fred Gray went to Darwin where he bought a block of land that he called Little Umbakumba. Ironically, he ran boarding kennels there. On Groote Eylandt he had convinced the Aboriginals, on health grounds, to have no dogs — the only time I have ever seen that achieved, more's the pity. I hate blackfeller dogs. A few of his 'Aboriginal family' travelled to Darwin with Fred and his wife Marjorie. Fred Gray gave me encouragement and unstinting support for more than 30 years as I researched a series of related incidents known as the Caledon Bay and Woodah Island killings of 1932–3. Fred had been involved. I eventually presented my research in 1994 and was awarded a Masters Degree. Then the story was published as a book titled *Justice All Their Own*.

In September 1932 Fred Gray was harvesting trepang at Caledon Bay, in north-east Arnhem Land. Aboriginals call trepang *dariba*. Another common name is *beche de mer:* it is the sea cucumber *Holothuria edulis*, highly prized in Asia as both food and aphrodisiac. Two Darwin-owned luggers, crewed by Japanese and Aboriginals from other regions arrived, and began to gather trepang in the same waters. There was a dispute between the Japanese and the local Aboriginals and on 17 September 1932 five Japanese were speared to death. Fred and his crew buried the Japanese, took their luggers back to Darwin and reported the killings. In July 1933 a police party travelled from Darwin to investigate the killings. Unbeknown to the police, in March 1933 two white men named Traynor and Fagan had been killed at Woodah Island, 100 kilometres south of Caledon Bay by a different group of Aboriginals, for stealing Aboriginal women. In the mistaken belief that all Aboriginals in the region were of the one tribe, whom the police called the Balamumu, the police landed on Woodah Island on their way to Caledon Bay when they saw the smoke of bushfires. The police party captured four Aboriginal women. It was ironic that one of the women captured by the police was Djaparri, the 17-year-old wife of a man named Tuckiar. Tuckiar and another man had killed Traynor and Fagan for stealing their women, including Djaparri, and now a police party had captured their women. Tuckiar killed a police constable named McColl by spearing him in the heart. The police withdrew to Darwin and plans were formulated to send out a large party to 'teach the blacks a lesson'. It was only four years since the last police-led massacre of Aboriginals in the Northern Territory, so Prime Minister Lyons, heeding the protests of various bodies and individuals in the south of Australia, and indeed the prime minister of England, gave permission for a party of missionaries to investigate the killings and seek to make recommendations about ways to bring peace to the region. The police and the people of north Australia were angry that 'southern ratbag organisations' had usurped the role of the white man in the north, and were not appeased when Gray and the missionaries were instrumental in bringing to Darwin five Aboriginals who volunteered to travel, acknowledged that they were in each case the killers, but sought 'talks' on the grounds that they felt justified in protecting their own rights in their own country. So much for 'talks': as soon as they arrived in Darwin the Aboriginals were arrested, farcical court cases were conducted, and three totally different verdicts and sentences were delivered in the white man's court to Aboriginals who did not speak English and certainly would not have understood the proceedings. Mau, Natjelma and Narkaya, the killers of the Japanese, were sentenced to 20 years hard labour. Tuckiar and Mirera, the killers of Traynor and Fagan, were acquitted. Tuckiar, the killer of Constable McColl, was sentenced to death. Tuckiar was acquitted after an appeal to the High Court, was released from Fannie Bay Gaol, but disappeared the next day, never to be seen again. The strong rumour was that the police took Tuckiar out into Darwin harbour and shot him. When my book was published I did not claim it to be the definitive work, but I *was* the only person who ever interviewed Djaparri and sought her memories and opinions. She stated to me that she had been taken and raped by Traynor and Fagan, and told me how Tuckiar speared McColl. She was in a good position to comment on McColl's spearing, for she was chained to McColl's wrist at the moment when her husband emerged from the bush, signalled to her to move to one side, and killed the policeman. It was alleged in court that Constable McColl had also raped her, but in a statement to me Djaparri said that was not true. One day the story will become a great film.

I dedicated my book to Fred Gray, and was proud when, shortly before his death in 1995, he wrote saying he was pleased the story had been told so comprehensively and accurately. Fred was 95 when he died. The Aboriginals of Groote Eylandt demanded that he be buried at Umbakumba with full tribal honours. A great man, he had a huge influence on my life and my attitudes to Aboriginal affairs.

I was never the same again, after my time at Groote Eylandt. I began to realise the complexity of issues where I and other people like me had awesome power and control. I started to think about Aboriginal land ownership, the ethics of the intrusion of church and state into their lives, the question of morale, the value of preserving their language and ceremonial life, the need for a meaningful self-sufficiency in the inevitable, regrettable association with the white man, a new lifestyle where Aboriginals had no control.

And the marriage promises? All I could do was pass over to CMS the list of marriage promises, and ask them to commence dialogue with the Aboriginals to seek to reconcile their various positions. I hinted at a biblical approach and immediately saw the lips begin to purse, but I put my suggestion nonetheless. I remember it vividly, sitting on the verandah of the superintendent's house, the brash young Native Affairs bloke about to make scriptural suggestions to people who several times since my arrival had reminded me they had Th. L after their names — I think it was short for Licentiate of Theology — people who reinforced their every opinion with a specific scriptural reference, people who suggested a word of prayer to mark the least occasion.

I was hesitant, tentative, watching the assembled eyes as I launched into my own attempt at a parable. 'Many of the younger men are paying for additional wives because it's the done thing, but most people, especially women, support the principle of monogamy. Why don't you seek to be arbitrators, face-savers? Seek to cancel out the promises with goods, even money where it's been paid? Where money has changed hands it seems to be trivial amounts, because they don't have access to money. More often than not the promises have been covered by services rendered. Why not apply Christ's Parable of the Vineyard as a guide? You know the one I mean?' The missionaries' lips are really thin now. I continued. 'A man engaged a worker for an agreed fee of a denarius to work a full day in his vineyard. Then, throughout the day, he engaged other workers at different times, but paid them a denarius also. The first worker complained, but the master said, "You were happy with the fee I agreed to pay you. I am showing you that the last shall be first and the first last."'

I was getting more confident. 'Perhaps if you establish which is the most extensive and expensive promise, and work out a satisfactory economic payout figure whereby everybody can save face, that would put you in a safe bargaining position to discuss other promises.'

My suggestion went down like a fart in a lift. There was useful dialogue though, and for the first time the CMS staff was forced to acknowledge that many of their senior churchgoers were involved in arranging traditional marriages. Things got better, rather than worse.

The control of the CMS was much attenuated, in any case, by the arrival of BHP in the next few years to exploit manganese deposits on the island. Black manganese has always been the base colour for the unique Groote Eylandt bark paintings. The island has one of the biggest and richest manganese deposits in the world.

Today the Aboriginals are recognised as the owners of their land, and derive hefty royalties from the mining. Economically affluent via royalties, wages and social services, the Aboriginals may now freely accept or reject the Christian way, where once they were coerced into becoming flour-tea-and-sugar Christians. They have excellent opportunities in employment, education and access to very good living standards. Previously, they had no choice other than to have their lives dominated by an unsought one-sided intrusion into their lives.

They'd still be better off without any whites or any mining on the island, for there are huge social and health problems. It would be good to take them back to a pre-white lifestyle. But bring back the *inugwamba?* I'm not sure that would be a good idea.

8
Desert Rat

I parked the truck outside the Native Affairs office in Hartley Street, Alice Springs, walked inside and introduced myself to Bill McCoy, a little jockey-sized bloke saddled in an executive chair and riding a huge, very empty desk. A pipe, a tin of Borkum Riff tobacco, a dozen boxes of matches, and a little name plate that announced he was District Superintendent.

'Ted Egan, Bill,' I opened with, and shook his reluctant hand with Top End vigour. He wasted no time setting me straight. But first I had to wait as he went through the routine of filling his pipe, clenching it tightly between his teeth, lighting it, and then talking to me through impressive clouds of smoke. Harry Mulumbuk would have approved: I narrowed my eyes.

'Hmm, yes, er . . . Ted. Well, you're going to find things *puff* very different down here. The old desert blackfellow *puff puff* is very slow to give his loyalty to anybody who doesn't *puff* have grey hair.'

He didn't say that counted him in and me out but I got the message.

I was no sooner back in Darwin from Groote Eylandt, reunited with Rae and the kids, than I was promoted to Superintendent — a big promotion, as I was only 25, same age as Ned Kelly when he was hanged — and posted to Yuendumu, 300 kilometres north-west of Alice Springs. I had never worked in The Centre, and we Top Enders referred to our contemporaries in that part of the world as Desert Rats. Suddenly I was to be one.

I travelled to Alice by truck on my own. Rae and the two kids stayed with Rae's parents until they flew down a month later. During a couple of days in the town of Alice Springs I found the whitefellers very hard-nosed in their attitudes to blackfellers. Among other things, there wasn't the Asian presence and genetic admixture that I was used to in Darwin. It was 'them' and 'us' as far as local whites were concerned. May 1958 was freezing cold in Alice at night, and cool, but sunny, during the day.

Strange to see everybody, especially Aboriginals, wearing overcoats, jackets, long trousers. The policemen wore brown serge uniforms, southern style. Indeed, the town of Alice Springs was nothing like Darwin. Neat streets and South Australian style houses, snug brick buildings with blinds on the verandahs, citrus trees and grape vines in the yards, and a general air of conservatism. Such a pretty town, nestled in the amphitheatre created by the spectacular Macdonnell Ranges. I had only been to Alice twice before, once passing through on my first trip to Darwin, and again in 1952 when we travelled down (or should it be 'up'?) from Darwin to beat Alice Springs at football. I hadn't had much of a look at the town then: now there was more time.

I realised that I would have to handle Bill McCoy with care, but when he misread that as being my due deference he became more expansive. Would I *puff* like a drink? He took me to the lovely old Stuart Arms pub, a charming stone building in Todd Street. It was full of cattle men with big hats and horny hands. Most of them were drinking rum, and Bill McCoy ordered a drink I had never heard of — rum and black currant. I had a beer. It was immediately obvious that Centre blokes were as disdainful of Top Enders as we were of them. Bill wore a big *puff* broad-brimmed hat but then carefully counted out his money *puff puff* from a little leather purse, and I bit my finger to knock the grin off my face. I was substituting John Wayne for Bill. Rum and black currant!

Bill drove me to Yuendumu, a five–hour drive on a reasonable dirt road. He was a good driver, and was very happy to answer my many questions. There had been recent rain, and I was amazed to see how green everything was. Indeed, the country about 100 kilometres from Alice was lush. Rolling Mitchell grass plains stretched out like an emerald carpet below the azure hills of the Macdonnell Ranges. Thereafter the country became flat, featureless, spinifex, mulga, limestone and not very noteworthy. But I was impressed by the excellent condition of the cattle at the various bores and waterholes along the track.

Yuendumu was a government settlement to serve the needs of the Warlpiri Aboriginal people. In those days it was spelt Wailbri. It was a neat but small place with five houses for white staff, a couple of Sidney Willams huts — 'the ration store' and 'the workshop' — a new hospital, quarters for the two nursing sisters and a new school. One of the houses was occupied by a Baptist missionary, Reverend Tom Fleming, and his wife Pat. They were pleasant, feet-on-the-ground people. Tom had been a prisoner-of-war of the Japanese, and did not expect any miracles in his religious work among the Aboriginals.

As I had been permanently appointed Superintendent of Yuendumu, Bill McCoy was intent on starting me off on 'the right track'. He did not seem to have much confidence in me, and spoke disparagingly of my predecessor, a bloke who had been there only about six months, and had made the big mistake, in Bill's opinion, of 'being too soft on the blackfellows'.

'They're tough, these desert blackfellows,' Bill told me for the umpteenth time. 'They'll only respect you *puff* if you are hard, but fair. In particular, you mustn't, *puff puff* you mustn't give rations, or any government goods to any able-bodied people who don't qualify. If you do, *puff* you'll find that nobody will work, and they'll run over the top of you.' I more or less understood that, for that had basically been Fred Gray's policy, a system that Aboriginals accepted as a 'fair go' but Bill was annoying me a bit, assuming that because I was from the Top End I'd be a softy.

I was glad when he went back to town and I had the chance to talk to a few people, white and black, and develop some ideas about how to run the place. I had a very good offsider named Don Busbridge, who, to my relief, was a super mechanic. I am hopeless with engines or anything mechanical. As well, I immediately liked Don and his wife Beryl. A wonderful Aboriginal couple, Tim Jabangardi and his wife Uni Nambijinba, announced that they would be working to me on a personal level, and they became friends for life. In fact I was given the skin name Jabangardi to make me a classificatory brother to Tim, and they told me that Rae would be a Nambijinba woman, a sister to Uni. Bill McCoy had warned me against taking on a skin name. 'They'll only do it to compromise you,' he told me. But I preferred Tim Jabangardi's approach. 'We have to call you something. You might as well be my brother.' I'm still just Jabangardi to the Warlpiri. There are family compromises to accept and honour, like sharing food and money, which make things a bit one-sided if you are an affluent (by Aboriginal standards) whitefeller, but I accept that. I know they would share anything they had with me if I asked them to. I would never turn down a request from one of my Aboriginal family for food. I often give them money. But if I say '*Laua*' [Nothing doing] in respect of money they accept that I either have none, I have none to spare or it's a straight-out refusal.

The first thing the Warlpiri have to do is establish the skin or sub-section of any person they are in contact with. It determines who you can marry or not marry, and basically establishes your entire behavioural program towards every other person. While white people are not taken into the kinship set-up, they are nonetheless given an identity. It is one of the most fascinating things worked out in Aboriginal culture, and certainly an absolute requirement for people living with one another for thousands of years in small isolated communities. It is vital to prevent inbreeding. The royal families of Europe, who have suffered badly in genetic terms over the centuries from inbreeding, could have learned something from a comparable system. If there are marriage mistakes things are corrected the next generation, for a person's skin is derived from the mother, not the father, as there is genetically no doubt who the mother is. The chart on the following page shows the genius of the skin system.

There were about 800 Warlpiri living at Yuendumu, in primitive conditions. There was nothing that even resembled a permanent shelter from the elements for them, let alone a house.

WALPIRI SKIN GROUPS

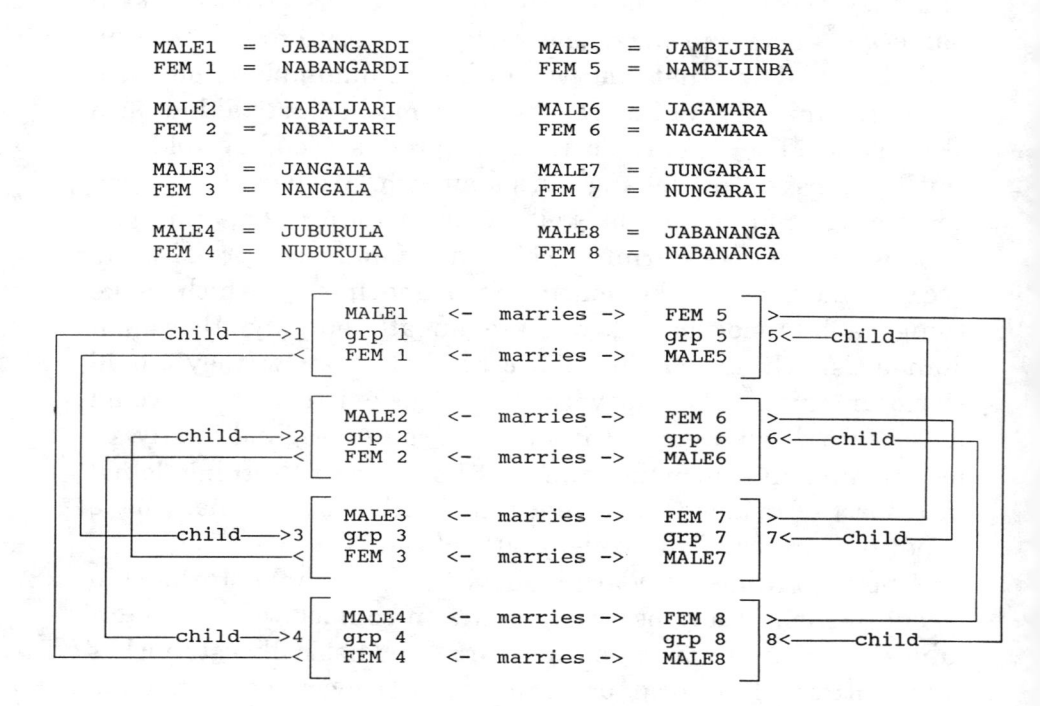

```
MALE1  =  JABANGARDI        MALE5  =  JAMBIJINBA
FEM 1  =  NABANGARDI        FEM 5  =  NAMBIJINBA

MALE2  =  JABALJARI         MALE6  =  JAGAMARA
FEM 2  =  NABALJARI         FEM 6  =  NAGAMARA

MALE3  =  JANGALA           MALE7  =  JUNGARAI
FEM 3  =  NANGALA           FEM 7  =  NUNGARAI

MALE4  =  JUBURULA          MALE8  =  JABANANGA
FEM 4  =  NUBURULA          FEM 8  =  NABANANGA
```

```
                  ┌ MALE1   <- marries ->  FEM 5 ┐
    -child--->1  │  grp 1                  grp 5 │ >--
              <─│  FEM 1   <- marries ->  MALE5 │  5<----child--

                  ┌ MALE2   <- marries ->  FEM 6 ┐
    -child--->2  │  grp 2                  grp 6 │ >--
              <─│  FEM 2   <- marries ->  MALE6 │  6<----child--

                  ┌ MALE3   <- marries ->  FEM 7 ┐
    -child--->3  │  grp 3                  grp 7 │ >--
              <─│  FEM 3   <- marries ->  MALE7 │  7<----child--

                  ┌ MALE4   <- marries ->  FEM 8 ┐
    -child--->4  │  grp 4                  grp 8 │ >--
              <─│  FEM 4   <- marries ->  MALE8 │  8<----child--
```

All Walpiri people are related to one another. Every person is identified, primarily, by being a member of one of the eight 'skin' groups: if you don't know a person's skin name, you ask, '*Nyiya nyiya?*' — what's your skin group? Note the repeated word *nyiya* — literally, what's what? Unless you know what's what you can not begin to have dialogue.

Sons and daughters born into, say, Group 1 have Jabangardi or Nabangardi as their names, respectively. All males take J names, all females N names, in all groups. Kinship law insists Jabangardi marry a woman of Group 5, someone called Nambijinba. Their sons will be Jabananga, daughters Nabananga, Group 8 skin. They must take Group 4 wives and husbands. Nabananga marries Juburula; her children become Jagamara and Nagamara, Group 6 skin.

A five-generation cycle will see Jabangardi and Nabangardi reappear. Maximum genetic mixing. Add inter-tribal genetic infusions and corrections — the real father may not always be known — and it adds up to an ingenious inbreeding defence system. No enduring Hapsburg jaw overshoots or haemophilia in Central Australia.

No toilets, no showers, no water to the Aboriginal camp. Women filled 20–litre tins from one water tap and walked to their camps with these huge loads balanced on their heads. They camped on the ground, in the open, on two sides of the 200 metres square settlement. There was light mulga scrub on three sides of the settlement, and the airstrip on the fourth side. The Warlpiri sheltered behind little mulga windbreaks at night, using tiny fires (and dogs) to keep warm. And yet, on the first couple of nights, when Tim Jabangardi invited me to visit the camp and talk to some men, I noticed several old people sleeping naked alongside these little fires. It was about freezing point at night, and I quickly formed the opinion, which I still hold, that the Aboriginals of Central Australia are about the toughest people in the world. Perhaps I should say they *were* the toughest, although I usually don't go for past tense talk about Aboriginals. It infers that they don't exist any more: it's a device whereby a lot of people deny Aboriginals their rights. They were the toughest in the world. Today they are not coping well at all.

Bill McCoy was correct. They were very different from the Top End people. They were brown rather than black, and many were quite big in build. Like the Groote Eylandt people, they were not quick to smile, and seemed to be summing me up before they committed themselves in any way. The women were used to hard work, but most of the men were not that keen on the work ethic. The weather was cold, even through the day, and below freezing at night. A chilling wind straight on an uninterrupted course from Antarctica chiselled away at your bone marrow. At every opportunity men sheltered from the wind and huddled on the ground around little fires. There were notable exceptions, especially Tim and two wonderful young blokes who quickly attached themselves to me and displayed cheerful, absolute unswerving loyalty for the rest of my stay at Yuendumu. Johnny Jungarai and Sandy Jabananga were both excellent drivers, mechanics, and prepared to have a go at anything. With those three men and Don Busbridge, I was in good hands and quickly began to enjoy this fascinating chapter of my life.

There was no electricity when we went to Yuendumu, but

the ritual of lighting five or six Tilley lamps at 6 pm was no novelty to me. Kerosene fridges were still a pain. A lighting plant was installed in 1960. The road to Alice Springs was a graded dirt track, good most of the time, but likely to be 'out' for weeks after rain — not that it rained much. We had to order our supplies at stores in town, but as there was constant traffic on the road it was easy to organise deliveries. There were no telephones, and our contact with the outside world was via the Royal Flying Doctor Service radio network. We all had Traeger transceivers, battery-operated versions of the pedal wireless sets invented by Alf Traeger. There were medical 'skeds' (schedules) twice a day at 8 am and 4 pm, followed by 'general traffic' in the form of inward and outward telegrams sent at normal PMG rates. Urgent medical calls could be made at any time during the day. At other times people could use the radio for what were called 'galah' sessions, chats about cattle, recipes, social arrangements.

The Alice Springs RFDS base covered a huge area, 800 kilometres in every direction. This meant that clients closer to Alice Springs had the strongest signals, and were usually first to be heard by the operators, George Brown, Margaret Baker or Sonia Rieff. It was frustrating for those with weaker signals, further out, to have to spend hours on the radio waiting for their turn for telegrams or medicals. A bloke named Bill Lavington had a cattle station named Kurrundi, 600 kilometres north-east of Alice Springs. He was very much a cattle man, not a desk man, and he used to get very short-fused about the radio sessions and the long queues for people like himself. One morning, after waiting about an hour on the end of the list, and probably fuming as he sat by his portable radio in the stockcamp, with a bit of fencing wire for an aerial, Bill finally got through to George Brown:

'Go ahead with your traffic, Bill.'

You could tell from Bill's voice how angry he was. 'About bloody time,' he muttered. 'One telegram, George. Here it is:

ADDRESS: ELDER SMITH ALICE SPRINGS TEXT: PLEASE FORWARD EARLIEST FIVE BAGS FLOUR ONE BAG SUGAR ONE CASE TEA ONE CARTON

PLUM JAM ONE CASE NATIVE TOBACCO TWO ROLLS FENCING WIRE ONE PAIR PLIERS TEN BUNDLES STAR PICKETS ONE PAIR R M WILLIAMS BOOTS SIZE TWELVE. ALSO SEND SOME GROG. SIGNED LAVINGTON.

'I'll just check to see if you got that, George.'

The Royal Flying Doctor Service was started by John Flynn, a Presbyterian minister. It has always been understood that gambling and booze are not to be mentioned over the sacred air waves. George Brown decided to play this one tongue-in-cheek.

'I got most of that, down to the Williams boots. What was that last item, Bill?'

You could sense the smoke coming out of Bill Lavington's ears. His voice went up a few decibels.

'Grog,' he roared. 'Grog.'

'Not reading you too well, Bill. Try spelling it for me. And use the radio alphabet please, Bill.'

'The what?'

'The radio alphabet. Alpha, Bravo, Charlie. Over.'

There was a short silence, followed by a fiery snort. 'Right, here goes. Grog. G for Jesus, R for Arsehole, O for 'Opeless, G for Jesus. GROG you dopey bastard.'

There were cattle stations on each of the four boundaries of the 2200-square-kilometre Yuendumu Reserve. On the west was Mt Doreen, owned by Bill Braitling, his wife Doreen and their son Wally. On the north was Mt Denison station, owned by the Martin family, and jointly managed by Leo Martin, his wife Thelma, and Norman Hagan, a renowned cattleman, related to the Gadens of Darwin. On the east was Mt Allan station, owned by the Smiths, and managed by David (Did) Smith and his wife Dawn. And on the south was Mt Wedge, owned by Bill (Wallaby) Waudby. Bill's wife, Pat, had contracted poliomyelitis and had only recently returned to the station, having spent six years in an iron lung. She had in fact given birth to her second son, Bob, in the iron lung. I visited our neighbours, and could spot immediately that Rae and I would get on well with all of them. Each neighbour ventured the opinion that Yuendumu should be capable of being stocked with cattle, and offered to give me some advice and help if and when I elected to do something about that.

'It'll give us the chance to pinch some government calves,' said Did Smith with a bit of a grin.

He and the others were good teachers. Eventually Yuendumu did its share of branding *their* calves, but I suppose they were doing the same to us. It's the oldest game in the bush, and part of the custom in open range cattle country. You never eat your own beef. Having studied Fred Gray at Umbakumba, I was determined to make Yuendumu as self-sufficient as possible, so I immediately began to ask a lot of questions about cattle. If ever any of the neighbouring stations were mustering when I had 'days off' I'd go into their stock camps with them. I quickly came to know a little about cattle in general, and a lot about butchering, branding and how the best stock yards function. We eventually built on the Yuendumu Reserve some wonderful stockyards out of desert oak, and Norman Hagan gave me invaluable advice about how to cater for the prevailing winds, where best to locate gates, the size of races, all knowledge derived from his lifetime of experience as a drover and stockman.

In earlier years Yuendumu had large vegetable gardens, and we got these back into production. Central Australian soils are very good if you put some fertiliser back into them. We had a herd of goats, and began to fertilise the gardens with burnt goat shit: it's too strong if you use it neat. It took no time at all for the gardens to flourish. At the outset we used to buy five bullocks a week from Mt Doreen, shot and quartered on the ground, and brought in by truck to be hung in our meathouse. It's surprising how hygienic this operation is when done properly. You use the hide of the animal and lots of green bushes to keep the carcass clean. This meat was distributed to various spots around the settlement, where communal meals were cooked each lunchtime. Each day a good healthy stew was available for all workers, women with babies, school kids and pensioners. Don Busbridge had a formidable collection of rifles, and had been a Queen's Prize shooter, so, at his suggestion, we went each Friday night, with Sandy and Johnny, and shot kangaroos. Don was a fantastic marksman, and I was above average, so we easily got 20 kangaroos each week. Some Aboriginals had their own .22 rifles, kept in my office, and they often hunted kangaroos on a recreational basis. Many of the older blokes still hunted successfully with spears. On weekends a lot of the Aboriginal people walked out to get bush tucker. Many of them were still mobile, likely to disappear for weeks at a time for ceremonial reasons, or, particularly in the winter months, to go 'puppy dogging'. There was a bounty of £2 a head on dingoes, and the blackfellows tracked down the dingo bitches that had recently whelped, and took all of the litter except one, left to suckle the mother: they certainly had no desire to eliminate the dingo as a species. They brought the little grey scalps, with the telltale white tip on the tail, to me, and I paid them the bounty.

Don Busbridge and I worked out a token system whereby each eligible person received a stamped metal washer each day to indicate they had fronted up for work or attendance at the baby clinic or the hospital, whatever, in order that we knew who should receive a weekly ration each Friday. These washers were tied on a string by the recipients and quickly became known as 'Yuendumu two bobs'. Five tokens, full ration. About 2 pm each Friday we distributed rations, which consisted of flour, tea, sugar, a tin of something — preferably meat, but more often than not treacle or jam. Workers, men and women, got a stick of chewing tobacco each. Twice a year workers and pensioners received an issue of clothes — nothing fancy, just a dress for women and trousers and shirt for men — and a blanket. Kids were issued clothes through school, pre-school and the hospital. It was all terribly feudal and I immediately realised, with some degree of shock, what power I had over the lives of so many people just because I had the key of the ration store. I vowed not to abuse that power, and in hindsight I know I didn't. Not to a culpable level.

The ceremonial life of the Warlpiri was still intact, and there were always signs of last night's activities. The punctual principal workers fronted up each day at about 7 am, for a shower and breakfast wherever they were located for work. More often than not they would still have blood, feathers and ochre mixed into their hair and on their faces and bodies. It was all kept fairly secret though, nothing like Borroloola, where whites were welcome at corroborees. I quickly realised how serious the ceremonial business was in The Centre. I did eventually go to quite a few men's ceremonies, which were spectacular. But I was always sworn to secrecy. 'Don't tell anybody what you see here,' I was told in no uncertain terms. In those areas I was no longer 'the boss': I was just an uninitiated whitefeller they were prepared to tolerate. Nowadays, I regret that I did not spend more time studying the various procedures and ceremonies, and learning the Warlpiri language, but I was a bit too imbued with the work ethic during my time at Yuendumu, and looked on the ceremonial business as something that took workers away from their jobs.

I did not realise at that time the enormity of the level of dispossession that had taken place among those original owners of Central Australia. Just one generation earlier they were independent in their own admittedly harsh environment. When whites rode into the country west of Alice Springs in the 1920s the government with a stroke of the pen encouraged the alienation of the Warlpiri land. Pastoral leases and grazing licences were given to practically any whites who asked for them, on the basis that it was Crown land. After the Warlpiri killed a white man named Fred Brooks in 1928 they became the victims of what has since been called The Coniston Massacre. A police party led by Constable Murray, sent to avenge the Brooks murder, acknowledged that they killed 31 Warlpiri: reliable witnesses assert the number killed was more like 80. Constable Murray and his party were exonerated by the internal police commission of inquiry. The Warlpiri were dispersed by this punitive action, the last officially organised massacre in Australia. They went in every direction, thereby allowing the white settlers to validate their claims to the land on the basis that the Aboriginals had abandoned it.

By 1950 almost all their country, with the exception of the Yuendumu Reserve, was taken up with cattle stations. The Aboriginals could still access their country, and many of them did, for relationships with individual station owners were generally good. In reality they were discouraged from moving around too much by the enticement of the white man's commodities, supplied to them at places like Yuendumu at great risk to their health and well-being by a government that today professes to be mystified when vilified as the principal agent of Aboriginal dispossession.

I acknowledge that I did not raise too many objections about the system, of which I was a vital cog at that time. The dispossession seemed a *fait accompli,* and irreversible. I did not start to develop even a glimmer of the truth until the middle 1960s. Those who scream for extinguishment of native title over pastoral leases, following the Wik High Court judgment, do not know what they are talking about. They need to be told some historical facts. They mouth nonsense stimulated by sheer greed, political opportunism, lust for land or the paranoia provoked by the guilty knowledge that we shafted the blackfellows in this country. But even the presentation of historical facts will not convince some whites of Aboriginal rights: I have heard seemingly intelligent white people say that there were no blackfellows in Central Australia until the whites drilled the water bores. Fair dinkum.

If Aboriginals in places like Central Australia are denied access to the cattle stations on land once indisputably theirs, it is removing their right to freedom of worship. For the land holds their beliefs. Deny Catholics access to Vatican City? Keep the Jews away from the Wailing Wall? Sadly, many Aboriginals in other parts of Australia have lost the secrets of their country, lost their language and thereby any claim to Native Title over land. They must accept some blame for that themselves, if language and culture were not sufficiently meaningful to warrant retention and preservation, even in the face of persecution. The blackfellows of Central Australia cannot be accused of loss of language and culture. Not yet anyway. Deny them access to their land, though, and it is bound to happen. Their opponents know that and seek to engineer it. Fortunately there are plenty of pastoralists prepared to acknowledge traditional ties to land. If they had any sense they would start individual negotiations with Aboriginals now. A benign Aboriginal presence on these vast areas of land might provide for the pastoralists a free caretakership of cattle and property. Where it is possible the operative word should be *share*, not *extinguish*. The alternative is centuries of litigation and confrontation.

At Yuendumu I began a running feud with the policy-makers and senior public servants in Darwin, who sought to make the lives of field officers a misery with their constant stream of requests for stupid statistics and futile form-filling. I decided to do as little office work as possible and was pleased to overhear people say on quite a few different occasions, 'He's not your typical government bloke: he's got callouses on his hands.' I refused to fill in forms that I knew had no practical value. I wrote short but scathing one-line letters to people who ordered me to do foolish things.

For example, we were desperately short of water at Yuendumu. We had two sub-artesian bores, and the old engines and pump jacks constantly broke down. Even at best we could get no better than 200 gallons of water—900 litres — an hour. Often Don, Johnny, Sandy and I spent an entire night trying to get engines going or pulling the columns and casings of bores to repair pumps, desperate to have a tankful of water to start the next day. In summer we had 1000 people at Yuendumu. We had good gardens, but the watering was done frugally, with watering cans. Out of the blue, this twerp in Darwin sent me £10,000 worth of irrigation piping, with a brisk memo to tell me that I had to give him figures to indicate what level of improvement to our 'horticultural areas' — what bloody horticultural areas? — had been achieved. A Top End settlement was having success with a banana plantation, and this idiot had decided that all the places would have similar enterprises. He was furious when I wrote to tell him we had cut up all the galvanised piping to make stockyard gates and rails, but thanks very much.

They had nothing better to do in head office, Darwin. Another joker had read some fancy magazine about restoring the Sinai Desert with plants like mulga. He wrote to me, telling me to 'immediately forward' some mulga seed.

I wrote back a polite (for me) letter, 'We are in the grip of the worst drought experienced in Central Australia for fifty years, so there is no mulga seed.'

He sent me back a scorcher, saying it was 'an order' that I must send him some mulga seed asap.

I told him (literally) to get stuffed.

He threatened to 'have me disciplined'.

I told him to go for his life.

A year later it rained, and rained . . . and all the mulga trees were in seed. I got all the old women together and offered them a stick of tobacco each for one billycan full of mulga seed. In no time I had five 44 gallon drums full of seed. I sent a telegram:

FIVE 44 GALLON DRUMS MULGA SEED AVAILABLE ADVISE DESPATCH DETAILS.

He came back with a letter saying that he only wanted 10 pounds — under 5 kilos — weight. I was furious, but nonetheless sent him 10 pounds of seed.

In great glee he came back to me three months later to say that the seed I had sent him was 'inferior, of poor quality, and totally unsuitable for anything'. Now I was mad. I'll show you, you bastard. I wrote to the United Nations, New York. 'I have a substantial amount of harvested mulga seed, *Acacia aneura*. Are you interested?' Were they ever! They offered £1 per pound weight, 500 pounds at first, and re-orders if successful germination ensued. They would pay the freight. Reafforestation agencies in Libya, Israel and Egypt would welcome the seed. We eventually sold the lot, and the UN people's word for the results was 'superb'. I divvied the money up among the old women, who got about £15 each, at a time when the top wage for Aboriginal women was 10 shillings a week. I returned from my next trip to Alice Springs with dresses, bloomers, toys for the kids, crates of lolly water, fruit, and we had a big party. I sent a copy of the UN letter to the chap in Darwin, but he never acknowledged it. Eventually the UN asked us to send them different seeds, in small lots, for experimentation, and we had good sales of spinifex seed. Spinifex is the spiky grass that stops Central Australia from blowing away.

I put my career on the line on another occasion when a truck arrived, full of crates containing the components for demountable houses for Aboriginals.

'Take them back to town,' I told the driver. I had seen these monstrosities in other places. They were called Kingstrand houses, with meccano-set frames and galvanised iron walls and roof. The worst feature of them was that part of the deal involved getting gangs of white blokes to come out and erect them. Ice boxes in the winter and furnaces in the summer to boot. I quickly wrote to the director in Darwin, for I realised how seriously he would view my refusal to take delivery. A big lie was called for.

> After intense and delicate consultation with the local elders we have just started to work out the detail of a self-help scheme whereby the Aboriginals will begin to quarry stone, erect a lime kiln, and build some simple basic shelters themselves. Anxious to show you progress when next you visit us.

Fortunately, I got on well with him, and he respected me as a doer rather than an office type.

The director gave me some leeway and we then started to do what I had said was in hand. I selected a site for a stone quarry, and a team of men began to stockpile beautiful, pink, flat sandstone. At the same time I put a hunter 'on the books' as a paid member of their team, so they were never short of kangaroos to eat. Groups of old women used to enjoy taking the small kids on the truck for a ride out bush to a limestone outcrop. There they sat in a ring, chatting away, singing songs, as they used little crowbars to stockpile limestone in bags. At the same time, some of their group would gather bush tucker. It was a picnic, easy stuff for these women, who were magnificent workers. I couldn't offer them much money, but was always able to supply plenty of tucker and tobacco, and that was more important than money. We built a lime kiln, and burnt the lime for mortar, so we didn't need to import costly cement.

It didn't happen overnight or easily but eventually we built some attractive little buildings, totally out of local material. Stone walls and fireplaces, desert oak roof frame, spinifex thatch roof. Designed for indoor-outdoor living, they are still standing going on 40 years later. We stockpiled the stone for the Yuendumu Museum, the next project. It is a fine building, still operational.

It sounds cruel and paternalistic to say it, but about the worst disservice nowadays done to Aboriginals in Central Australia, people who still speak their language and basically are required to adhere to the traditional ceremonies, is to provide them with western-style housing. Basic shelter from the elements, yes, but their whole system screams for mobility, not a sedentary lifestyle. And the sheer economics of housing projects in Central Australia are appalling to contemplate. Millions of dollars are wasted, time after time, on building houses for people who know they must vacate those houses if somebody dies. Can't somebody else take over the house, people ask? What, among all those evil spirits! No way! It's like offering the offending leg of pork to the other Jew. No. The white man will build us some more houses. Aboriginals are blamed because places like Yuendumu nowadays have rows of empty wrecks of vandalised houses, and people still living in wurlies. And our international critics love it.

The whole approach to housing on Aboriginal places is riddled with political skullduggery, and with outsiders imposing their views. It usually costs about $300,000 to build a standard 3-bedroom house out bush, because white contractors are engaged. They take bricks, sand and cement from Alice Springs, they cart concrete from Alice Springs in Readymix trucks. The blackfellows sit and watch the white builders. Many of the contractors, in turn, despise 'the lazy coons' for whom they build the houses. Members of the various clubs of Alice Springs are often regaled with tales about the 'ungrateful bastards' who wreck the beautiful houses 'we taxpayers' build for them. During the period that houses are occupied they in many instances are cesspits, with dogs and humans shitting and pissing inside, and the most dreadful squalor. What they need are clever shelters from the elements: nothing more, nothing less. Windbreaks, sensible spinifex shades, fireplaces and waterproofing. Dismantleable and transportable. In Central Australia mobility is the operative word for the Aboriginal people and their belongings.

It's all very well to insist nowadays that the policy for Aboriginals must be one of self-determination. That assumes people are going to make wise decisions and plan their own economy. But our system has robbed Aboriginals not only of their land, but of their decision-making processes, to the point where many of them couldn't organise a two-seat dunny without running out of paper. They need help from all sections of our system, but not as a means of us again controlling their lives. At the moment there is no sense of reality with money. This country has such a sense of guilt about the shafting of the Aboriginals that there is always a preparedness to shovel lots of taxpayers' money at their problems. Most Aboriginals never seem to have money or derive benefit from it: but as a group they are the victims of white vitriol because billions of dollars are allocated to the 'Aboriginal industry' each year, largely to allow whitefellers to do jobs that Aboriginals should and could do on their own behalf. At the same time the problems get worse. Self–determination? Self–destruction?

And it is all so tricky, so devious, so political. For the hidden agenda of those opposed to the Aboriginal cause is that if they maintain the means of despising Aboriginals their dispossession can be justified on the grounds that that is all they deserve.

At Yuendumu fights usually occurred during the summer months. The long, hot summer indeed. And sometimes they were fair dinkum donnybrooks, all in, no holds barred, the end result of coercing people who should live in small groups onto overcrowded institutions where they were required to be near those they had been reared for centuries to avoid. Fighting among the men was often achieved as a duel, but instead of pistols at forty paces at dawn, it was stone knives at sunset. In a system called *karintjukara*, if two men had a grievance, they met at sunset with appointed referees. The combatants crouched, facing one another and appointed seconds stood behind them. On 'go' the fighters then traded blow for blow, cutting into one another's backs and shoulders with *junma*, stone knives. Old Warlpiri blokes had stripes of ragged, calloused, shiny scars on their backs as cherished mementoes of being ripped apart in these brutal duels. When honour was satisfied, after fairly hefty cuts had been inflicted on both sides, the seconds called a halt. All very honourable stuff.

Women had no such niceties. If women argued to the point where blows were to be struck, they went for the *watiya*, mulga sticks about a metre in length, and 10 centimetres thick. Every self-respecting woman has one nearby at all times. They beat shit out of one another, broke arms, busted shins, cracked skulls, to the point where you marvelled that nobody was killed in the process. All-in brawls were common, men and women involved, and it was important for me, or any other potential arbitrator, not to arrive on the scene too early, otherwise they 'saved face' at your expense. 'If that *gadiya* [white man] hadn't turned up, I would have killed you.' Fighting was like a lot of other things in small communities: it was better to get a grievance out of the way, rather than have it fester. We had some eventful summer Sundays I'd as soon forget: if I could.

Tim Jabangardi advised me when to turn up at a fight. 'Wait until they've had a good go, then drive in and pick up the fresh meat,' he said, so that became my practice. I would drive into the middle of the fight with the Land Rover and shout, 'Anyone for hospital?' and those with serious wounds climbed or were lifted aboard. Sometimes people who'd been in mortal combat five minutes ago laughed and went over the detail of the fight as I drove them to the hospital, where the patient nursing sister did the stitching. When we had a sister. It was always important that people retained some sort of scarring, for scars were badges of honour, to be fingered in later years as they recalled the exploits of their tempestuous youth. Tough people.

Occasionally injuries were so serious I had to drive people to the Alice Springs hospital, a five-hour drive, and invariably at night, for most fights occurred at sunset. We had an airstrip and a radio link with the Aerial Medical Service, but they could not operate at night.

On the worst night I had, there were five people on an old mattress on the tray of the Land Rover utility, three with the spears still in them, for nobody was game to extract them. We had no nursing sister at the time, and, as I wasn't prepared to put any other white person in the invidious position of being blamed for inadequate or incorrect attempts at treatment, I took responsibility for the decision to take the patients to Alice Springs. I felt sure my five passengers would all be dead on arrival. One woman had a *kularda* — a barbed throwing spear — about a centimetre from her heart, embedded about eight inches into her chest. The fight had started when her own brother speared her. I expected her to die first. Two blokes had *mangulpa* — huge mulga spears made for thrusting rather than throwing — right through their thighs, in one side and poking out the other. When I reached them they had run out of weapons, and they stood toe to toe throwing haymaker punches and occasionally hitting one another. They were totally thrown off balance by the 2-metre-long spears through their legs. I sawed both ends off the spears to enable the men to get on the Land Rover: they laughed and joked as I did it. I put tourniquets on their thighs. A woman had her skull split open and her brains were showing. I filled the hole with cotton wool and bandaged her head. Another man, the one who had speared his sister, had been beaten unconscious by her husband. I wrapped him in a blanket.

It was a memorable drive. Freezing cold all the way — and I was wearing warm clothes, inside the cabin, driving: they were totally exposed on the back. When I stopped to give them a drink of water, the speared woman vomited all over me. What with driving slowly, and all the stops I had to make, to check the rude dressings and the tourniquets I had applied, it was pale dawn light as I drove into the Native Ward at Alice Springs Hospital, where the experts relieved me of the dreadful responsibility.

I went to have breakfast at Freddy Woods's cafe.

'Jesus, mate, you look crook,' said Fred. 'You should have more water with yer rum.'

Amazingly, my passengers all survived.

We had no mechanical diggers and any drains, post holes or other excavation had to be dug by hand. Desert soils compact like concrete in dry times. I caused a lot of laughs after we had a decent fall of rain.

'Let's dig some graves.'

They all looked at me as though I had gone nuts.

'Nobody dead.'

'That's right. But if we dig the graves now, when the ground's soft, they'll be ready when somebody does cark.'

Up there for thinking, Ted. I had been caught before. An old woman had died and sorcery was suspected, so everybody had left. Gone bush. Only Sandy Jabananga remained, and he and I had to dig the grave for the old woman and bury her — she didn't get the regulation six-foot deep job. I wasn't going to be caught again. We dug six graves after the rain.

Not long afterwards a bloke named Wokulgari died. He was a huge oafish retarded fellow. When he died, we took his body to the hospital for the sister to check him out and get permission to bury from the Alice Springs Coroner. A few women asked if they could cut off his hair.

'Why?' I asked.

'Oh, him very danger that man,' they told me. 'We gotta make string from his hair and sing big mob song.' They cut his hair, and again, everybody left. Even Sandy went bush. Don Busbridge was in town. Only one young bloke, Anzac Juburula, himself a bit slow, volunteered to help me with the funeral. The dead bloke weighed over fifteen stone. We wrapped him in a blanket and a piece of tarpaulin, and I asked Tom Fleming if he would do the normal Baptist service at the cemetery. Tom agreed. We loaded the body on the back of Tom's utility and went to the cemetery, where, fortunately, the grave was dug. We put the body on the side of the grave, and Tom said the prayers. Then we had the job of getting the body, as gently as possible, into the grave. We felt we couldn't just roll him in. So I climbed into the grave to be handed the body by Tom and Anzac, both fairly slight fellows. Something went wrong, and all of a sudden I am in the bottom of the grave, with the dead and I mean very dead weight of the corpse on top of me. Tom and Anzac began to laugh.

'What we do, Egan? Leave you here, dead feller?' asked Anzac.

I told him what he could do, and even Tom Fleming, old army padre, professed later that he was 'a bit shocked, Ted' at my intemperate outburst. You try getting all that dead weight off you, when you're in the bottom of a narrow grave, regulation six feet deep. It took them five minutes, lots of false starts, and a few laughs towards the finish before I was back in the land of the living.

'I'll walk home,' I said to them. 'It's bad luck for you two. You don't drink, Tom, because of your religion, and the law doesn't let you drink, Anzac. But I'm going home to have a bloody good go at the rum bottle.'

You drink rum Mistegan? I bloody well did that day.

9

The Brunette

'You know, I've been a drover and cattleman all my life, but I've never been to the Brunette Downs Races,' said Norman Hagan.

Say no more, Norman. I hadn't been to 'the Brunette' — as the ABC race meeting is called — either, and it's the most important bush race meeting in the Territory. Leo Martin, Norman and I decided to go in 1959. ABC stands for Alexandria, Brunette Downs and Cresswell, big cattle stations on the Barkly Tableland. The meeting, for bush horses and bush people, was first organised in 1908. We'd travel in Norman's utility.

On the way we stopped at the Aileron pub, where there was a meeting of the Barrow Creek Race Club Committee. The three of us were on the committee. It was a good excuse for some of the local white blokes to have a good drink and a yarn as well as attend the meeting.

Bob Purvis from Wood Green station was on the committee. We called him 'The Sandover Alligator'. He claimed to be the greatest eater in Australia, and on principle was given three times the normal serving of food at the pub. He said to me, 'Only once was I beaten in an eating competition. I'd had a lot to eat one day, but then this Norwegian sailor challenged me to a butter-eating duel. I'm not going to pass up the challenge, but I'm not strong on butter, and you know how it is when you eat a lot of butter, you get clogged up, sort of. I managed to force down nineteen pounds of butter, but the big Viking did twenty. I wasn't full, mind, it was just that I couldn't force down any more butter. I ate a leg of a goat to demonstrate that I wasn't full, but I had to concede to being done on the butter.'

Wallaby Bill Waudby, our next door neighbour, big, jet black beard, renowned rum drinker, was on the committee too. And Jack Dowler, from Pine Hill, an old Kidman man, who told lots of stories about the legendary SK, as Sidney Kidman was called. Jack was working for Kidman on a cattle station near Oodnadatta in South Australia one time. There was a demand on the southern markets for meat suitable for smallgoods, so Kidman ordered his stockmen to muster all the wild donkeys in the region and send them to market. Kidman himself was supervising the loading of the donkeys on a freight train at Oodnadatta, when over walked a very smug station master, anxious to take a rise out of the cattle king.

'So, what are we sending away today, Mr Kidman?'

Kidman had three guiding principles in life. Leave your cheque book at home. Keep your branding iron hot. First one to talk loses. The cattle king-hit was a Joe Louis bolo punch.

'Train load of stationmasters.'

Drinking got serious at Aileron, so Norman Hagan and I decided to sneak away early, about 11 pm. Leo Martin and Bill Waudby, who were going to camp with us, had a taste for the rum, and said they would come along later.

'Light a big fire on the side of the road so we can spot you,' said Bill, whose nickname Wallaby was changing to Wobbly. Norman and I drove about 10 miles north and set up camp in a bit of mulga scrub. We lit a big fire by the road, and then drove into the scrub for about half a mile, lit another fire, and unrolled our swags. It was below zero, so we had a quick pannikin of rum each and turned in. I am always at peace camped under the stars and slid into a fulfilled sleep. Three hours later, a rude awakening, although I didn't let on I was awake: Bill and Leo arrived, both very drunk, but Leo was legless as well. Bill had to help him out of the truck and unrolled his swag for him.

'Now go to bed and shut up,' was Wallaby's terse command.

'I'll just have a smoke and one more rum. A nightcap.' The words were as staggered as Leo himself. I cocked my head a bit, heard Bill's immediate snores, watched Leo puffing away as he slurped a little song into his pannikin of rum. I dozed off.

'Jesus Christ!' Norman and I blasphemed in unison and leaped from our swags. There was Leo, incandescent, his swag on fire. You have to see a swag ignite to believe it. The waterproof canvas campsheet is impregnated with very flammable material. Not only does it burn easily, there's a 'whoomph' as it ignites. We both dived for Leo and rolled him around on the ground until the flames were extinguished. He had no hair, no eyebrows, but was as stoical as ever. He gave us a silly grin. We hadn't noticed Wallaby, who had jumped from his swag, filled a bucket of water, raced to us — and threw the icy water over me! Leo got the joke.

'A bit of water to go with the rum,' he roared. 'Whose shout is it?'

'I'll shout, you bastard,' I shouted. 'Let's get back to sleep.'

'But my swag's gone,' said Leo. 'Where's a man going to camp?'

'Here,' responded a generous Wallaby. 'Hop in with me.'

'Good onyer Bill,' said Leo, and climbed into Bill's swag, not forgetting to croon: 'If I give my heart to you, will you handle it with care, will you always treat me tenderly . . . ?'

I don't know how long I slept. But I woke to a roar from Wallaby. His swag was aflame. Leo must have had a spark on his clothes. Wallaby hurled Leo into the open and I jumped out of my swag, threw a blanket over Leo, and stifled his flaming trouser leg. We emptied a jerry can of water over Bill's swag, and stoked up the campfire. Norman got out of his swag and joined us. Bill rubbed some rum into Leo's burnt scalp, just what the doctor would have ordered. Norman looked at me.

'Not much point trying to get back to sleep. I might cook a feed and we'll get an early start to Brunette.'

It was a 1200 kilometre drive, and we did it in two days. Leo was only a little subdued, for he was one of the toughest blokes I ever met. He had been a fine horseman when younger but had gradually developed a very painful, unfixable back problem which was slowly turning his spine into a steel block. He assured me that once the total fusion was achieved there would be less pain, but in the meantime his life was an agony, although he never solicited pity. He worked as hard as anybody else and was a very ingenious fellow on the station. You have to be if you live on a cattle station. If the engine breaks down you fix it. If the plumbing goes you repair it. Most Territory station blokes are masters at innovation, and Leo Martin was well above average talent. He was a great mate, but the poor bloke drank too much rum, and mixed it with painkiller tablets, which wasn't clever at all.

Leo, Norman and I got on very well, for we were great sports lovers and talked endlessly about racehorses, cricket, football, tennis. I loved to spend time in the stock camp with them, for by day we worked hard with their capable Aboriginal stockmen, and at night we yarned around the campfire about Bernborough, Bradman, Laver, Marjorie Jackson or any other Australian greats.

Norman was one of the famous Hagan family, renowned as cattlemen in a unique part of Australia that contains, in my opinion, the essence of 'inland' settlement. Draw a line on your map linking Marree in South Australia, Newcastle Waters in the Territory, Julia Creek in Queensland, and Bourke in New South Wales. Exclude the towns of Alice Springs and Mt Isa. The people, black and white, who live on stations inside that area have no connection with, or thoughts of the coast and they look introspectively inward. They speak differently, they are more laconic, they move slower, they are more resourceful and more generous than other Australians. Norman Hagan embodied all of those qualities.

The Barkly Highway links Tennant Creek and Mt Isa, and when you turn left to go north to Brunette Downs you get straight on to the Barkly Tableland, good but cruel cattle country. Huge Mitchell grass plains where you can travel 50 kilometres without seeing a tree, a shrub, a bush. It's the excesses of weather that make it cruel country. Searing blinding heat in summer, zero temperatures and biting slashing winds in winter. In the summer some milky white surface water gets trapped in *gilgais,* but mainly the cattle stations depend on bores, and the ground water is hard and salty. Those who work on Tableland cattle stations become as hard and salty as the elements. Tough, uncompromising people to those not like themselves.

Brunette Downs is one of the biggest cattle stations in the world. It is not a sweet property in terms of fattening cattle, but it is good breeding country, so the main exports are store cattle. These beasts, usually four-year old or older bullocks, were formerly walked by drovers but are now transported by road trains and rail to Queensland to be fattened.

The ABC race meeting is traditionally held on the Friday, Saturday and Sunday closest to the full moon in June so, in the days before electricity, bushies could hold their important nighttime activities, using the moonlight. It is a great meeting, and most station people spend a week to ten days at the course, living in comfortable camps that have holding yards for their horses, tents for women and kids, and a communal bough shed under which people sit, cook, eat meals and chat before and after the races and other festivities. Usually a station will have a full carcass of beef hanging up, and people, most of them good butchers, cut off the meat they want to cook on the hotplate. Meat left hanging in the shade in cold weather will stay fresh for a week. It is greatly enhanced in quality if not refrigerated. Stations kill the best beef their neighbours can produce, so the steaks are superb. Station cooks make bread or damper. Campfires never go out, so tea and coffee are always ready to drink. Early morning coffee is spiked with rum.

Preparations were well in hand when we arrived on the Wednesday. Everybody knew Norman Hagan, so we received several offers to camp with different stations. We decided to camp with Norman's nephew, John Hagan, who was a drover at the time. John had 1200 bullocks 'tailed out' near a bore a few miles away, and he would walk them on to Queensland after the races. I had known young John in Darwin when he was a kid. He was still not much more than a kid, about 19, and it is an indication of the reputation of the Hagan name that he was entrusted to walk 1200 bullocks 1500 kilometres to the railhead at Dajarra. John was a wild young bloke when away from the job, and he joined us in some hectic sessions around the bar, where I remembered my mum's sound advice and became a 'good listener'.

Around the bar crusty weather-beaten faces framed bright, alert eyes. Hands were like shovels — I thought there must be a competition to see who could have the most skin knocked off knuckles. A cold, relentless, piercing south–east wind made you drink rum, crinkle your neck under your hat and keep your shoulders hunched into the big jackets we all wore. There were 44 gallon drums with fires burning inside, and we slowly pirouetted around these as we warmed first the front, then the arse, and in between drinks a quick rub of the hands. The drinks came fast and furious, mainly rum, and the stories became more lurid.

'They only talk about four things,' Norman Hagan confided. 'And they all start with b. Bullocks, blackfellers, booze and bores.' He was dead right. Bullocks were rushing over the top of us as we stood around the bar that day. Blackfellows weren't as good as they were in the old days: they 'knew their place' then. Huge drinking sessions were re-enacted, days, weeks non-stop on the rum if you could believe it all. The discussion about sinking a particular bore became so heated and involved one laconic bloke was moved to say: 'I wish you bastards would finish puttin' down that bore. I've got the bloody contract to put the windmill on it!'

Aboriginals, not allowed to drink in those days, sat, watched, and shook their heads at the antics of the white blokes as they swigged, swaggered, swore, shouted and sometimes fought one another in their mad quest to have a good time. Nowadays you go to the Brunette Races and other bush meetings, and the white blokes drink lolly water and light beer and deplore the behaviour of the blackfellows. We taught them well. And sad but true, one white bloke gets drunk and he's a 'character', a 'dag'. One blackfellow gets drunk and the race is vilified.

I took time out from the drinking to see a few of my Aboriginal friends from Borroloola who were working on the big Tableland stations. They had their own camps, with plenty of tucker, and it was a wonderful opportunity for them to get together for a break in the busy mustering season on the various stations. They, too, talked of little else but their 'b' stuff. Bullocks and blackfellow business. It was part of the enigmatic cattle station life, so tough and so exploitative of them, but nonetheless a lifestyle that turned many of them into talented, capable, healthy people. There was a real meaning to their lives on the stations, for their traditional skills and knowledge of the country were invaluable assets in the cattle industry. The sinister aspects were deplorable: the cruelty, the prostitution of their women, the neglect of their medical needs. But there were good elements of that lifestyle that are gone forever.

One meeting with an Aboriginal was fortuitous. I had briefly met a bloke named Limerick at Borroloola a couple of years before. People had remarked that he was a top stockman, but apart from noting that fact I had had little contact with him. But we got talking at Brunette and he told me he had ridden most of the horses that would be competing, and had a fair idea of who might win the various races. Those he hadn't ridden he'd observed. He agreed to meet me on Friday and pass on some information. We set up a pact that if I won on any of Limerick's tips a component of £1 of my bet would be deemed to be wagered for him.

Brunette is a grass–fed meeting. Horses are put into a paddock at the station a month before the race meeting. They are not fed any grain until they come out of the paddock a couple of days before the races. This is to establish an even system where a simple stockman can race a horse on equal terms with a rich station owner. Most of the races are for district–bred horses, removing the opportunity to import quality racehorses from other regions or 'ring-in' horses under assumed identities. The whole idea is to have a good fun meeting for the local people with local horses and riders.

There are eight races on both Friday and Saturday. It wasn't stated outright as a policy, but for six of those races the jockeys were all white men. Then there were two 'blackboy' races at the end of each day for Aboriginal riders only. It was, and is still, a regrettable feature of station life that whites feel they must use derogatory terms in respect of Aboriginals. It's brought on by peer group pressure, a general sense of insecurity, a belief that Aboriginals must be 'kept in their place'. So Aboriginal men are always 'boys' or 'bucks', women are 'girls' or 'gins', children are 'picaninnies' or 'pics'.

The main race on the Friday is the Ladies' Bracelet, and the Brunette Downs Cup is the feature on Saturday. Sunday sees the sports, gymkhana and the rodeo (once known by its Australian name, the buckjump show). There is a Calcutta sweep on both the Bracelet and the Cup, whereby tickets are sold and drawn, as in a raffle. The money from the ticket sales goes into 'the pool'. Names of winning ticket holders are listed as 'drawers' of the various horses. The horses are then auctioned, individually, and all the money from the auction also goes into the pool, which becomes the stake for the outcome of the Calcutta. A percentage of the pool money goes to a bush-approved charity like the Royal Flying Doctor Service. During the auction the 'drawer' of the horse can either bid for and 'buy' that horse, and then get it for half the auction price, or else get paid half the sum bid by the 'buyer' of the horse. When the race is run the allotted prizes from the pool are paid to the placegetters. I always take a lot of tickets in Calcuttas, for it puts you in a strong bargaining position if you draw a good horse. I have won a lot of money on Calcuttas over the years, but had no luck that time at Brunette.

Luck came from another quarter. Limerick met me before each race, and would say 'Try number three' or whatever.

I backed every winner on the first day. At first I was just betting £1 on each of his tips. But by the time I walked into the ring for the first blackboys' race at 5 pm I was confidence itself: Limerick had picked every winner ridden by white jockeys, and was certain he knew the winners of the races for Aboriginal jockeys. By this time I had come to the attention of the four bookmakers and many punters, and quite a few punters followed me into the ring where I had my biggest bet ever, £50 on a 3/1 horse, whose odds immediately went to evens. The horse bolted in, and I had another £50 on the 2/1 winner of the second blackboys' race. By the end of the day Limerick and I had won fortunes. I was £450 in front, and I'd won £50 for Limerick. It was almost a year's wages for each of us. I went to the bar, he went to the card game.

In 1954 the Northern Territory Aboriginals Ordinance was repealed, replaced by new legislation, the Welfare Ordinance. It was tricky political stuff, engineered by Paul Hasluck, on the grounds that Australia was under scrutiny in the international arena for having discriminatory laws based on race. Hasluck had also been heavily pressured by the AHPA, the self-styled Aboriginal Halfcastes' Progress Association, on the grounds that they should not be subject to laws designed for 'tribal blackfellows'. Hasluck organised the framing and passage of new laws, purported to be based on need, not race. The new Welfare Ordinance provided that 'people who stood in need of care and assistance' could be declared to be 'wards' within the meaning of the Welfare Ordinance if they could not 'without assistance manage their own affairs'.

With a stroke of the pen in 1954 almost all 'full bloods' — as supposedly 'real' Aboriginals were described: around 17,000 in number — were declared to be 'wards' within the meaning of the Welfare Ordinance. The new legislation had basically replaced the word *Aboriginal* with the word *ward*. Henceforth 'wards' were not allowed to drink alcohol, be in town between sunset and sunrise, own property, marry without permission, travel interstate, earn award wages, and were subject to all the other bits of petty apartheid prevailing at the time. Life was unchanged for the 'full blood' Aboriginals, most of whom did not know that they were now 'wards'.

At the same time 'part-Aboriginals' (as people of mixed Aboriginal descent were called) were not declared to be wards, and were thereby automatically exempted from any discriminatory legislation. In Hasluck's terms they had become 'like whites', the stated objective of his nowadays much-maligned assimilation policy. A handful of 'full-bloods' were not declared to be wards, on the grounds that they had very clearly demonstrated that they *could* 'without assistance manage their own affairs'. Prominent in this group was Albert Namatjira, the great painter. Another to be exempted was Smiler Major, an outstanding Jingili bloke who had worked for many years as a yard-building and fencing contractor on the Barkly Tableland. He was a big powerful fellow, and he was at the Brunette Races in 1959.

After the races each day there was a two-hour drinking session for the white blokes, while the white women and their Aboriginal helpers looked after and fed the kids, and the white women then got frocked up for the dance. The bar was a little galvanised iron building set out on its own for safety's sake, to 'give the drinkers room'. It was freezing cold that Friday night, and the bar was surrounded by about fifty white men, all in big hats, wearing winter clothing topped up with big jackets or overcoats, standing in clumps around the fire drums. The talk was about the day's racing and tomorrow's prospects. As the biggest winner I was required to shout for the bar, and was happy to oblige. Mine's a rum.

The light was fading to a sickly grey as Smiler approached the bar. But even in the gloom everybody could tell he was an Aboriginal just by his style of walking. He was dressed in similar gear to those at the bar. He was a big bloke, weighing about fifteen stone, and the army overcoat made him look even bigger. The conversation stopped as he strode to the bar. This was going to be interesting.

'I'll have a rum, Scotty,' he said, as he placed a £5 note on the bar. Little Scotty, the barman, didn't know what to do. He licked his lips and furtively looked around for guidance. No blackfellow had ever had a drink of alcohol at Brunette. Smiler sensed the silence, and he too looked around. Every eye was on him and the barman.

'Come on Scotty. You know me. Smiler Major. I got the citizen right,' he said, good-naturedly. 'I'll have a rum.'

Up stepped a bloke named Jim Marshall, from Bing Bong station. He made sure everybody was watching him, and he moved aggressively to the bar. He grabbed the £5 note and dropped it on the ground.

'Fuck off, boy,' said Marshall. 'You don't drink here.'

Smiler stood his ground. 'I got the citizen right. I can drinkit the grog, just like you mob.' Then he made his first mistake. He stooped to pick up his money, and Marshall whacked him on the side of the jaw, a big haymaker. Smiler grabbed the money nonetheless, stood erect, and eyeballed Marshall: 'You try and stop me gettin' a drink.' As he spoke he began to unbutton his overcoat.

That was his second mistake. He was wide-open. Marshall dropped him. But there were no more Major mistakes.

Smiler got up, took the overcoat off and they got stuck into it. It was slow and ponderous, for neither of them was a good fighter, but they were both big and powerful, and felt they had a lot at stake. They stood toe-to-toe, slugging away at one another, probably for only three or four minutes, but landing heavy grinding punches to the head. Marshall began to waver and Smiler was devastation itself as he slammed a couple of big right handers to the jaw, and Marshall was out cold.

Smiler put on his overcoat and walked to the bar. His face was a mess, and he was bleeding at the mouth. Scotty served him a rum. A few of us clapped in approbation, but most of the drinkers just turned their backs on the scene. Smiler threw down the rum, and walked off into the darkness. Nobody went to Marshall's assistance. After a couple of minutes he staggered to his feet and slinked off in the opposite direction.

It finished Marshall in that part of the country. It was the unfair opener that did it. One of the gnarled old blokes at the bar said: 'You don't king-hit anybody. Not even a blackfeller.' Marshall left the district soon afterwards. Bessie, the Aboriginal woman who had put in years of hard slog helping him to run his cattle station, and bearing his children, returned to her people.

The next day I went looking for Limerick to repeat the onslaught on the bookies, but I was told he was in a big card game down by the creek, so I left him to it, and spent the day just walking around and soaking up the atmosphere of Cup Day with a few quiet beers. It was an excellent day of racing. That night we went to the ball, which was held in the tin shed called 'the hall' and watched the distribution of trophies, known in the bush as 'the settling up'. Leo Martin was still on deck despite being in shock from the burns. People kept asking why he had his hat on in the dance hall. After the ball we all adjourned to our camp for a few rums, and Norman Hagan cooked us a beautiful beef curry on the coals, using a Number 8 shovel as a wok. We drank right through the night, and sang songs around the campfire. There was a bloke named Sam Hordern drinking with us. He was from the famous Anthony Hordern family who had the big store in Sydney. Sam had a tape recorder, and none of us had ever seen one of these before. He taped me singing a few songs, and must have passed the tape on to RCA in Sydney, for I had a letter from them a year or so later, asking me to call on them one day. I promptly forgot about it.

We waited up until sunrise, for it was full moon, and we knew we would see the breathtaking spectacle of the full moon and the rising sun as two fiery balls on each side of the horizon. When you have seen that on the Barkly Tableland, with no trees to impede the view, when all around you is a 360 degree golden Mitchell grass emptiness, then you have been in the great Australian outback.

We had a few hours in the swag, and then showered to get ready for the sports. On the Saturday everybody had nominated one another for Sunday's bullock ride, the saddle horse or the bareback buckjumping events. Most of us were thrown off easily, but John and Norman Hagan both rode time on their horses, as we thought they might. John Hagan had nominated a team in the tug-of-war, but we reckoned we had no show of winning as the red-hot favourites were the huge Darcy boys from Mallapunyah. Their father, the redoubtable George Darcy, used to train his sons for the event by making them pull tree stumps as they gradually cleared an airstrip on their station. As it turned out we beat them easily, but John Hagan was quick to call for 'two out of three'.

'What are you on about?' I asked him.

'Just have a look at old George,' John hissed out of the side of the mouth. 'He's furious. He'll sool the big bastards on to us. I don't want to fight the Darcys. Do you?'

'Shit, no.' I'd seen Jim Darcy fight, and he could really go.

'Well, prepare to lose gracefully,' he said. We did just that. Old George even bought us a beer. John Hagan has always had an old head on his shoulders.

10
Mean Bugger Egan

I sent £100 to my parents in Melbourne, and put a deposit on a car with my winnings at the Brunette races. Rae and I settled into the hectic life at Yuendumu. I concentrated on getting cattle and got support from my director in Darwin and the Animal Industry Branch in Alice Springs. The Commonwealth government through its various agencies owned cattle here and there, and the local heads of department were happy to supply us with 500 breeders, as they knew I would co-operate with them in any research work they wanted to undertake. We began a big fencing and yard-building project, and I went with a team of men for three weeks to Mt Wedge station where, with Bill Waudby's permission, we cut desert oak posts and rails. As a means of access we established a road from Yuendumu to Papunya which went through Mt Wedge. Desert oak is wonderful timber for stockyards, and I didn't feel too badly about cutting the trees, as Mt Wedge station has thousands of them, and they generate prolifically. It is one of life's great pleasures to camp under a desert oak tree, for it is a member of the casuarina family, similar to those on the Arnhem Land coastline. The sighing wind cuts thin slices through the needle leaves of the desert oaks at night, and brings echoes and reminders of the inland sea that was in Central Australia when desert oak trees were born.

We had three gangs of fencers putting in a boundary fence and building a horse paddock. Norman Hagan selected a couple of sites for dams for us, and work started on the construction of one of these. Dams are a good idea in Central Australia, for cattle will walk past a bore to get to a dam for a drink, and it provides a good opportunity to spell the country around bores, which gets flogged from constant usage in all seasons. Dams are dependent on rain to keep them full, but when the dams are dry you fall back on your bores. Yuendumu is quite good country for cattle. Most of Central Australia is. The vital thing is not to overstock. When there are big rains you could run thousands of cattle if they were available, but the enigma is that big rains usually come after long dry spells, so you see the country lush while there aren't too many stock to eat the feed. But the country derives the advantage. The only way to run cattle is to keep your numbers right, and have strategic waters and fences.

Yuendumu was looking good, neat, tidy and well-organised. Don Busbridge was transferred to Papunya, promoted to Superintendent, as he had passed his public service exams by studying at night. We got in Don's place a mate of his named Max Trenowden, a wonderful offsider to me for the remainder of my time at Yuendumu. We were a good combination. I would articulate my outlandish ideas and Max, after a mandatory creasing of the brow, would bring them into effect. He was a mechanical genius, and he had a tremendous ability to teach young Aboriginal blokes his many skills. His wife Beryl was a happy person and fitted in immediately. We were very fortunate in this respect, for one of the features of life on most government settlements in those days was friction among white staff members, many of whom were inept bastards who wouldn't get a job anywhere else. The policy of the department in respect of bush settlements was to have lots of white 'instructors' to enhance the skills of Aboriginals, but I kept imploring the director in Darwin not to include Yuendumu in all of this nonsense. I had seen too many of the so-called instructors on the job, and the vast majority wouldn't work in an iron lung and needed a course of instruction themselves. Besides, I was a Fred Gray follower, and I could see that if there were lots of whitefellers the blackfellers were happy to leave the work to them. But one of the worst features of having lots of whites on Aboriginal settlements was that they had nothing to talk about except the Aboriginals, and often these mindless parish-pump chats deteriorated into harangues about 'how ungrateful the bastards are'. Some of the most racist statements about Aboriginals came from people employed to help them out of their supposed problems: the main problem for blackfellows was and is the sheer presence of outsiders in their midst. I was quite happy to have just Max Trenowden and a bloke named Arthur Hutchins as my two white staff. Arthur was a retired stonemason, who was teaching our Aboriginal blokes to do simple building jobs. He was a great tradesman himself, but he was also a born teacher, who demonstrated the skills and then made his trainees do the work.

I began to train the younger blokes to play football, and it was a good means of keeping fit myself. We couldn't afford jumpers or boots, so the blokes all played barefooted, and our uniform was white singlets and shorts. Max Trenowden cut us a stencil, and we painted YUENDUMU inside a boomerang on the singlets. With their black skin the young blokes, who were all very fit as a result of strenuous ceremonial activity, a good diet and the football training, looked superb in their outfits. They were quick to develop good skills. I was a bit dismayed a few years later, when proper jerseys and boots became the norm, to hear that Yuendumu settled for the Collingwood colours, to maintain their loyalty to the black-and-white. What would my father, staunchest of Richmond barrackers, have thought of a son who was seen to encourage anybody towards support of Collingwood?

We challenged other settlements to football matches, and thrashed them all. It was good fun travelling to the 'away' games, for we piled as many blokes as we could on the truck, and drove off on the Friday night before a Saturday game. A camp in the bush was always a good experience with them. We always shot a couple of kangaroos on the way, and this ensured a happy camp and high morale.

In 1960 at the first Bangtail Muster festival in Alice Springs the Yuendumu Aboriginals led the parade. Our athletics team members were sparkling in their white uniforms, and they were led by about twenty scarred old warriors, painted up and bristling with spears, boomerangs and shields. The old blokes were a big hit posing for the cameras, as they had all put *marabindi* bones through their pierced noses. Our athletes cleaned up all the sports. My offsider, Johnny Jungarai, won the mile race, and Peter Jangala won the main race, the 120 metres Gift, and £30 prizemoney. A couple of weeks later, Peter Jangala received an invitation to compete in the famous Bay Sheffield race in Adelaide, but he had ceremonial obligations at Yuendumu, so he declined. He was a beautiful runner, but it was good to see that the culture came first with him.

Considerable drama surrounded the birth of Mark Egan on 7 December 1959. Mark has since become a tough, good-looking, easy-going bloke, but he was quite sickly for his first couple of years. He was born prematurely and Rae had to be evacuated to hospital a few weeks earlier. She had a threatened miscarriage, but this was averted by skilful attention from the staff at Alice Springs Hospital. At the same time she had a blood transfusion. This caused a dramatic life-threatening reaction, only arrested after some daring treatment by our mate Dr George Tippett, who packed her in ice and gave her cortisone injections. I was at Yuendumu, blissfully unaware that all of this was going on, but George came on the radio the next morning when I inquired after her.

'Er, yeah, she's . . . well, she's OK Ted, but you'd better come into town, and we'll tell you all about it.' That was his laconic way of letting me know how serious it was. He never told me the number of hours he and the nursing staff had stayed awake to save Rae's life.

George Tippett and I are lifelong friends. He later became one of Australia's top anaesthetists, as well as doing great work for the Royal Flying Doctor Service. He has been awarded top honours by Rotary International for work in south-east Asia, and is a close friend of the Dalai Lama. He is a member of the Order of Australia. He was a talented, exuberant, wild young man when I first came to know him in Central Australia, and was the very first to organise a comprehensive medical service for bush places, for both whites and blacks, a system based on good organisation rather than the former hit-and-miss methods of treating people in the bush.

George was one of the better visitors we had. He visited once a month, and after a busy schedule over a couple of days at the hospital we would always settle into a good meal, a few drinks, a profound chat and a laugh. He has a colourful way of putting a precise finger on things. Into our third rum one night he had this to say: 'When I started at university I did engineering for the first couple of terms. Then I had this vision of myself, ten years later, wearing a hard hat, covered in grease, and eating dry sandwiches out of a plastic box. So I switched to medicine. And look at me! I've been up to my armpits in piss, poop and puss ever since.'

Most of the many visitors we had were a pain in the arse. Lots of boring public servants who expected to be looked after hand and foot. Often they were just out to bludge on the people in the bush, and were paid handsome rates of travelling allowance as well. You could always spot the good travellers. They would arrive with precious little gifts — in those 'pre-freezer' days — like a loaf of fresh bread, sausages, or fruit, things you couldn't get away from the towns. But the freeloaders bowled in with nothing. We had to shuffle kids around to provide spare bedrooms, share showers and toilets with them, and feed them. And some of them would make demands as though we were required to provide five-star accommodation and service. Bloody visitors. They were the biggest single problem at Yuendumu.

Another lifetime friendship didn't start all that promisingly. I went into Alice Springs one day and my diminutive boss, Bill McCoy summoned me into his office. There was a stranger sitting with him. Bill lit his pipe, and the visitor and I were supposed to be impressed at being allowed to watch The Grand Old Man of Aboriginal Affairs going through his rituals. A couple of clouds of smoke and he was ready to impart his great wisdom in a series of grunts and puffs.

'Hmm, . . . er, Ted.' He still couldn't develop any warmth for me: the feeling was mutual. 'I want you *puff puff* to meet Colin Tatz. Colin *puff* is a PhD student and he's here to do some research on Aboriginal administration. I've suggested to him that he might *puff puff* put in some time with you at Yuendumu.'

Thanks very bloody much, you old arsehole, I thought. How much time? Just what I need, another bloody visitor. My thoughts must have been reflected on my face, but I muttered some pleasantry to this newcomer who did not seem the least reassured. He was genial enough, but was watching me closely through his intense brown eyes.

'How do you do?' he inquired in the best Oxfordese I had ever heard. It was in fact an educated South African voice, but he sounded like a pommy first up. Things were getting out of hand.

'How do I do?' I said. 'Well, I do all right, really, but it's just that . . . well, I'll level with you, mate. Visitors are a bloody nuisance.'

Colin gave an embarrassed shrug, and I started to feel bad about my attitude. After all, it wasn't his fault. It was the system. We had no visitors' quarters, and McCoy should have known better than to impose so many visitors on a busy bloke with a young family. Visitors to Alice Springs did not front up for accommodation with Bill McCoy, they stayed at one of the pubs. The department never made any attempt to screen or discourage visitors. And every Tom, Dick, Harry and Johnny-come-lately was happy to grab the opportunity to go bush, get free accommodation and tucker, and look at some primitive blackfellows.

Colin Tatz proved to be a visitor with a difference. First, he suggested we have a few drinks and get to know one another. Then he bought some brandy and wine, a bottle of rum for me, a couple of chickens, chocolates for Rae and little books for the kids. In two hours we were good mates, have been ever since, and always will be. Colin has gone on to be a renowned academic, a scintillating writer on sport, and a prominent lecturer on Holocaust studies. Meeting him provided my first encounter with a big intellect. I'd met lots of smart people before, but nobody with a worldly overview, nobody who could put English together so well. And nobody who could cook like he could. We had Chicken a la Tatz on his first night at Yuendumu, washed down by a bottle of fine wine, an introduction to South African politics, a spirited argument about cricket, and the prospect of some research that just might have long-term meaning. Some bloody visitors were OK.

The health of most of the Aboriginals at Yuendumu was good, notwithstanding the fact that they were now herded onto a small area of land and forced into a more sedentary lifestyle than was good for them. Their intrinsic toughness helped, and I often wondered how 1000 whitefellers would cope if forced into the same situation. There were understandable problems that had always been a feature of their lives — things like sore eyes caused by flies, smoke and dust, exposure to the elements, the wounds from fighting, the 'sorry cuts' — self-imposed gashes on heads and thighs when relatives died. But their Spartan existence in their harsh environment for so many thousands of years, their strict marriage laws, their healthy traditional protein-rich diet, their life in the open air, all contributed to an impressive group of people. None drank alcohol, because the law forbade it. Access to tobacco was minimal, and they mainly chewed tobacco in the same way they had traditionally chewed *pituri* — the only drug in their background. *Pituri* is a wild tobacco-like plant, and the traditional method was to pound it, mix it with ash, and then mould it into wads like blocks of chewing tobacco. There are four types of *pituri* in Central Australia, and I guess it is no coincidence that the species with the highest nicotine content, *Nicotiana gossei,* is the most popular. The chances are it was beneficial if used in the quantities they were able to attain. The old blokes told me that when they were on the long walks in the pre-whiteman days the *pituri* they chewed lulled them into a sense of well-being. Make you happy, they said.

Women still gave birth in the bush, attended by their own midwives, who rolled the baby in ashes immediately after birth as a sterilising precaution. Most Warlpiri women were *wiri nabulu,* big-breasted, and the vast majority of young babies were well-fed and happy. The big danger period for them was from the point of weaning — usually at about twelve to eighteen months, although you often saw four-year-old kids seeking attention from their mothers by having a go at the *nabulu* — to about two years of age, when they could demand and eat proper food. In the meantime, given the institutionalised life of the parents, the babies in the danger age tended to be fed damper soaked in tea, and given water out of billycans that dogs also drank out of.

My two great phobias in life are bikies and blackfellow dogs. There are great similarities and we'd be better off without both species. I developed a hatred bordering on paranoia about dogs when I was at Yuendumu. It was infuriating that Aboriginals could not or would not realise that their mangy dogs were the source of much illness. The old women especially insisted that the dogs were great for hunting, but from what I saw they were an impediment to any hunting that went on; and furthermore they ate most of the food, hunted or otherwise. Dogs might be all right in a society where people sit on chairs, babies sleep in cots, and food is kept on tables, shelves, in pantries or refrigerators. They are a distinct health hazard in a society where people, food and utensils are at ground level. The point at which I came closest to abusing the great power I possessed at Yuendumu via the key of the ration store related to my seething anger when a baby in the danger age died. In almost every case they died from gastro-enteritis, or 'green one *kuna* [shit]' as the Warlpiri called it. If you check through the records of children born at Yuendumu you will find that there are years where *every* child born in a given year died before it reached three.

Whenever a baby died I demanded the right to shoot at least 20 dogs before I opened the ration store on a Friday. It didn't take long, because we chased after them in a Land Rover and shot them with 12–gauge shotguns — no fancy head shots, just blast them away. There were so many dogs that even the constant shooting failed to reduce their numbers to a manageable level. Max Trenowden, like Don Busbridge before him, was a crack shot, and I got total backing from both of them. It would have been unfair for us to ask any of the Aboriginal blokes to assist other than by driving, for they would get embroiled in all sorts of trouble if they did any shooting. Given the horrendous third-world state of affairs on most Aboriginal places nowadays, a starting point to any improvement might well be a campaign to convince Aboriginals that dogs are about as bad as alcohol in their lives.

I tried to establish a policy of encouraging people to live away from the main settlement area, to reduce the health problems, the fights, the general overcrowding. I referred to my policy as 'decentralisation': today it is called the 'outstation movement'. We built a little show, 6 kilometres away at Penhall's Bore, another at Konaji (White Point Bore) a further 3 kilometres, another at Kerridy, a semi-permanent waterhole 15 kilometres from Yuendumu. At each place we planted a few citrus trees, and established small vegetable gardens, but the main idea was to set people up as eventual 'caretakers' for cattle in the region and to relieve the pressure at Yuendumu, where we constantly had water problems. It took a lot of supervising, but I was sure it was the way to go, especially if we could get people back to the actual country they belonged to. That was not possible in those days. It is difficult even today, for the Warlpiri traditionally covered a large area, but were dispersed in 1928 by the Coniston Massacre. Pastoral leases were granted to white settlers, and the Warlpiri were encouraged to move. Sometimes they went to regions not traditionally theirs. I hear nowadays of Warlpiri claims to land that was certainly not theirs traditionally. At the same time they have lost access to land that was theirs. It's very complex, and politicians should be barred from making arbitrary decisions about Aboriginal land: it might take hundreds of years to sort things out, and in the short term is best left unresolved, with the onus on all interested parties to be reasonable, and carry on with whatever is their lifestyle. The trouble with politicians is that they want the quick fix, the populist action that will win them votes in their short period of office, three years. There's plenty of time. Let's talk things through.

One motive for my decentralisation policy was a desire to be rid of trouble-makers. A particular problem for me, and for every other person who had dealings with him, was an old bloke named Wally Jabaljari. He was a big tough old fellow, with the best-scarred back I have ever seen, to indicate that he had been a warrior, fighter, trouble-maker or thug, perhaps all of these, all his life. I encouraged him to be 'in charge' of the garden at Penhall's Bore, and he certainly took all the credit for the success of the project, but it was really his brother Paddy, and the wives of the two brothers who did all the work. It got Wally out of my hair, or at least removed him to a place where he had a long walk before he could annoy me. I sent his rations to him rather than have the weekly confrontation at the store, where he always demanded much more than his allotted ration on the grounds that: 'You gubmen [government]. You gotta give it long me: me Abridgin' [as he pronounced Aboriginal].' I graduated, or deteriorated, however you want to look at it, in his estimation as he called me in turn, a 'mean bugger', a 'cheatin' bugger', and eventually a 'mingy bastard'. That suggested a good command of English, but he only had a few English words in his vocabulary, all similar to those encompassing his opinion of me, and he flung them at every white person he met. I admired his toughness, but his approach was not about throwing off the white man's yoke on behalf of his people, it was absolutely self-centred. Many of the other Aboriginals hated him: he was the classic bully. He constantly demanded that I 'lend' him things, but 'lend' meant more than that. 'You, Egan, you mean bugger, you lendim Land Rover,' meant, 'I am ready to be driven somewhere. Now!' 'You lendim *wailguru*,' meant, 'Give me an axe to keep.' I established a much better relationship with him when he was at a distance.

One of the outcomes of my contact with Colin Tatz was the decision to take up some tertiary study. I had always been critical of things and people academic, for most of the people in our Darwin head office with university degrees seemed to have no practical savvy at all. I envied Colin's grasp of things, his ability to articulate valid opinions about most subjects, and the learned listening that enabled him to ask searching and discerning questions on particular topics. I began to realise, too, that while I enjoyed the social drinking scene that surrounded me, it could become mindless on occasions, and lapse into getting drunk as we reminisced how we got drunk last time. I thought it wouldn't hurt to stretch the brain cells a bit and read some books I might otherwise never experience. I was flat out all day, every day on the job, but applied for and got the papers for a Bachelor of Arts external degree course from Queensland University. I felt confident I could manage one unit of study a year, in a 10 unit degree, studying at night. So I enrolled for English 1 in a course that would achieve majors in English and Australian Studies — English 1, 2, and 3, Australian History, Australian Literature, Australian Government, Political Science 1 and 2, Public Administration and Anthropology.

Ever since I left home in 1948 my parents had written regularly, and I was a fairly good return correspondent. Nowadays I, like most people, have lost the drive for letter writing — especially hand-written letters — but I guess that is understandable given all the other means of communication. My dad, Joe, always wrote bright and breezy letters, packed with perception, but Grace, my mum, tended to write lectures rather than letters. Her missives were fired somewhat tongue-in-cheek, for she knew she had an image to maintain, and would laugh with us about her own foibles while still feigning shock at our 'lack of respect'. As she used to say, with a twinkle in her eye, 'When I'm in my coffin with my hands folded over my little bosom you'll all regret you made fun of me.' Little Bosom! Come on, Grace.

I got a real blister from Grace. It happened like this. I had received a letter from a mate of mine, Tom Ellis, a New Guinea patrol officer — *kiaps* they were called — who had attended the Australian School of Pacific Administration Course with me in Sydney in 1956. Tom was much older than most of the other blokes on the course, and he had many years of experience in New Guinea before he attended ASOPA. He had done the course with very bad grace, considering it a lot of academic garbage, but completion of the course was a promotional barrier he had to overcome. He and I got on very well. We drank a bit of Negrita rum together, he told me hair-raising tales of New Guinea pre-war, and I was a reasonable all-rounder in the ASOPA cricket team which Tom captained. It was inconceivable that anybody else would be captain: Tom certainly knew the meaning of the pidgin word *masta*.

He was back in New Guinea in 1961 and promoted to the rank of District Commissioner, which was not quite God but certainly Archangel Gabriel — or maybe a Satanic metaphor would be more appropriate for Tom. He was a tough, no-nonsense bloke, a real achiever, and he wrote to me asking if I would be interested in a job in New Guinea. I did not take it too seriously, although I was flattered he had asked me, but I mentioned in a letter to Grace that I had been approached and was considering my future.

In the late 1950s two New Guinea patrol officers had been killed by natives, and there were reports that parts of their bodies had been cannibalised. Grace knew that I had once been a patrol officer in the Northern Territory, but was very proud that I was now promoted to superintendent. Her letter came by return mail, and I knew I was in for a lambasting when it started 'Dear Teddy' — she only called me that when it was really 'on'. She started: 'Don't you dare even contemplate going to New Guinea. Didn't you hear what those savages did to those two patrol officers? If they would do that to a patrol officer, what in the hell do you think they might do to a superintendent?'

Father Stephen Worms, a German-born Pallotine priest, visited Yuendumu. He had spent many years working on Catholic missions in the north-west of Western Australia. He was in his late seventies, a trained linguist and anthropologist, and had considerable knowledge of the Gogadja people whose country is not far from the northern parts of Warlpiri land. I took Father Worms to meet the old Warlpiri men. Billy McCoy had told me of the respect desert elders have for grey-haired old men, and it was obvious that Father Worms made immediate impact. When desert Aboriginal men sing or talk about secret or sacred things they tend to speak or sing on the inward breath, rather than the normal outward breath delivery. Father Worms went straight into the same style, in a language that not only made the old men listen to him, they then took him to a place where they sat down and had a private session. I did not seek to accompany him. I did not wish to intrude on this meeting of the wise old men. The priest obviously made a huge impression. That night there were a few visits to my house, announced by a peremptory cough somewhere in the darkness, as men came to show him various objects, some of which they gave him.

Father Worms stayed only one night, and I never saw him again, but I will never forget him.

Not that such visits at night were unknown to me. I am intrigued nowadays at the openness of the display of ceremonial objects. You see Aboriginal people offering for sale things that were definitely not for general exhibition forty years ago. You see women and young men handling things they would not have dared look at. I made it known in the late 1950s at Yuendumu that I would like to collect some artifacts, and pay good money for such things. I made no attempt to coerce people in any way, but was not going to knock back anything offered to me. Things like *tjuringa*, which are stone 'story boards' (I stress that I did not seek, or get any sacred objects: paradoxically, the sacred *tjuringa* are made from more perishable wood), *kuridji*, bean-wood shields painted to depict a story, and *tjunma,* the stone knives used in fighting, were offered to me on the understanding that no Aboriginal women or children were ever allowed to look at them. They were invariably brought to me at night, always wrapped in a towel or similar, and always handled with absolute reverence. I stored them very carefully, and still do. Today similar objects are flogged around the streets of Alice Springs. Today's dot paintings, so popular all around the world, relate in many cases to stories once considered to be very dangerous if seen by the wrong people. It must all be contributing to an attenuation of the status of the old people who were once custodians of the culture. If the elders thereby relinquish or lose their control, who will provide the wisdom necessary to resolve the huge problems confronting Aboriginal people?

It must be obvious to everybody involved in Aboriginal affairs that solutions to those problems must be found from within. The many different imposed systems introduced by white people have all failed. Including mine. My approach at Yuendumu was based on the Fred Gray inspired belief that if everybody subscribed to the work ethic the place could become virtually self-sufficient, and surely Aboriginals would see the good sense of that. They didn't. Forty years later there is only one indication that I spent four years at Yuendumu and flogged my guts out. Yuendumu has some fine footballers, and it is always acknowledged that I taught the game to their fathers and grandfathers. But gardens, housing projects, stone quarries, cattle station? Why bother?

Yet we must not simply blame the Warlpiri. It is too easy to say the obvious, the 'if only' stuff. If only they'd get off their lazy black arses and do some work the problems would all resolve themselves. If only the government stopped shovelling money at them they would be forced to do something other than just sit around and contemplate their navels. They might not articulate it, but they probably rationalise their position in terms of prior occupancy — we have been here for thousands of years and our system enabled us to survive. It's our land. We didn't ask you to come here. We're bewildered by the problems, too, but they are not of our making. They must be in charge of their destiny, but we must give them a hand.

While I don't regret the many physical programs I started and developed at Yuendumu I wish I had done more to learn language. I wish I had adopted a co-operative rather than an authoritarian style. I should have used Tim Jabangardi as a Warlpiri equivalent of my Tiwi mentor, Aloysius Puantulura. If only.

11
Desk Jockey

After four years at Yuendumu I transferred back to Darwin with mixed feelings. It was good to return to the dear old town, but I could now walk down Smith Street quickly: I didn't know everybody any more. The population had quadrupled, to about 20,000

I was appointed superintendent at Bagot settlement, the place that housed Aboriginal town workers and itinerants in Darwin. The big plus was the best house Rae and I had ever lived in, one of the lovely old pre-war bungalow homes, 50 gracious spacious squares, built up on high stilts with living space underneath. The big minus was the job, sterile after Yuendumu. All the superintendent had to do was sign the many pointless forms I had resisted in the bush.

People had been given leases over land and buildings, rather than fortnightly tenancies, in Darwin post-1956, and the old town not only had a facelift, there was quite a bit of building activity, none of it very impressive in architectural standards, but including a lot of new houses. I resumed my connection with St Mary's Football Club, and had a few games. I enjoyed coaching the juniors in the 1962-3 season. In the St Mary's colts team at that time were three talented young kids destined to become national names: Maurice Rioli, Pat Dodson and Mick Dodson.

I was working — well, attending the office — from 9 to 5 each day so there was plenty of time for socialising. And I was able to study for the BA course at night. I began to realise how unique the pioneering Territory lifestyle was, and started to interview and keep notes about a few individuals with a view to developing my mental archive: the store of knowledge from which I now write songs and books like this. The Territory's history has been orchestrated into a boisterous, colourful (in the true sense of the term) symphony by the Aboriginals, Europeans, Asians and Pacific Islanders as they interacted as miners, the overlanders of cattle, the pioneers of the huge stations — single properties sometimes bigger in area than countries of Europe — pearlers, trepangers, buffalo and crocodile hunters. Even the early administration officials look larger than life when one studies this intriguing region called the Northern Territory — one of the last frontiers in the world.

Let me present four human works of art. Four larger–than–life people. People who are parts of the great pageant I will write one day. There is a painting, a photographic essay, a song called 'Eileen', and a hilarious comic strip.

When I first went to Darwin one of the most memorable personalities was an old Aboriginal woman named Alyandabu. I didn't know her name was Alyandabu then: like everybody else in Darwin I knew her as Lucy McGinness. She was tall, about 180 centimetres, and had that regal erect carriage only achieved by people trained to carry things on the head, hands free. She was Top-End black, which is blacker than jet black by a couple of pigments. She puffed on her pipe as she strode each day from Salonika, down Vesteys Hill, past the government gardens and the old cemetery, into town. She walked straight out of a Russell Drysdale canvas. I came to know her through her five children and her many grand-children, most of whom feature somehow in the sporting history of Darwin from that day to this.

Alyandabu was one of the last of the Khungarukung people of the full descent. I came to learn she was born in the 1880s in the Finniss River region, south of Darwin, in today's Litchfield Park area. Like most other tribes in Australia the Khungarukung, otherwise known as 'the paperbark people', suffered at the hands of white settlers: they were shot, given poisoned flour as the standard 'present' of the day, and their numbers had been decimated, their people dispossessed and in many cases demoralised. Alyandabu should have hated white people. She didn't, for in 1898 she met and married a white man, a young Irish adventurer named Stephen McGinness. Legal marriage between blacks and whites was rare, perhaps unknown in the Territory prior to the union of McGinness and Alyandabu. Stephen McGinness was a strict Roman Catholic, and must have been a man with high principles. He and his wife represent a wonderful combination, the best of their different worlds. That is apparent when one knows their many offspring, inheritors of magnificent genes.

McGinness was employed on the north Australia railway, the meandering line between Port Darwin (or Palmerston as Darwin was known in those days) and Larrimah (later Birdum), the line along which Xavier Herbert set his racy novel *Capricornia*. The McGinness family's story prompted the eccentric Herbert to confront the literary world with the colourful lifestyle of north Australia.

By 1904 the couple had three children, Barney, Jack and Margaret. They left the railway job after McGinness was blamed for an accident, and the family trekked off through the bush with their herd of goats. Alyandabu showed her husband, something of a prospector, some interesting rock which McGinness recognised as tin-bearing ore. They took out a mining lease over the area and began to mine and stockpile tin. Their claim came to be known as the Lucy Mine and life was good for them. They had two more sons, Valentine and Joe. In the awareness that life would be complex for their children of mixed Irish-Aboriginal descent, the parents did a fine job of rearing their family. The father, a knowledgeable man, taught the children to read, write and speak excellent English: to this day crossword puzzles are grist for the McGinness mental mill. The mother, a consummate bushwoman from a 'warrior class' family, taught the children her language and how to live off the land.

The good times came to a sudden end in October 1918 when Stephen McGinness died in Darwin hospital after an operation on his leg. The dramas of her childhood were bad enough. Without her white husband Alyandabu reverted to being a 'non-person' in those unenlightened days. As an Aboriginal she could not own property, so she forfeited the mining lease to the government. A mother of mixed-race children could have them taken from her on the grounds that life in one of the institutions for their supposed care and protection was better than Aboriginal society could create for them. Her two young sons Valentine and Joe, then aged 8 and 4, were taken from her and placed in Kahlin compound, Darwin.

Most Aboriginal mothers lost contact with their mixed-race children at that point. But not Alyandabu. She followed them to the compound and found work there so she could be near her boys and ensure that they were not fretting for her. Eventually, through her presence, prescience, persistence and pure determination she regained custody of them. She more or less lived happily ever afterwards, until she died in 1961, in her eighties. If she was white they would name a suburb of Darwin after her.

Xavier — or Frank, as Francis Xavier Herbert was known in those days — worked for the Health Department in Darwin. He was a pharmacist, but was put in charge of the Kahlin compound for a short period in the mid-—1930s. Valentine McGinness worked at the compound, and the two men became friends. The rest is *Capricornia.* When Xavier died in Alice Springs in 1984 Valentine McGinness travelled from Darwin to deliver the funeral oration in the Khungarukung language. Joe, whose Aboriginal name is Pumeri, is the only survivor of Alyandabu's children. Joe fought for Aboriginal rights long before it was fashionable, as did his brother Jack. Joe lives in Cairns, a cherished mate of mine, a mighty man.

Henry Lee was known in Darwin as 'The White Chinaman'. He was born in 1916 to a single mother who had problems surviving herself let alone looking after her baby, so the little Caucasian boy was given to the Lee Hang Gong family and placed in the loving care of Selina Lee, a lovely demure 16-year-old girl. He was reared as a Chinese boy, spoke only Chinese for the first ten years of his life, and was named Lee Kim Hoong. As is the custom, the family name Lee comes first in a person's Chinese name. The Lee family felt that poor little emaciated Henry deserved and needed the strongest possible name, so they chose Kim, 'gold', the most valuable metal, and Hoong, 'red', the strongest colour. Later in life the Darwin Chinese gave Henry the affectionate nickname Fung Quee Doy Hoong, which translates roughly as White Devil Red.

Henry was reared in Cavenagh Street, Darwin, in colourful pre-war Chinatown. He went to two schools, one for Chinese children only in Cavenagh Street, and at age ten to the Darwin Primary school in Wood Street. As a result of his upbringing his speech patterns were unique. Later in life mystified people would ask, 'What are you Henry, Swedish or something?' Henry delighted in replying, 'No, I'm a bloody Chinaman. And don't you forget it.'

I got to know Henry well, and loved to talk to him about the old days in Darwin, the balmy 1920s, the turbulent 1930s, through the Depression and leading up to the war.

'But what are you, in your heart, in your mind?' I asked him one day. He pondered the question.

'Well, by the time I was 18 I was knocking around with all the other young blokes in Darwin, and I thought I was just another whitefeller. But one day I was swimming in the Daly River and got into difficulty. I thought I was going to drown. When I found myself screaming to my Lee Hang Gong ancestors, I knew I was in fact the White Chinaman.'

He told me a funny story about his enlistment in the army during the war.

'I'm working out bush and I come into Darwin and go to the hut where I living. Two military police there. They say to me, "You know any boy name Henry Lee?" I say to him, "That me, I'm the Henry Lee." Silly bugger, Henry. They say, "We take you RSL. You gotta join the army." So I go. The man he say to me, "Orright, you swear on the bible, we put you in the army." I say, "I can't swear the bible, I'm Confucian." He say, "You not bloody Confucian," and you know what, he put me in the cage. All my mate, Donny Bonson, all that mob, they come laugh at me. They say, "Henry, join the army, you get a uniform, beer ticket, tobacco ration, leave pass, everything." So I join the army. And you know what they make me? They make me military police. Orright, they send me Melbourne, training, Melbourne Cricket Ground. So I think, Melbourne, hmmm. I got Uncle mine there Little Bourke Street. Chinatown. I go visit my uncle. Well, I walk the Little Bourke Street, I hear click, click, the fan tan game. I got my military police uniform. I walk my uncle house. I knock the door. Little shutter open. This Chinaman he scream, "You go away, you white man not allow." So I give him the good burst Cantonese, *"Ho nhe fah sung, far how kai-ai-ah."* That mean, "Listen, you peanut, you prawn-headed bastard," and I tell him my name, Lee Kim Hoong. He say, "Ah, Fung Quee, come in, you our boy from Darwin." That how I meet my uncle family.'

Henry once gave me a photo, taken at Wing Cheong Sing's studio in Darwin in 1917. In it a beautiful serene young Chinese girl, his aunt Selina Lee, stands behind the malnourished little white baby, Lee Kim Hoong. Henry's eyes are like hubcaps on his pinched little face. On Henry's seventieth birthday we were both in Melbourne, and we went to the home of his aunt, 86-year-old Selina, now Selina Hassan. I organised a repeat photograph. The eyes still had it. Selina was as tranquil as ever. The loving relationship between them was a delight. The two photographs tell me much of my beloved Darwin, and are among my most prized possessions.

'My dear old dad always called me Eily.' She burst into her renowned, bosom-bursting laugh as she said it, and her eyes danced with an even sparklier flash. Eileen Fitzer and I have been mates for many years, and I guess the focus of our friendship has always been that we were both reared in happy families where music was pervasive and singing came easily. We've been known to burst into song together on the odd occasion, whether it's needed or not..

'Dad was a lovely singer, and when we were kids Walter,

Gertrude and I would sing with Dad. Lilian played piano and Myrtle played accordian. Tragically, my wonderful mother died when I was 7.' She takes you back to precise memories of pre-war Darwin, pre-World War 1 that is. Eileen Styles was born in Darwin in 1902. The Styles family lived in Mitchell Street, between the Club Hotel and the Masonic Lodge, opposite today's Plaza Hotel. After her mother's death Eileen was cared for and educated at the Darwin convent, and so strong was that influence she later in life converted to Roman Catholicism. Her father went to work at the now famous Zapopan gold mine at Brock's Creek, and took his young family with him. Eileen considers that those years at Brock's Creek were vital in her life because she developed the level of tolerance that is her greatest asset apart from her laugh. Europeans, Chinese and Aboriginals mixed at Brock's Creek, not always harmoniously, but always as part of the great frontier development that took place in those heady days. Her eyes turn on the lights again as she recalls the Chinese New Year celebrations.

'Yes, darling, I can still see the dragon, smell the fireworks, and, oh, those great ceremonies at the joss house. Those lovely pumpkin seeds we used to eat, and the salty plums. I can still taste them darling. Honestly I can.' And then another of her infectious, head-swinging laughs, as she takes you back, and makes you wish you had been there.

She trained as a nurse in Darwin and then Melbourne after her brother Walter was killed at Gallipoli. As a triple-certificated sister she was put in charge of the Aboriginal compound at Alice Springs, then became Matron of the Pine Creek hospital. Life was busy. She stops laughing for a time when she tells you of the deaths of three young miners in quick succession at Pine Creek, and her involvement.

'One chap, screaming his innocence, was shot by a revenging father after the rape of a 13-year-old girl. One was crushed to death in a mine accident. The third died from massive head injuries when thrown from a railway quad he had borrowed to go to Pine Creek to get booze. I had to do what I could for all of them. They were all alive when they were brought to me.'

But it wasn't all work. The pretty and very sociable Eileen

Styles had never seriously considered marriage, only because the suitors were too numerous to choose from. She recalls with a passion the old bush dances, the picnic race meetings, and the social atmosphere in the frontier pubs where good manners usually prevailed, and fights among men were conducted outside. 'I feel sorry for today's kids,' she says. 'Surrounded by gimmicks and gadgets and video games, and they tell me they're bored. Bored, darling, I don't know what the word means.' I share her position. I have never known boredom. It's just not on.

Eileen was the first and only nursing sister at the mining rushes to Tennant Creek and Wauchope in the 1930s and returned to Darwin just in time for the 1937 cyclone. Cyclones were not named in those days, but Eileen is adamant that the 1937 cyclone was every bit as severe as Tracy in 1974. She should know. She survived both.

Finally she married. His name was Harry Gribbon, and he was known in the Territory as The Mad Irishman, a renowned charmer.

'My God, Ted, I've been lucky with husbands,' she said to me one day in her Darwin flat. 'I married two exact opposites, but they were such wonderful blokes in their own way. Never a dull moment.' Mind you, it's an important fact that the fun-loving, gregarious, roll-with-the-punches Eileen would have made married life a bit of a Laugh with a capital L. Harry was working at Zapopan, but then Eileen had an SOS from two old mates at Alice Springs, Joe Costello and Mona Minahan. They had opened a store at the Wauchope wolfram field. Would Harry and Eileen manage it? Of course. Eileen could also be the nurse. Let's go. Off they went, on Aunty Jess Chardon's truck. The formidable Jess up front with the driver, and Harry, Eileen — wearing her topee and flyveil — together with Johnny Gribbon, Harry's Aboriginal offsider, sitting on the back surrounded by swags, supplies and crates of chooks. No bitumen road in those days. Sunburn, plagues of grasshoppers attacking their faces, the chooks falling off at regular intervals. A memorable trip. Eileen has a tumultuous laugh when she recalls that one. Oh, darling, what a trip.

In 1940 Eileen and Harry came back to Darwin. Harry opened a butcher's shop and Eileen became matron at the Channel Island Leprosarium. She recalls it as 'the most rewarding time of my entire nursing career. Those poor darlings, with that awful sickness, yet so cheerful, and so grateful for anything I did for them.' Next she was posted as matron of the Bagot Hospital for Aboriginals in Darwin. As well as running the hospital Eileen got together a group of Aboriginal singers, and trained them to sing for Lord Gowrie, the Governor-General. One of her singers was Betty Fisher, who won Australia's *Amateur Hour* a few years later.

In 1941 Eileen and Harry decided they should put down some permanent roots, but just as they opened refreshment rooms and a pub at Adelaide River the Japanese attacked Pearl Harbor. All civilians in the Northern Territory were ordered to be evacuated. Harry was deemed unfit for active service. The Gribbons went to Sydney. Sadly, Harry died. Because of her nursing qualifications Eileen was allowed to return to the Territory before other civilians. In 1945 in Darwin she met the dashing Tas Fitzer, arguably the best-known and most popular policeman the Territory has ever had. They married at Tipperary Station and settled into fifteen years of postings at bush stations, principally at Timber Creek on the Victoria River. When Tas retired from the police force they settled at Avalon, Sydney, and began extensive travels. Eileen drove across the Golden Gate bridge in a Cadillac. She climbed the Leaning Tower of Pisa — 'With my bulk, darling, that's why it's leaning.' She had a birthday party in Jerusalem. There's a saying among her mates in Darwin, started by her Aboriginal friend Lalla Miller: 'Don't mention any place. Auntie will say she's been there.'

After Tas died in 1966, Eileen returned to her other love, the Northern Territory. In Darwin she plays Grand Old Lady and laughmaker to her many friends of every colour and creed. She lives alone, but is never lonely. To me she embodies all the qualities of the mythical Territorians we others pretend to be. She's warm-hearted, fun-loving, innovative, generous. She's bequeathed $2000 in her will for champagne for her mates after her funeral. She's no myth. Not Eily.

I wish the critics of Asian migration to Australia could meet some of the people I have known. Take Jamesy Yuen, the self-styled 'Mad Chinaman'. He's dead now and the world's a poorer place. He worked for many years at Haritos' store in Daly Street, and he was one of the funniest blokes imaginable. He was straight out of Bluey and Curley, that sort of humour. He wasn't mad at all, in the lunatic sense, but he was mad ha-ha. Fair dinkum funny.

He said to me one day, 'I am the youngest of three brothers. My oldest brother has a big dick, and we call him Hang Lo Dong. My other brother is a plumber. His name is Lee King Pai.' When I was a young bloke in Darwin we used to have a party at Jamesy's place about once a month. He was a superb cook. The arrangement was that we supplied the grog, he put on the tucker. What shows they were. He insisted on lots of singing, which suited me, and the highlight of each party was that, on the stroke of midnight, Ronny Chin and Jim, The Flying Chinaman, and The Mad Chinaman, would get on the table and sing the Chinese national anthem, or their version of it. Move over, you Three Tenors.

It was November and I was walking along Woods Street for some reason. The Wet had started early and suddenly there was a drenching downpour. I was getting soaked, but it's of no concern in Darwin, it's good fun to be out in the rain, to get cool. Jamesy, sitting under his house, saw me and sang out, 'Hey, Ted, come in out of the rain, China. Come and have few beer.' I thought that a bit incongruous, him calling me China Plate, mate, but needed no second invitation, and we sat down to enjoy a few cold glasses and have a yarn. Being a good listener I steered the conversation his way, and got him talking about the old days. He told me of his great-grandfather who had come to the Territory in the 1870s as a coolie working on the Darwin to Pine Creek railway. There was a shortage of government funds, and the daily rate of pay for the Chinese labourers was cut from fourpence to twopence a day. So the Chinese hacksawed the blades of their shovels in half.

I remembered that Jamesy had been working on the Darwin wharf on 19 February 1942 when the Japanese bombed Darwin

Harbour and 243 people were killed and 300 injured on that first day.

'What was it like?' I asked him.

'Christ!' He paused for a bit, and you could see his mind was rewinding as he sipped his beer. 'What was it like? What was it like? Mate, it's 10 o'clock in the morning and I'm just knocking off for smoko, and in they come, the Japs. Well, they hit the main wharf, and the *Neptuna,* tied up alongside, goes up with an almighty bang. She's full of fuel and explosives, see. I'm knocked sky high and thrown into bloody Darwin Harbour. I surfaced about twenty yards from the wharf, and the water's alight, there's oil and shit everywhere, especially in my bow wave, and I'm not a real flash swimmer. I start breast-strokin' for the wharf, but I've got no way of climbing up, have I? Suddenly, through the smoke I see a dinghy being rowed madly by two of my mates, Ernie Koosney and Tom Flynn, two jokers I've been working with on the Darwin wharf for the last fifteen years. Saved, I thought. I started swimming towards them, and got within a few yards of them when Ernie spots me. But are they going to save me? No bloody way. Ernie passes his oar to Tom and shouts, "Quick Tom. There's a Jap. Hit the bastard!"'

My career as a jockey was short-lived but spectacular. Billy McGill and I decided to go to the Fannie Bay St Patrick's Day meeting in March 1963, and we bowled up just wearing shorts, singlets and thongs. Dress is casual at Fannie Bay, and we were a bit overdressed, as we both sported a bit of green ribbon as well. There were six races, and these had been run so Bill and I were settled into the bar, yarning with a few blokes. Brian Egan rushed up.

'Quick, Ted, they've organised a "selling race". We've just paid big money for a nag, and we've nominated you as the hoop.'

'You're joking.'

'I'm not bloody well joking. We've paid six hundred quid for the horse, and it's a bloody certainty. We've backed it to win two grand.'

'About the only certainty is that I'll come a gutser,' I said. 'I've had about fifteen schooners.'

He wasn't going to be put off.

'Come on. You're nominated.'

A selling race is usually run to raise some money for charity. They get a pool of horses, 'auction' them, whereby the 'owner' is the owner of the horse just for the one race. The proceeds of the sale go to the charity. This one was for the Red Cross. My only consolation as I was being dragged to the mounting yards was that it was all for a good cause, and that various other blokes were being hauled from the bar to be jockeys, and I reckoned some of them were in worse condition than I was. I kicked off my thongs, but was aware that riding barefooted and just dressed in shorts was hardly clever, an affront to the racing game. It wouldn't have done at Ascot. Or even Brunette Downs. I looked across to the betting ring. Alec Fong Lim, who on St Patrick's Day always wore lots of green ribbon and had his name on his bookmaker's stand altered to Alec O'Lim, had the starters listed according to their jockeys, and I realised the gravity of my position when I saw in bold red letters EGAN 3/1 ON. I'm riding an odds-on favourite!

My horse was obviously good class. Brian Egan hovered by me, just like you see at the big meetings, the trainer giving last minute instructions to the rider.

'If you fall off, don't expect any of us to pick you up, you bastard. And don't forget, we've got a packet on this nag.'

'Thanks, cousin.' To this day we always refer to one another as 'cousin', but thank Christ we're not related. Brian Egan is a dangerous man. He legged me up into the racing saddle. My God, it's no bigger than a postage stamp. And those little stirrup irons cutting into my bare feet. I've got soft feet at the best of times. Then, he bent towards me, and whispered the real inside information.

'Tommy Gorle, the starter, is with us. Don't take your eyes off him.'

We trotted out onto the track, and I could tell straight away that the thoroughbred I was riding was a real goer, the best horse I had ever ridden. It was a big bay gelding, about 16 hands. For all I know they might even have given it a needle to enhance its performance. Maybe I should have asked them to hit me with a jab? I knew that I could ride a bit, and was confident I wouldn't fall off — well, reasonably confident, but I had not had such an adrenalin run in a long time. Suddenly I was sober, or thought I was anyway. My reflexes were good, but all drunks say and think that. It was only going to be a five-furlong race. We trotted towards the starting line, and my horse was rearing to go.

It was a walk-up start. Remembering Brian's instructions I got as close to Tommy Gorle as I could. I needn't have bothered. Tom rode up alongside me, and spoke quietly out the corner of his mouth.

'You OK, Ted?'

'I hope so.'

'Watch my hand.' He indicated the handkerchief in his right hand, and obviously he would 'drop' that to start the race. The other riders were having a hell of a time getting their mounts into line. Suddenly, Tom gave me a wink, roared 'Go' and dropped the handkerchief. In the same motion he gave my horse a whack on the arse. I was off, flying. Nobody else caught the start, and it was immediately obvious, five lengths in front, that I was going to be hard to catch. The big imponderable: would I still be on the horse when it reached the post?

I got so far in front I became confident, and as I turned into the straight I looked around for the others. There were horses bucking everywhere, riders strewn all over the track. There were only a couple of other riders still on board, and they were twenty lengths behind me. I roared past the post, the easiest of winners, and managed a big Darren Beadman wave to Brian Egan and the rest of the gang, jumping, cheering with delight.

But then I realised that I had to stop the horse. Maybe they *had* hit it with a sting? All I knew was that the horse was looking for at least one more lap of the track, and I was not in control. I remembered everything Norman Hagan had taught me. Saw on the bit. I did. No result. Dig your boots deeper into the irons and pull his bloody head off his shoulders. But I'm barefooted, and he's stronger than I am, by a mile. I'd gone about another two furlongs, with no possible chance of stopping the horse, and I imagined myself finishing up at Humpty Doo. But suddenly, inspiration.

It was March, the end of The Wet, and the spear grass on the outer perimeter of the track was about two metres high, and thick. I couldn't slow the horse down, but I steered him with a savage rein towards the long grass. We ground into it, blinded, grass seeds flying and we went through it like a crashing helicopter, the horse's legs and my arms flailing into the wall of grass. Gradually the horse ground to a halt, and realised that the race was over. It was content for me to turn it back towards the grandstand and the crowd. I was still hanging on to the reins for all my worth, holding as tight a check on the horse as I could muster. There was a burning sensation in my feet but I wasn't game to look down. I rode triumphantly back to scale, expecting a tumultuous welcome, but by the time I got there everybody had adjourned to the bar. Everyone except the real owner of the horse that is. He savaged the reins from me, and gave me this black look. His disdainful gaze roamed to my feet. Just a shake of his head. I looked. Stuck between all of my toes were these bloody great tufts of spear grass. I slid from the saddle, and unpicked my toes.

'I hereby resign,' I announced at the bar. We all had a good laugh. Around the bar there were my fellow jockeys, with skin and fur off every part of them. There had never been so many falls in one race. Ronny Smith, my old Melbourne schoolmate, who had become a bookmaker, suggested nominating for the *Guinness Book of Records*. Peter Fogarty sang, 'When autumn leaves, start to fall.' A mate of ours named Jim Newell was in a hell of a state. His face was covered with blood. You'd have thought he'd been on Springfield beer, but no, he had just come the greatest buster off his horse. And he had told us in the mounting paddock what a great rider he'd been, back in Scotland. His wife, Jessie, was in the hospital, and silly Jim could not be talked out of going to visit her that evening. He told us later, 'I walked into the hospital ward and wee Jessie burrst intay tears. An' burrst her stitches intay the barrgain.'

Riding racehorses and assembling your archive is great Ted,

but what are you going to do with your life? I'm back in Darwin, promoted out of the bush forever, I'm 30 years of age, married with three kids, wanting to stay in the Territory, no real skills or talent, can sing a bit, but can't everybody? I'm a permanent public servant, and good at relating to Aboriginals, but desk-bound forever? The present job is hopeless, but next step will be worse, promoted again, into town to head office with the silvertails. Never see any blackfellows at head office. I'm going to finish up like those other bastards. I'll be ordering the superintendent at Yuendumu to send me mulga seed in the middle of a drought. I agonised about things as I went through the motions as superintendent at Bagot. One good aspect was that I did not tire myself on the job too much, and was able to put a lot of night-time hours into study. I was going well with my English studies with Queensland University, getting great marks for assignments, and often remembering to think kindly of Colin Tatz, who had given me the jump-start.

I was having a few beers and talking about study to my mate Jim Gallacher one day. Jim had been a teacher in Aboriginal bush schools as a younger bloke, and was now in head office, in charge of Aboriginal education. Although we were the best of friends, with lots of common interests in sport and politics, we often had stirring arguments about the effectiveness or lack of it of some of his fellow teachers. Many of them in my opinion did nothing other than teach Aboriginal kids to clean their teeth and sing songs, and supervise them on bush walks. There were notable exceptions, like himself, and he knew that I had the highest respect for him. He agreed that there were many misfits and bludgers among teachers in the bush.

'When are we going to get some Aboriginal matriculants?' I asked Jim one day.

'When are you going to do something about it?' he fired back.

'What do you mean?'

'Come on, Ted, you hate it at Bagot. You're a bush bloke, and you know it. I've just kicked off a system to encourage mature-age people to train as teachers for bush schools. You'd be a champion teacher. Put up or shut up.'

'Tell me about it.'

He did. I thought about it. I warmed to the idea. I would have to almost halve my salary, but as the training would be in Brisbane I would get a good allowance to rent a house. I would still be down in cash, but Rae was prepared to give it a go, and I thought I could probably take a spare job to make some extra money. Do a bit of singing perhaps?

I enrolled.

12
Chalkie Ted

We rented a good house in Red Hill, Brisbane, handy to the Kelvin Grove Teachers' College. There were 1000 student teachers on the course, most of them straight out of high school. There was a handful of 'mature-age' students and I was the oldest at 30. It was good to mix with so many young people, and rewarding to find that I could more than hold my own with them at study and in the college's comprehensive PT and sporting program.

It was a two–year course, and I was lucky in that I knew exactly what I would be going back to, a posting in a one-teacher bush school. So I decided from day one to plan my activities not so much to accommodate what the college wanted from me, but to get what I wanted from the college.

Win the hearts and minds first, Ted. I met a bloke named Coll Portley, an art lecturer at Kelvin Grove. He was the brother of a mate of Rae's and mine, Margaret Portley, who had been a sister at the Alice Springs hospital when Mark Egan was born there. Coll and I quickly became good friends, and have stayed that way. Coll told me that the Principal of the College, Dr Greenhalgh, was an Aussie Rules fanatic, but had never been able to get a team going at Rugby-mad Kelvin Grove. Dr Greenhalgh, I'm your man. Ted Egan was quickly appointed captain of the newly-formed Teachers' Australian Rules football team. That set up all sorts of privileges, the main one being that I asked Doc Greenhalgh for a lot of practical experience at Ascot, where a one-teacher 'demonstration' school was set up within the organisation of a normal 500–kid primary school. The essential difference with one-teacher schooling is that the one teacher takes a group of kids through their entire primary schooling. The Ascot school has for many years demonstrated the value of that type of approach, for among its past pupils are doctors, professors, engineers, architects, top musicians, Olympic athletes — levels of achievement far above average.

The two years sped through. Lectures were for the most part boring, as the policy of the Queensland Education Department at that time was to reward faithful old teachers with posts as training college lecturers. They were as dull and conservative as their clothes. Some of the art lecturers were dashers who did things like drink and play sport with the students. Dreadful! But by and large I felt that the students were not being allowed to leave school, and they in turn, as teachers trained under the same system, ran the risk of perpetuating the 'safe' Queensland line. Don't rock the boat, seemed to be the general policy.

I passed all the exams with a sprinkling of distinctions, most-prized being a High Distinction for Class Teaching, was awarded a Full Sporting Blue for Aussie Rules and basketball, started a few lifetime friendships, and won the Best and Fairest in the Brisbane Aussie Rules competition, largely as a result of being honed to the highest level of physical fitness I have ever attained. All the PT and cross-country runs did the trick. All the lunchtime volleyball. All the extra footy training with my mates Neil Davies and Frank Brennan. Playing my first games of handball since I left school, in fierce competition with Frank Brennan, who had been the champion of Gregory Terrace College. Frank and I were about even as players, and played it fast and hard. And working three nights a week cleaning telephone boxes, with young Frank as my offsider, involved lots of physical work, and brought in the extra money that made up for the massive reduction in salary. Singing at pubs on Saturday nights helped, too. I don't ever remember getting more than £5 for an engagement, but it was good experience, and I was learning that some of the techniques that worked with kids in a classroom applied also to working an audience in a pub. Rule number one, never seek to get 'discipline' or 'order' by raising your voice: a whisper works better.

I had a couple of chances to sing on TV on a program called *Brisbane Tonight*. I sang 'Rambling Rose' and 'Wolverton Mountain'. I also went in a TV talent quest, and was 'gonged' out after only three bars of 'No One Will Ever Know'. That's showbiz.

Brisbane was good for Rae and the kids. It's an easy city, and the weather is great. The house was comfortable, and the kids saw TV for the first time. They attended the local Catholic school. We became very friendly with all of the Portley family, who also lived in Red Hill, and Coll Portley introduced me to that great game, Rugby Union. In 1964 young Jacki Egan was born. She was a little dynamo from day one, a lovely baby, and she gets better as the years roll by. She is fierce about her Queensland origins, and don't you ever talk to her about any Rugby League team other than the Broncos.

At the end of 1964 I got my posting back to the Territory. I would start the 1965 school year at Newcastle Waters in a one-teacher school. After spending Christmas on the Gold Coast, Rae flew back to Darwin with baby Jacki, and I had the wonderful experience of driving my dad, Joe, from Queensland, where he had joined us for the holidays, by road through western Queensland into the Territory. Joe had never been further from Victoria than Barcaldine, Queensland, when he was a young fellow, and he lapped up the trip. The three older kids were great company, and my dad and I yarned away incessantly as the kilometres changed into miles. I'll never forget the look on his face one day somewhere near Hughenden in Queensland. We came over a rise, and there, before, beside and behind us was a 360 degree expanse of Mitchell grass. We stopped, got out of the car, and had a celebratory beer together.

'Now I know why they call it The Big Country,' Joe said.

When we hit the Territory, heading for Darwin, we stopped for a day at Newcastle Waters, to check out my new posting. There were only two houses on top of the rise in the old droving township, one for the teacher, and one for the PMG linesman, Brian Cornelius. Brian and his wife, Dee, were very pleasant people. They had the key for the empty teacher's house, and showed us over it. My kids were thrilled to bits. It was in fact the old police station, a spacious two-storey home, with old-fashioned phones linking upstairs and downstairs, and lots of little nooks, crannies and cupboards to excite the imagination of kids. I met an Aboriginal couple, Duncan and Elsie, who told me they were waiting for our arrival in a few weeks, when school would re-open. 'We look after you,' Duncan informed me. We travelled on to Darwin, feeling confident that it was going to be a good experience, and better still, back in the bush.

We arrived in Darwin in January 1965. The big change was that Aboriginals had been given the right to drink. In the pubs I now saw Aboriginal 'full-blood' and mixed race people drinking together, something previously denied. Mixed-race people had been 'freed' — ironically, that was the word used in respect of rights to drink alcohol — in 1954. I could now spot the physical resemblance that identified people as brother and sister, and the paradox was that alcohol had reunited them. The biggest concern was the frenetic pace of the drinking. Even though I was established as a 'bloody good drinker' in Territory terms, drinking must only be a positive social exercise. The alcohol is the catalyst that allows people to spend harmonious time with others, an accompaniment to chat, laughter, celebration, mourning, eating, conviviality. Here I was seeing people drinking to get drunk, to make up for lost time. It was bound to inculcate all sorts of wrong ideas about alcohol. I remember saying to Ted Evans, a big drinker like me, 'This is not going to work. It will take three generations to sort this out.' I said that in 1964. I still hold to it. The irony is that Aboriginals developed over milennia a system that did not need props like alcohol, drugs and social services, but they were dragged into a lifestyle that by its very nature made them dependent on all three. I have never met one Aboriginal whose life has been enhanced by alcohol, whereas I think mine has. It's not biological, it's the social system that dominates different lives in different ways.

When we returned to Newcastle Waters a few weeks later, to start the school year, I checked the place out more comprehensively. There were a few little shacks, all perched along the same ridge above the high water mark of the Newcastle Waters

Creek, which is renowned for massive flooding. A few Aboriginal and mixed-race Afghan families lived in these. The old pub's licence had only recently been renewed after many years, and the new licensee was an old Vesteys station cook named Jack McDonald, called Mac. He was a good bloke, a big-framed fellow, always stripped to the waist to display a hairy barrel of a beergut that he delighted in lifting onto the bar. It turned him into an imposing sentinel as he served you your beer. I always felt like drumming on his exposed gut. It looked taut enough.

I got a good insight into Mac during my first couple of days. School was to start the following Tuesday. I strolled up to the pub at 5 o'clock one day, and sat in the corner sipping a luke-warm stubby. Mac was busy out the back. Mac had no refrigerator, and cooled the beer in the old-fashioned way, putting a wet bag on top of it. It was the end of January, stinking hot, but I was used to hot beer, so I was happy enough.

'Motor car,' came the voice of an Aboriginal from somewhere outside. I went to the door. Sure enough, there was a cloud of dust to indicate that a car had left the bitumen highway and was undertaking the 3–kilometre trip into Newcastle. They must be mad. Nobody did that. Why would you?

Of all things the car turned out to be a little Austin A 40. It stopped, and out stepped two trim little old ladies, both about 70, obviously tourists doing an intrepid circuit of the outback. They checked their hair, patted down their skirts, and slowly worked out how to access the pub. They were beautifully groomed, the hazards of the trip notwithstanding. I slipped further into the corner. It was getting on to dusk, and I was hardly noticeable. This was obvious material for my archive. They moved gingerly into the bar, which seemed empty. Mac was stacking some gear in the shed. There was a little handbell on the bar, and one of the women gave it a nervous tinkle. Out stormed old Mac, sweat glistening on his huge gut. He lifted the Foster-child in one impressive heave onto the bar where it confronted the women like the arse-end of a huge hairy-nosed wombat.

'Yes,' roared Mac, and the little old ladies took a pace backward.

'Er, do you, do you serve . . . beer?' asked one of the travellers.

'It says "pub" on the door, don't it?' said Mac. He wasn't a fierce bloke at all, but there's an unfortunate attitude in the bush that tourists, often called terrorists, are dangerous, a bit like snakes: if you don't hit them first they might get the upper hand and take advantage of you. But the intrepid old ladies had a bit of spirit to them. After all they had driven across Australia in an A 40.

'Well, we'll have two glasses of beer, please.'

'We don't serve it in glasses. It comes in stubbies.' Mac had already reached under the wet bag, and plonked two of the hot stubbies on the bar with a bounce that was bound to have consequences.

'Right, stubbies it is, then.' The customers might not be right, but they were not daunted.

As the lady agreed to the deal Mac was already ripping the scabs off the tops of the bottles. They were hot to start with, but his treatment of them caused the two stubbies to overflow, fizzing, foaming onto the counter. The old ladies raised their hands in horror, nonplussed.

'Well, drink your bloody beer, don't spill it all over my counter,' roared Mac

The two ladies gallantly grabbed the stubbies, slapped their mouths over the eye of the volcano and stopped the flow. They heaved a sigh as they swallowed half the stubby in one go. Mac had a good laugh.

'By Jesus, you city sheilas are fast drinkers,' he shouted. But the ice had been broken, if my inappropriate metaphor is to be excused.

'You seem like good sorts,' said Mac, now his genial self. 'Let me buy you another beer. And will you stay for tea, ladies? A nice bit of corn beef — stolen of course — some spuds and a lovely white onion sauce? Sound good?'

'Sounds wonderful.' The two ladies finished up staying the night, swapping yarns and sharing a bottle of rum with Mac and a couple of other locals who drifted in. I guess it was one of the highlights of their big adventure.

'Every journey starts with a single step'. Me, 17, on the doorstep of the family's Coburg home, 1949, on the start of the journey to South America.

Me and Ron 'Smithy' Smith (*left*), the other prospective gaucho, snapped in Darwin

Post-war Darwin

Bombed out flats on the site of today's Uniting Church

Gordon's Don Hotel, bombed and strafed, before its conversion into a hostel, Abbott House. Site of the ABC's studios today.

Darwin Hotel, miraculously unbombed, intended Japanese HQ rumour had it

The freighter *Neptuna* lay in the harbour until the 1960s, when Japanese salvage crews retrieved it for scrap!

Opposite page, from top: Parap Police Station - beyond here was considered bush. The United Church Club, typical pre-war Darwin architecture. Looking from Raintree Park to where Woolworths now stands was A E Jolly's general store. `The Vic', from which my songs were banned. The Don, where footballers drank after the game. Darwin Railway Station, a thing of the past - and future?

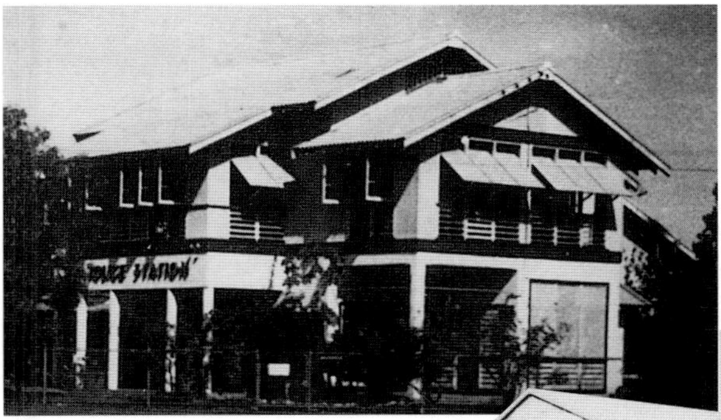

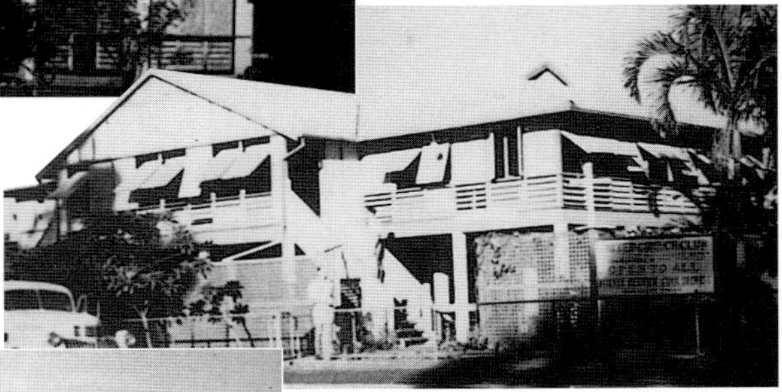

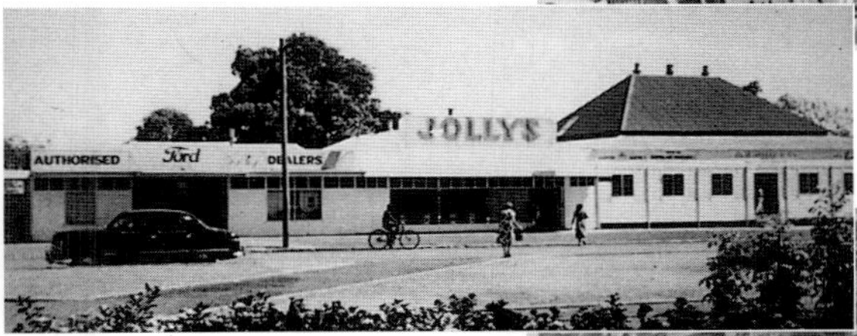
JOLLY'S
AUTHORISED Ford DEALERS

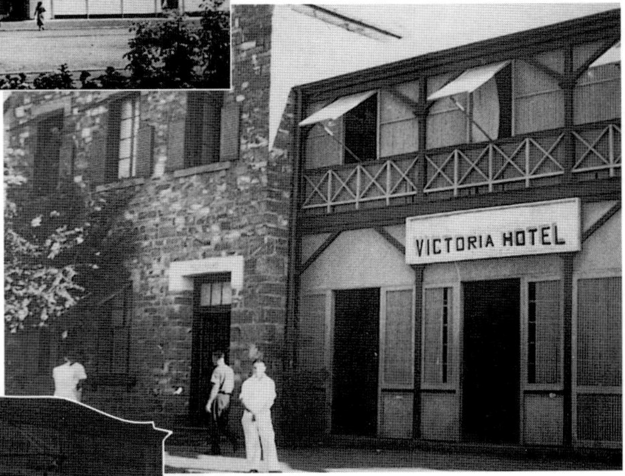
VICTORIA HOTEL

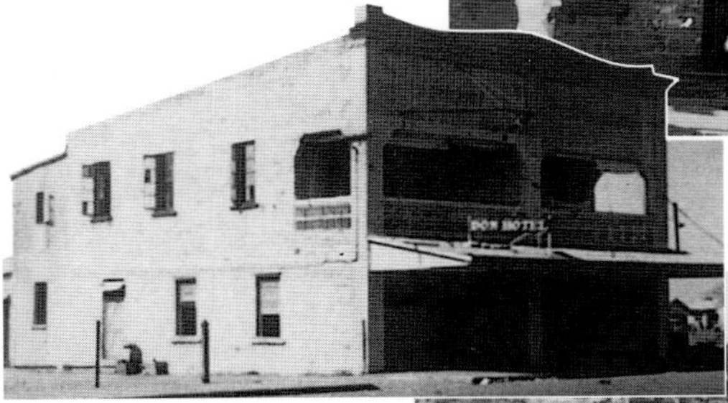
DON HOTEL

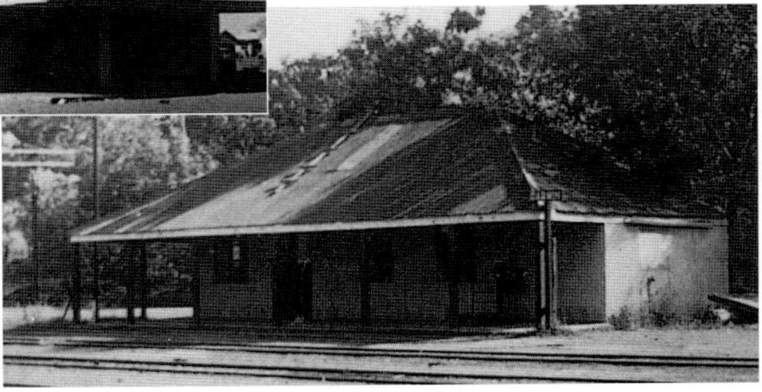

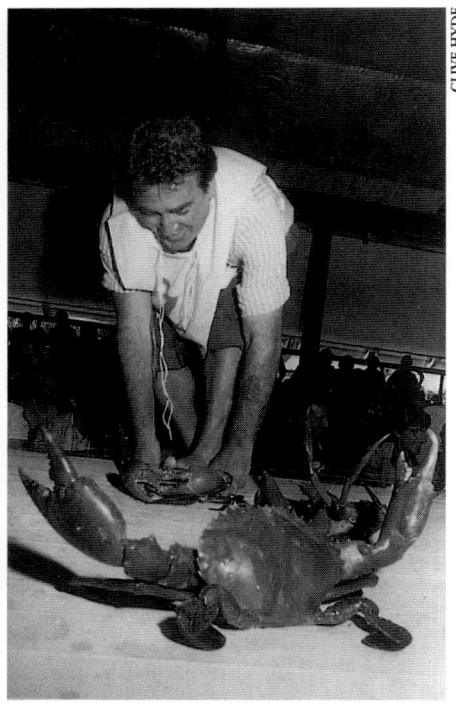

Top left and left: Every inch a most proper patrol officer in my head office tropical gear, at 'Belsen' and on Casuarina Beach, 1950

Above: But there was time enough for truly serious pursuits, like trying your fingers in a crab-tying contest

Northern Territory Basketball Team, September 1954, about to depart for the Australian championships in Brisbane. *From left:* Ray Yee, George Sarib, Bill Roe, Terry Lewfatt, me, Don Bonson, Rim Gasiunas, Johnny Mayo, Phil McLaughlin, Jacko Angeles, Cedric Chin, Joe Sarib, Welly Chin, Albert Cahn. It was the first Territory team to compete in an interstate competition.

St Mary's Football Club, 1954 Darwin Premiers. *Back row, from left:* Harry Sherlock, Benny Cubillo, Arthur Smith, Terry Lewfatt, Ken Bowman, Bill Roe, Terry Connollly, Brian Pobjoy, Gordon Roe, Anastasius Vigona, Bill Power. *Middle row:* Edmund Johnston, Urban Tipiloura, Philip Babui, me, Saturninus Kantilla, Jerome Tipuamantumirri, Raphael Apuatimi. *Front:* Jacob Pautjimi, Bertram Kantilla, Dermot Tipungwuti, Paul Kerinaua.

Young Captain Ted being chaired off after the big win in 1954. Dermot Tipungwuti in front, Steve Cubillo behind.

'We'll teach you to drink, Ted.' *From left:* Cousins Frank and Bill Brennan, me and cousin Leo 'Sandy' Brennan on the deck of the m.v. *Dulverton*, Darwin, 1950.

Cashed-up and fit after labouring on the West Australian wheat harvest, young Ted samples Perth's department stores, city life and the Golden West, 1951

Above: The Mad Chinaman, Jamesy Yuen: 'You too can have a body like mine.'

Left: With my mate The Flying Chinaman, Ronny 'Hoonga' Chin, at Melbourne's Luna Park portrait stand on a visit in 1951

Below: Fred Gray and me in the 1990s. Fred was a trepanger, trader, and generously provided information and guidance in researching the Caledon Bay killings in the early 1930s, *Justice All Their Own*.

Bill 'Bilarni' Harney, bushman, historian and friend. The greatest storyteller I ever met

Below: Tiwi kids acting up. *'Madi yoi yoi krijini* - let's dance, kids.'

Island life in the Top End
Felix Kantilla and me sailing to Bathurst Island

Below: The motor ketch *Margaret Mary*

Below left: 'You know that Queen woman? Too much him want that Wallaby dance.' Aloysius ready to do it.

Below right: Bathurst Islander Tony worked for the army

Margaret Egan with sponsors Ted Evans and Hazel Gaden-McGill on her confirmation day. Ted was my boss in the Native Affairs Branch. Hazel is Rae's cousin.

Me. The only reason for including this photograph is that I can't remember ever looking this young.

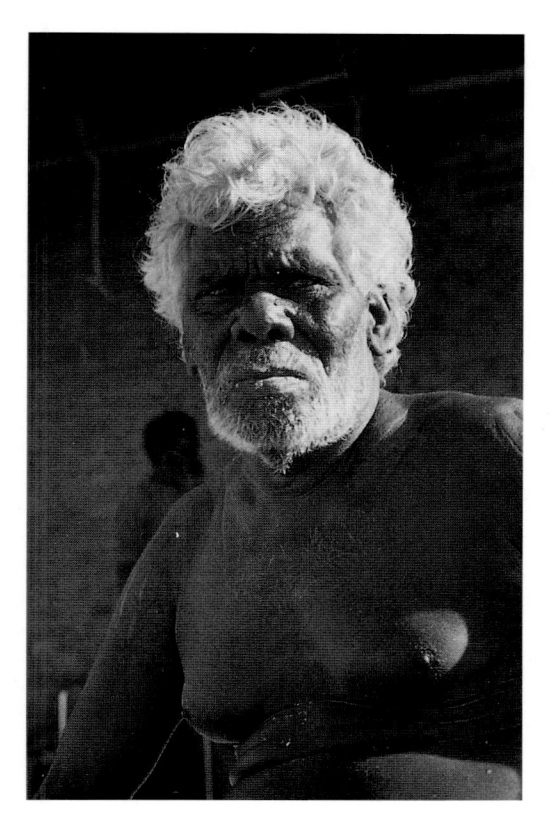

Harry Mulumbuk, paragon of Australian bushmen, the man who invented 'she'll be right'. 'You want to hop in, killim like a Tarzan?' he asked me - of a croc!

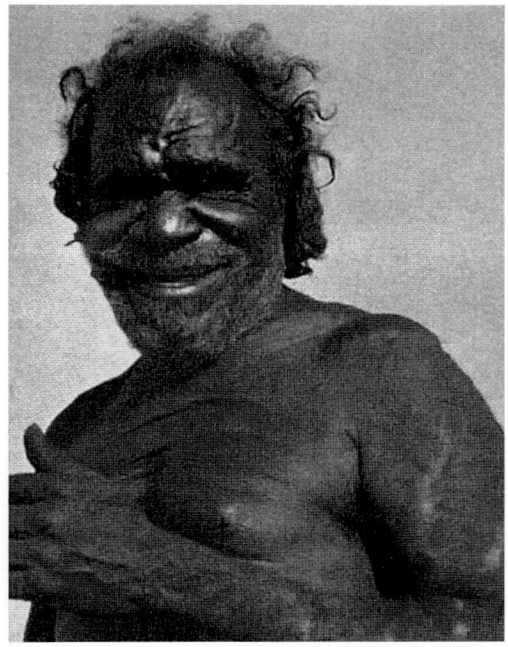

Old Wally Jabaljari. Whatever you call him - standover man, thug, warrior - there was never a dull moment when he was around. Dr George Tippett measured one scar on his back: 110 cm long.

Rae and me, 1972, in Edinburgh on long-service leave en route to the Munich Olympics

Me and my father, Joe Egan, on a too-rare trip to Melbourne. Ferntree Gully, early 1960s.

Egan offspring. *Clockwise from top left*: Jacki, 9; Greg, as mascot for St Mary's Football Club, 2; Mark, 8; and Greg and Margaret, 4 and 2.

Borroloola was an unlikely place to find scholars, but it had some, and they were among the most learned people I ever met

Above: two shots of Roger Jose, Borroloola's Socrates. Voracious reader, debater, anthropologist, experimenter with drugs, Roger was also a successful polygamist, metho-drinker and eccentric.

Left: Jack `Mull' Mulholland, postmaster. That's the post office behind him, the old Tattersal's Hotel.

Yuendumu stone housing project

Clockwise from top left:
Women singing while stockpiling limestone to burn for mortar.
A team break up sandstone blocks.
The blocks are loaded.
Then laid - a completed house is in the background.
A totally 'local' building emerges.

Top: Wallaby Bill, the late Bill Waudby, our neighbour at Yuendumu. Wartime airman, genial bush policeman, rum drinker and puftaloon maker of renown.

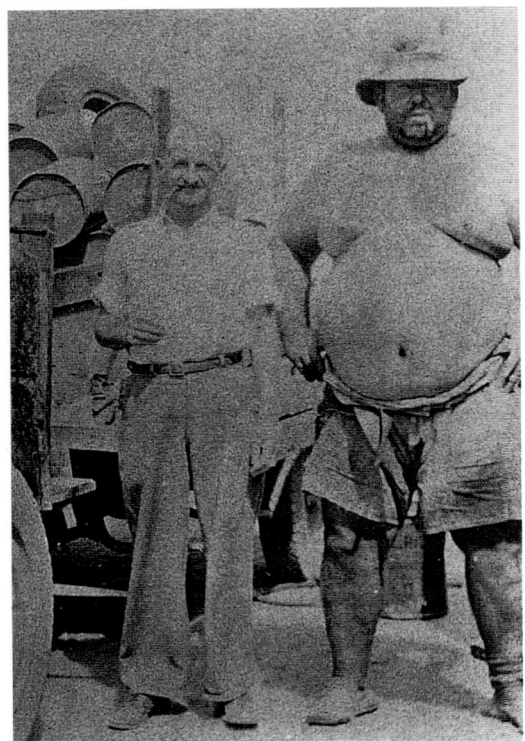

Right: Jack McKay, a cattleman who measured the seriousness of the bogs he encountered after The Wet by the number of bottles of rum it took to drink his way through. Tiny Swanson, biggest man in the Territory, a soft gentle fellow with a quiet voice, strong as a sumo wrestler. They lowered Tiny into his grave with a crane.

Below: Tuit's coach drops passengers at Banka Banka, on the road from Alice to Darwin, 1950

Right: Mawalan Marika, the artist of whom Picasso said, 'Ah, if I could paint like that...'

Above: Edmund Johnston, St Mary's full back, had Olympic teeth. At the 1956 Games Melbourne's dentists took time off to cast his rarely seen, perfect full complement of 36 teeth.

Above: The Kakadu Man, Bill Neidji, shows me around his born country

Right: The Junction Hotel, Newcastle Waters, where Mac the proprietor hung out and was propped up by the bar - literally

Above left: Alyandabu, Lucy McGinniss. Deprived of her sons (and the family tin mine) by her husband's death and stupid laws, she followed them to Darwin.

Above: Granny Lum Loy, grandmother of The Flying Chinaman. 'Watch her walkin' down Cavenagh Street...'

Right: Eileen and Tas Fitzer, a pair as good as they look, two hearts of gold

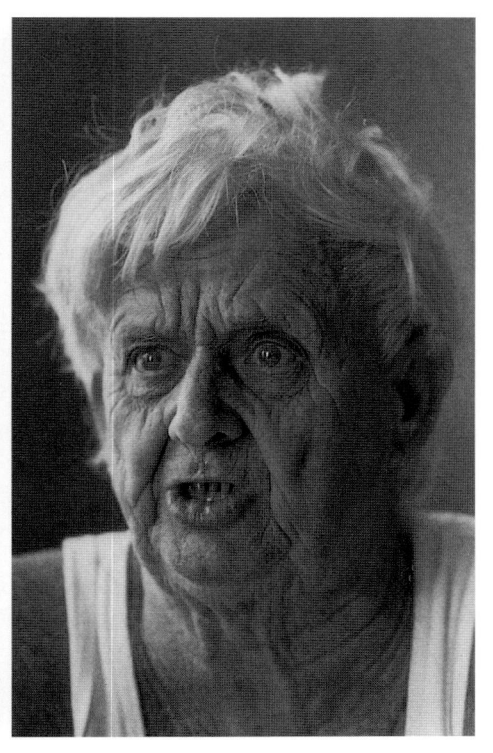

The photograph top left was taken in Wing Cheong Sing's Darwin studio in 1916, the one below in Melbourne in 70 years later. The people are the same in both, Selina Lee Hassan and her adopted nephew Henry Lee, generally known as The White Chinaman.

Above: Henry Lee, spinning a yarn, in 1980

Rotorua, New Zealand, Aboriginal-Maori cultural exchange visit, 1976. I am the whitefella sitting on the steps. In front of me, facing camera, is Eddie Mabo of land rights fame. Alongside him extreme left, in three-quarter profile, is James Rice, the plantiff in the Mabo case when Eddie died. Standing, addressing the assembly, is artist Dick Roughsey, Maori and paheka schoolchildren at his feet.

Aloysius Puantulura performs in ceremonial mode before a sculpture of a Maori warrior

Djaylama upstaged us all when he threw a spear over the crossbar of a rugby union goalpost and it came to rest after passing over the crossbar at the other end, over 100 m away. He threw his next over the grandstand and 40,000 people roared.

When the Nabalco bulldozers scarred the side of the Nhulunbuy Hill, the Yolngu men staged this angry demonstration, led by Mathaman Marika, who said, 'My heart is broken.'

Dhanburama, the sacred banyan tree, left standing in the middle of the Gove alumina plant following protests by Aboriginals over the destruction of another sacred banyan tree

Above: Alec Kruger (*left*), plantiff in the High Court 'stolen-generation' case. Les Humbert, a man of mixed descent, who was left with his people, at the insistence of a white pastoralist Charlie Schultz.

Below Left: Pincher Numiari, head stockman for the Gurindji Murramulla Cattle Co, Daguragu, Wattie Creek

Below: Dr H C 'Nugget' Coombs with Narritjan Maymuru. Nugget was Chairman of the Council for the Arts. Narritijan, a world-famous painter, was the great conciliator of Arnhem Land, as I came to appreciate.

Daguragu, 1969, during the Great Strike. *From left:* me, Donald Nangiari, Phillip Roberts, Jack Doolan, Vincent Lingiari, Ted Evans and Captain Major. Vincent Lingiari, 'proper old-law boss, called "boy" by the whites'. Phillip Roberts, subject of the book and film, *I, the Aboriginal.*

Galarrwuy Yunupingu, Roy Dadaynga Marika and Daymbalipu Mununggurr outside the the Supreme Court in Canberra, 1970. Galarrwuy was interpreter. Daymbalipu borrowed my coat for the occasion.

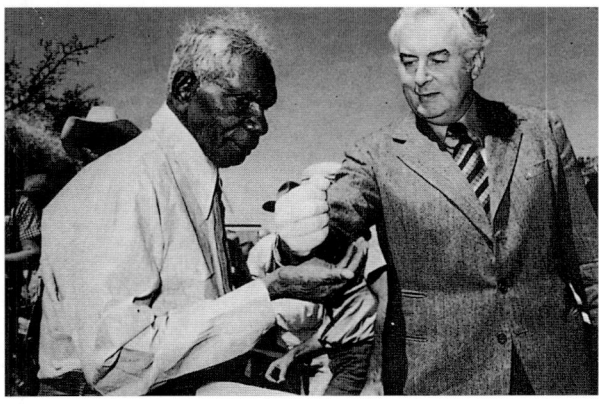

Prime Minister Gough Whitlam symbolically pours earth into Vincent Lingiari's hands at the ceremony to mark the handover of a large part of what was the Wave Hill pastoral lease to the Gurindji, 1975

Some great Territory faces and me. *From left:* Historian Peter Forrest, Aboriginal soldier Dick Butler, me, Torres Strait Islander Jaffa Ahmat (composer of the song 'Old TI'), Filipino-Aboriginal 'Babe' Damaso (Charleston champion) and The Flying Chinaman, Territorians all.

'C'mon, Rolf. Get the words right.' I try to teach 'Two Little Boys' to whatsisname 1969

One other day in the pub the Beetaloo boys were having a drink. They were the mixed-race progeny of the famous Bullwaddy Bates, who had taken a string of Aboriginal wives and produced his own work force for Beetaloo Station. The essential difference between him and other white settlers who did the same thing was that Bullwaddy acknowledged the children, and bequeathed the station to them when he died. Peter Bostock was in the bar that day at Newcastle Waters, and he went outside for a leak. The overseas jets had just started to fly and he must have looked up to see the vapour trail left in the sky. He charged back into the pub.

'Quick, boys, outside,' he roared. 'Spitfires!'

There was a system going in bush schools in the Territory, whereby at the end of each school year teachers had to pack their entire belongings and furniture, and store their goods in one room. That had been brought about by the high turnover of teachers. Teachers might be interstate, or even overseas, during the long school holidays, send in a letter of resignation, or be transferred, with the problem that their gear was filling up the house to be occupied by the replacement teacher, who would then have to pack the stuff and send it on. There had been all sorts of insurance hassles as a result of this, so now, even if you thought you were returning to the same posting after the Christmas holidays, you still had to pack your gear before the long holidays started, and the basic responsibility for its safety, in terms of suitable packing, was yours.

My predecessor at Newcastle Waters was Ron Gallacher, a friend of mine, a brother to Jim Gallacher, who had talked me into taking up teaching. Ron's gear was very neatly packed into one of the many spare rooms at Newcastle, and in my first couple of days there, in rolled a truck to collect it. The removalist did not inspire much confidence at all. He was an old cattle drover, out of work like most of the drovers who had been replaced by the road trains.

'I've never done any of this sort of caper, but I put in a tender for the contract and won it,' he told me. I offered to give him a hand with the paperwork.

'As I understand things,' I said, 'you have to make out an

inventory, and then we check that off against Ron's inventory. He's left a copy here, and he has a copy at his new posting. Should be easy.' The old drover was pleased to have some assistance, especially as his reading and writing skills were not so hot.

'It sounds a bit like drovin' cattle,' he suggested. 'Count 'em here, check the count on delivery?'

'A bit like that,' I rejoined. 'All you have to do is keep the condition on them on the road. No bruising.' He laughed, and we got to work. As we loaded the gear on his truck I called out the detail.

'One occasional table.'

'One occasional table. M and S,' he responded.

'One chest of drawers.'

'One chest of drawers, M and S.' The 'M and S' had me stumped. It's probably some sort of personal code, like checking brands and earmarks on cattle, I thought.

'One roll-top desk.'

'One roll-top desk, M and S'.

'What does M and S stand for?' I asked.

'Marked and scratched,' he replied.

'But there's nothing "marked and scratched".'

'There bloody well soon will be,' he assured me. Ron Gallacher told me later that the goods arrived in fairly good conditon, but I guess it's a good idea to hedge your bets if you're a cattle drover.

My pupils at the school were drawn from the many Aboriginal families living on the vast 3000 square miles of Newcastle Waters cattle station, the homestead of which was perched on the next rise above the creek, right above a permanent waterhole. It was immediately obvious it would be a joy to teach these kids, 20 of them, plus three of my own. They were delightful, friendly, and so were their parents. We had a substantial, two–room brick school, with a large verandah that doubled as either extra classroom or recreation area, a great idea in a place with such excesses of weather, ranging from scorching summer heat to icy winter winds. The kids fronted for school at 7 am each day, showered, had some milk and cereal,

Chalkie Ted

and changed into clean clothes. During the day Elsie washed their other set of clothes, ready for tomorrow. We started school at 8.30 am.

There were no problems with truancy or punctuality. These were station kids, reared on discipline, in fact very tough discipline in the case of Newcastle Waters. The station owner, Roy Edwards, whom I knew from Darwin, had a real fortress mentality. Big NO ENTRYs signs warned visitors off at the station gate. Roy lived in a mansion, but even his own workers did not dare go anywhere near 'the big house'. I was never once invited through the gate of the station, and one day, early in the piece, when Margaret, my daughter, innocently walked into the station to see one of the school kids she was ordered to go home, fast. I had never struck an attitude like it in the Territory, but Roy Edwards was a rich old turd who didn't deserve company anyway. He had a manager named Viv McLean, and Viv and his wife Molly were quite embarassed at the station's isolationist policy. They became good friends of ours, but their socialising had of necessity to be away from the station. They, like the Aboriginals, were not allowed to have visitors. It was a strict, unhappy life on the station for the Aboriginal people, and the kids certainly responded to our warmth at school. We settled into a lovely harmonious routine. My own kids benefitted greatly from mixing with such pleasant Aboriginal kids.

The key to success in one-teacher schools is preparation. The teacher is a co-ordinator, and to a large extent the bigger kids teach the little kids. This is a wonderful system, for schooling becomes a desirable extension of the family. Kids must be taught to think for themselves, to learn where to go or what to do if there is a problem. Don't wait for somebody else to get you out of trouble. Work out what to do, and do it. And activities must be organised so that the teacher can concentrate on one group while the others quietly work on some other project. While you are teaching fractions to the bigger kids, give the other groups writing or reading tasks to perform. The entire school comes together for music, or drama, or English as a second language, which was one of the major subjects, and mainly organised via meaningful drama and role-playing in any case.

I learned as much as I taught at Newcastle Waters. It was an advantage having my own kids in the school. Greg, Margaret and Mark were also enrolled for South Australian correspondence classes, which gave them an extra work load, but it also enabled me to have the Aboriginal kids follow as much of the South Australian syllabus as they could handle. It was also a big plus to have had a lot of general experience among Aboriginal people, and to have been subject to the discipline of Aloysius as he taught me to speak Tiwi. I could see how difficult it was for the Aboriginal kids to be encouraged to think in English, when their first language was Jingili. So I organised a couple of periods each week where my two senior pupils, Lena and Susan, took over the group. They put me in the front seat where they could keep an eye on me, and they taught us all in Jingili. Guess who looked dumb then?

I realised quickly that when we were doing oral English lessons the smaller kids very skilfully 'lip-read' the bigger kids, or performed the required movement a split-second after the bigger ones without necessarily understanding what was being instructed. So I developed the 'game' where the kids all blindfolded themselves, and then I could see who really understood, or, more importantly, who didn't. This was a lot of fun, and at the same time I learned as much as the kids. One thing I picked up from this activity was that I could not disorient the Aboriginal kids. Even blindfolded, I could spin them around and then say, 'Point to the north,' or, 'Where is Beetaloo station?' and they were always spot-on. I sometimes felt there should be some scientific analysis of this, but Aboriginals cop too many intrusions of that kind into their lives, so I didn't do any more about it.

It was difficult to broaden the horizons of children who had never been further than Elliott, 50 kilometres from Newcastle Waters. It was also annoying that we could not extend the school's activities into station life, for that was going to be the future of these kids, yet the acquisition of skills at school did not seem related. Better to count cattle rather than buttons, better to learn measuring through fencing and yard-building than measuring classroom doors and windows. Nothing was impossible for these alert kids, but what future was in store for them? I yearned for enough money to buy the station and help create a meaningful life for them.

Newcastle Waters is halfway between Alice Springs and Darwin, and only 5 kilometres from the bitumen highway. Yet we were isolated and marooned for three weeks when the creek flooded after late rains at Easter, and the creek was between us and the bitumen. The bitumen itself was cut by the same Newcastle Waters Creek, a 2 kilometre-wide stretch of floodwater, for two weeks at the same time. This was before the Redmond Causeway was constructed. The milky-white water came almost up to the school buildings, and the telegraph line was submerged. We used to get a weekly perishables order on the coach from Alice Springs, but for three weeks the coach couldn't get from Alice to Darwin.

You'd never believe this, but Roy Edwards was so paranoid about outsiders that he wouldn't sell beef to any local people. This from one of the biggest cattle stations in Australia, and thereby the world, running about 40,000 head of cattle at the time. Part of our standard weekly perishables order from Alice Springs therefore included meat. With the creek flooded, and nobody able to get in to or out of Newcastle Waters we had no fresh food at all. Plenty of tinned stuff, but certainly no meat or vegetables.

But with the rain there were plenty of scrub turkeys or bustards as they are more correctly known. It is an offence to shoot them, and I understand that because they are a threatened species, mainly because they are vulnerable and stupid. And they lay only two eggs. But I am prepared to acknowledge, all these years later, that I used to drive out a couple of late afternoons a week in our old Peugeot, and shoot a turkey. The roads on either side of the 2 kilometre-wide creek were open, it was just that the creek was between us and civilisation. We had the turkeys baked, in curries, in casseroles, with sweet-and-sour sauce. We had cold turkey sandwiches. Fortunately, they are lovely to eat — another reason why they are threatened. I promise I will never eat another scrub turkey. Unless. I should have rolled one of Roy's bullocks: I'm sure he'd have understood.

We had no electricity at Newcastle Waters, but I was used to the ritual of lighting Tilley lamps at 6 pm. It meant having kerosene around the house, and to my eternal discredit I had some kerosene in a similar wine flagon bottle to those we filled with water and kept in the fridge. Young Jacki Egan, a busy little twoyearold, prone to turning up at any moment naked in the school, forever inquisitive, grabbed my bottle of kerosene, upended it, and had a good swig. Goodness, was she crook. She foamed and spluttered, and we filled her with milk until it was running out of her ears. She's a tough one, and she quickly responded, but it makes you aware of the hazards of isolation which are as everpresent as the joys.

Some of the kids were just so bright. Using Cuisenaire rods one day, and in the belief that he was just playing a 'game', I had an eight-year-old Aboriginal boy named Kevin establish, and tell me, using these precise terms, that 'x squared minus y squared = x + y times x — y'. In less precise terms, but nonetheless establishing the 'facts', he demonstrated for me that the square on the hypotenuse equals the sum of the squares on the other two sides of a right-angle triangle. Mind you, I was out for a bit of learning, too. I still don't know the real application of 'meaningless' things like that, other than that if you're wanting to 'square' things like buildings you measure 3, 4 and 5. I took the kid through the exercises simply by having him construct 'squares' with the rods. I remembered the 'formula' but had never had it demonstrated to me when I was at school. It was just one of those things I was 'taught' by rote. Don't ask why, son, just learn the facts and pass the exams. Just as well Kevin didn't ask me 'Why?' But then, I told him it was a game, didn't I? I still think Cuisenaire rods are wonderful 'toys' for children, in that they really help kids to understand fractions and decimals, and to develop good number concepts.

Speaking of Cuisenaire rods, I had a memorable experience with the Aboriginal adults, the parents of the kids. It was 1965 and decimal currency was to be introduced in 1966. The adults asked me if I would explain the new money to them. So we organised for them to come to the school a couple of nights a week thereafter, for adult education lessons. As the new money was to be based on decimals, I thought I'd use the Cuisenaire rods as an aid. The first thing you do with Cuisenaire rods is to just tip a heap of the coloured sticks on to a table and let people, or kids, 'play' with them. Make something. Anything. The majority of people build flat patterns: those with artistic talent or possessed of better number concepts build 'upwards'. None of the Newcastle Waters adults could read or write, and none of them could count beyond 'two hand'. Their numbers thereafter were 'mob' and 'big mob' and 'little bit big mob'. But what they did was to create, with the rods, the shape of every cattle brand from every station within 500 kilometres of Newcastle Waters. Things like TWX, YTR, or, in the case of Newcastle Waters itself the famous 'wine glass' brand — a flattened and rounded Y. They could not read back the letters they formed, but they knew where the brand came from, and whose cattle were whose.

We had lots of singing, for social studies is best taught to kids like that from pictures and songs from other parts of the world. They were good singers, and they quickly got off pat songs like '*Isa Lei,*' '*Pokare Kare Ana*' and '*La Marseillaise.*' Singing extended into the playground as well. The Beatles were all the rage, and although I keep telling people I missed the Beatles because I was out bush a couple of Beatles songs had filtered through, even to Newcastle Waters station. Greg Egan, Terry Jabada, Angus and Eric formed up as The Khaki Four. The boys used to wear khaki shorts and shirts to school. Every morning, before school, we got a burst of

> She lub you, yeah, yeah yeah [followed by]
> She look at me
> Under a tree
> In felly lub wid a ha
> I couldn't dance wid anudder
> When I saw her standing dere

Angus was on drums — two empty flour tins and a frying pan cymbal, Greg Egan, Eric and Terry Jabada gyrated frenetically as they sang and played tennis racquet or shovel guitars. That's showbiz. It was great fun.

Young Terry Jabada was a mighty little athlete. Like so many Aboriginal kids, he possessed acute mechanical skills. He was good at all ball games, and could spring like a kitten. The Fosbury flop hadn't been invented for high jumping at that stage, but I taught Terry how to do the straddle, and in no time he could jump well over his own height. We trained like demons for the local sports day, a three-way affair between Elliott, Beetaloo and Newcastle Waters, and we scooped the pool, especially in team games like tunnel ball, softball and corner spry. Then at the 'big' district sports at Katherine we repeated the dose, thrashing schools that had ten times our number of kids. I was so proud of the kids and they were justifiably proud of themselves.

I did not have a long teaching career, but I remain fascinated and dismayed when I think how little has been achieved in real terms in education for Aboriginal people in this country. I think there are a couple of basic flaws in our overall approach.

One of my beliefs applies right across the board, not merely to Aboriginals. I think it would be good if there was no compulsory schooling. At the same time I think education should be made so attractive that people would beg to be involved. There goes impractical, pie-in-the-sky Ted again. But it's worth thinking about. Can you imagine kids queuing up, as they will for rock concerts and the like, saying, 'Please, may I come to school?' I can.

I believe, too, that the one-teacher approach could be applied, even within bigger schools. What would be wrong with striking a contract between kids and a teacher they were prepared to work with right through their schooling? You'd thereby create the 'we're in this together' approach rather than the 'sit down and shut up and pay attention' style that we see in practice far too often. Again, my idea applies right across the board.

The main thing wrong with the education of Aboriginals is that we seem to have started from the bottom up. We assume that there is nothing to be done for the parents, and that the only hope for Aboriginal society in education terms is to take the kids and teach them new skills, language, habits. They are going to be better achievers in those fields than their parents.

So the parents look dumb and inept by comparison. We can not expect parents to enthuse about a process which is going to alienate them from their children, or have their children trained to despise them.

I am not talking so much about Aboriginals of mixed-descent, for many of them have had that dreadful 'new start' in life where the Aboriginal person in their lineage was stolen and put in an institution. There a rigorous white-style education was part of the process of de-Aboriginalisation, and many people, once released from the institutions found themselves on the one hand robbed of the Aboriginal positives in their life, but at the same time with a good command of English, and good basic skills in the three Rs. They were expected then to look at all the scruffy, uneducated Aboriginals back in the bush and feel superior to them. 'Become like whites' the assimilation policy told them. Then you can despise blackfellows. Some of them, in turn, realising that the only way back to the lost Aboriginality is to beat whitey at his own game, have grabbed the scholarships and gone on to activism via education. I understand that, and I think that if I was an Aboriginal person in the same position I would not only have sought the higher education, I would have done a few diploma courses along the way. In chemistry.

But for the so-called tribal Aboriginals, those for whom English is a foreign language, I really think there is a need to 'sell' education to the adults before we can expect to get any results from the education process. A good example was given by the great linguist, Beulah Lowe, when she worked in Arnhem Land. In learning the languages of the region Beulah worked with old people. Not only did she write down their languages and become fluent herself, she made her 'teachers' literate in their own language. Thereby she sold 'education' to the people that count, the ones who are going to encourage their children to go to school and better themselves. I think it is not insignificant that the Aboriginals who worked with Beulah Lowe are the parents of the Gatjil Djerkurras, Galarrwuy and Mandawuy Yunupingus and the Dr Kevin Djiniyinis of today. At the moment too many Aboriginals resist education. But go to a bank in Alice Springs on social services day. There they are, lined up, unable to fill out forms, sign their names, the butt of the behind-the-hand so-called 'jokes', a pathetic sight. Let's re-think education, and start with massive adult literacy programs. At the same time, if they are first made literate in the language of their thoughts we will have enhanced the already commendable process of recording these ageless Australian languages for posterity. Otherwise, in a hundred years time the brunt of activist complaint will not be that you stole my children: it will be that you stole my heritage.

Lesson number one for oppressed people comes from the Welsh: 'don't lose the language'. I acknowledge that the essential difference between the Welsh and the Aboriginals is that the Welsh were literate in Welsh, so the English efforts to kill their language failed. But it's not too late to start Aboriginal adult literacy programs. In that way we might sell education for their kids to them as a worthwhile process.

13
War Games

I had all sorts of things planned for the school at Newcastle Waters, counting on at least a three-year stay, by which time I was sure I'd achieve so much with those beaut kids. The Ulamari kids, Lena and Tim could have gone on to great things with a hefty primary school education behind them. Their lovely natures made them ideal to work with, and their social skills were developing as quickly as their academic achievement. So the arrival of a telegram two weeks from the end of the final term threw me out. It read:

> YOU ARE TRANSFERRED TO GROOTE EYLANDT NEXT YEAR AS HEAD TEACHER PACK ALL EFFECTS VERY REPEAT VERY SECURELY

I was terribly angry at first. Departmental shuffling of that type happened all too frequently in those days, throwing out plans and negating much of what a person had done. For new brooms always sweep clean, and the new teacher would probably start from scratch as I had done: it's one of the big problems for Aboriginals. You need people like Fred Gray. People who stay. People who understand. People who develop plans that work. People who sitdown in the country.

The removal was very complicated. We packed everything with great care, for our belongings were to be transported by sea, and there were ominous reports about damage to goods in transit. As it turned out we need not have bothered, for almost everything was water-damaged when it arrived a couple of months into the school year, delivered on a barge open to the elements and after being left exposed on the wharf for several days in The Wet. Six months later we were paid some compensation but it did not cover the annoyance of having personal treasures ruined. It was a fact of life in those days.

We decided to send Greg Egan to boarding school. He was 11, a bright kid, and we went along with the thinking, still prevalent, that Territory kids achieve best if they go 'interstate' for secondary schooling. We enrolled Greg at Adelaide's Rostrevor College, and friends of ours, the Vaughan family, agreed to have him for his *exeat* weekends. Margaret and Mark would attend my new school. Jacki was three, and would rule the world from home.

It was a minor consolation that the new position entrusted to me was not only a personal challenge but part of an important change in Territory history. The government was taking control of the Angurugu school at Groote Eylandt. There was no complaint about the teachers or teaching at Groote, for good academic results were being obtained. The new plan was to better service education with government funding and facilities, rather than impose on missions the responsibility of finding the money, for sometimes they didn't or couldn't. Jim Gallacher chose me to be head teacher, and my staff of five would be the women recruited by the CMS mission who had been teachers at Angurugu for years. The previous principal, Judith Stokes, would stay on as a staff member, but devote more time to her study of the local language. This could have been a very tricky situation for all of us, but Judith and I had become good friends when I was at Groote nine years before, and the handover–takeover of the school was not seen as a power thing, but a sensible change.

The women teachers themselves had sought the addition of a male staff member at the school. There were huge disciplinary problems with the adolescent boys. Groote Eylandt Aboriginals and their basic aggressive nature. I knew a bit about it. I would teach the senior boys and some of the senior girls. Anne-Marie Priestley, AMP as we called her, taught the majority of the senior girls. Judith Stokes and Deaconess Norma Farley taught the middle school, Mavis Ough the infants, and Lois Reid had a special class for better achievers. They were all formidable, sensible teachers, and we quickly developed good team spirit. Organisation and hard work were not a problem for any of us.

My family occupied a very good house, rent free — and we had electricity! The school's buildings were basic but satisfactory. Angurugu is a pretty place, with the timber buildings of the mission set among stringybark trees. The lovely Angurugu River ran through the middle of the mission. The Aboriginal people lived in quite reasonable houses on the other side of the river from the mission buildings. The kids all had a 'bogie', a swim combined with a wash in the river on the way to school. Groote Eylandt Aboriginals are scrupulous about cleanliness.

I established contact with the people I had come to know quite well in 1957 when I tried to sort out the marriage-promise problems. The support of parents would be vital I felt, and was proved right. I got great assistance at the school from my good friends, Nandjiwara Amagula and Nango — the man who had killed the crocodile with a rock. Both were members of the school committee. Strong men. Good blokes. Good families.

It was 1966. Decimal currency was introduced on 14 February of that year. A subsidiary of BHP, Groote Eylandt Mining Company (Gemco), started to mine manganese in 1963, and three mining camps had been established, one at the crusher, one halfway to the port, and the third at the port. The first buildings of Alyangula township were under construction. There were 200 white newcomers to the island, all male. Strict guidelines had been established between CMS, the government and Gemco to establish rules about things like access to places, and the tricky question of alcohol. A good working relationship had been set up by Col Brunker and Ian Gunn of Gemco, Colonel Mike Casey of the government, and Reverend Jim Taylor, superintendent of the mission.

I knew I would be under intense scrutiny from all quarters at Angurugu, so I played my cards with care. I took a long time preparing my first talk to the kids, for I was aware they would not be the only ones listening. At the school assembly on the first day I announced, among other things, that there would be no more floggings. It had been the practice on occasions for a male staff member of the mission to be called to the school to administer corporal punishment with the strap, to senior boys especially. Such things usually invite melodramatic discussion, and I was aware that among the Aboriginals these occurrences were called 'floggings'.

'If I was to flog any of you it would only prove that I was bigger than you, and we already know that,' I said, as sagely as I could. 'So floggings are out.' I noticed the look that circulated among the bigger boys, but went on with the next point, to outline the routine for the year. So far, so good. Into the classrooms.

My first morning was busy, sorting out kids, attendance rolls, seating arrangements, books and routine. Time for lunch. After lunch I appeared on the verandah — the school was built on stilts about 2 metres high — and looked down at my angelic pupils, sitting in two groups, boys and girls, in the shade of the many trees that grew in the school grounds. Nobody looked up.

'OK, time for school.'

Nobody moved. Ah-ha, the try out. Typical Groote Eylandt treatment. Come and get us, white man. Let's make him flog us.

'Coming in?' I was saccharine itself.

Heads down. The old Confucian–Kidman motto: first one to talk loses. I was not going to lose face, although I had no idea what to say or do that might be clever. I had plenty to do, though, sorting out stores, procedures, school records.

'Well, I'm busy,' I said, 'but you're welcome inside.' I went in, they went home. Come on Ted, you're the smart-arse. Tactics, son. Tactics.

The next day was a repeat performance. Time for school. You'll have to drag us in. A flogging would be nice. The white man speaks with forked tongue again. I had to admire them. But consider having to live in a system based on such intrinsic hostility. I'm glad I'm not a Groote Eylandt Aboriginal. It must be an awful existence. But this time I was prepared. I had a book in my hand.

'Well, I'm going in to school. I have this great book called *Sammy Going South*. It's about a kid who travels through

Africa. You probably wouldn't like it. It's all about black people and elephants and lions and that sort of boring stuff. I'm going in to read it. You're welcome to come in and hear the story. But I'm not trying to force you.'

I went in and sat at my desk. After an agonising two minutes a black face appeared at the door. Another.

'Come in.'

In that sort of situation, for Groote Eylandt people, it's one in, all in. They sat at their desks. Still inscrutable. Come on white man, entertain us.

It was one of the cleverest ideas I ever had — and I have lots of clever ideas. It started a pattern. First period after lunch each day I read a chapter or two of the strangest series of books. *Sammy Going South* is no great literary work, but it is a fascinating story about a nine-year-old boy whose parents were killed in the fighting around the Suez Canal in 1956. He felt he was all alone in the world. He remembered he had an aunt and uncle down south, in a place called Johannesburg, so off he went. A mere 5000–kilometre walk. He had amazing adventures, met an astonishing array of killers, kind people, robbers, poachers. It proved to be a great means of studying social studies, but I never told the kids that. We followed Sammy in our atlases, we had Miriam Makebe and Paul Robeson on the record player, we read about the construction of the pyramids. We considered slavery and apartheid. There was no end to the mileage we derived from the book. We even got the film of the same name starring Edward G Robinson, who played Sammy's main travelling companion. It was a hoot of a success. Round one to the white man.

The Groote kids were wonderful listeners. You can't get 'shamed' while you are listening, and I watched them furrow their brows in concentration, as they observed every detail of the epic journey. I could tell from their written work that they had taken on board immense detail about *Sammy Going South*. Again, with written work there was no risk of being ridiculed. They would never talk to me, or tell me what they had learned. But I knew I was winning.

My next choice was *Tom Brown's Schooldays*. Now there's

a challenge for you, taking Groote Eylandt kids into the stiff protocol, discipline and class distinction of a toffy English public school. But they loved it. It was about power, cruelty, lots of things in common. And the reaction? The senior boys started a fag system. You'd hear them in the playground. Somebody wanted something. 'Fag,' a senior boy would shout, and some little bloke would be given a job. I must admit the Groote Eylandt fag system was more light-hearted than the British, and it was one of the few times where I saw Groote kids actually having fun.

The senior girls that I taught were the 'upper stream', the brighter ones, and they were delightful pupils. They just sat there and absorbed knowledge, never the slightest problem in any respect. My boys were very different. Poor insecure little buggers, getting themselves ready for a lifetime of discontent based on the old Groote Eylandt system I had examined in 1957, where brother competes with brother for everything in life, including the same women in the marriage stakes. They couldn't accept me: they felt they just had to take me on. If I put any of the boys under real or imagined pressure they would stand up, on the toes, and try to eyeball me. A few of them were my height. It was always the same routine.

'This you island?'

'No.'

'You born here?'

'No.'

They'd beat the chest, like a turkey drumming. 'This my island. I born here.'

'Fine,' I'd say. 'I know it's your island. I'm glad you were born here. Now can we get on with things?'

More often than not they would sit down, and burn inside for the rest of the day. But if they were really angry, or someone sniggered at them, they would stalk out, giving the door an almighty slam as they departed, and stamp down the stairs. Then everyone else would close the glass louvres and hold their hands over their ears. For as sure as it was payday every second Thursday there would be a shower of rocks thrown in the general direction of the school. It was unfortunate that the walls of the school buildings had glass louvres. In the storeroom were boxes of glass louvres. I had wondered why but now realised that the practice was to keep replacing smashed ones. I organised metal louvres — much more appropriate where people insisted on throwing stones at glass houses.

'Groote Eylandt confetti,' I said, after the first shower of rocks. The kids were suitably mystified, but loved the explanation, and took the phrase on board.

The girls never walked out of my mixed class, only the boys. Girls would walk out of the other classes though, following the same routine. If the kid felt that the sniggers and snide remarks of the other pupils had been really offensive he or she would then go home and return with mum and dad. Mum would shout abuse at everybody in the school building. Dad would let go a couple of spears, anywhere, but more often than not over the top of the school, just to make his point. He was angry. Very dangerous stuff. They would then go home, the child perhaps conjuring up tears, the parents supportive.

'We are soldiers Mistegan,' the senior boys said to me, early on.

'So, what do you want me to do about it?'

'You teach us marching Mistegan,' they commanded. There were a couple of kettle drums in the school store, and the kids watched me hark back to my drumming days in the Coburg Central Band where I played the side drum for four years as a kid. I did a couple of fancy drum rolls, and they were impressed.

'Marching it is,' I announced.

Typical of the Groote boys, they stayed back at school for an hour each afternoon and I taught them marching. A little bloke named Mark Wurramurra was quick to learn drumming, and they copped me roaring commands at them, sergeant-major style, as they became formidable marchers. It gave me a good idea.

I had two towers of strength working with me at the school. One was a teaching assistant named Nanindjurrpa and the other was a gentle old bloke who used to teach the kids handcraft and traditional painting. The old man's name was Nandabida.

'How about if every fourth week we take all the senior boys to a bush camp for the entire week? Leave here Monday morning, camp out bush all week and come back on Friday afternoon?' The eyes of the two men lit up. Absolute approval.

It was easy. Jim Taylor, the superintendent, was enthusiastic, and made the mission truck available to transport us to the camp on the Monday morning, and pick us up on Friday afternoon. The other teachers relished the idea of a school without all those big aggressive boys. The boys themselves worked like slaves to prepare for the excursions, including preparations for their own quota of school work.

We chose the Amagula River, 20 kilometres away, as our camp site. A beautiful flowing stream, with sandy banks and shady trees, it was idyllic. Boys were rostered for kitchen and mess duties, and each had a daily quota of tasks, some academic — supervised by Nanindjurrpa or me, some traditional — supervised by old Nandabida, a consummate bushman and one of the best known Groote Eylandt artists and spearmakers. He had travelled with me on my month-long canoe trip in the Gulf, back in 1958.

When any boy had completed his allotted tasks, acknowledged by all three supervisors, he was free for the remainder of the day.

It was a lot of fun, but exhausting for me. The boys were up at daybreak, writing in their books, reading, hearing one another for rote tasks. Then they came to me. 'You check my reading Mistegan.' 'You mark my spelling Mistegan.' What they didn't realise was that they were doing a day's work in a third of a day, just because they were keen, and felt that they were in charge. As soon as they were all cleared, they played for the rest of the day. A bit of volleyball, which they liked, but mainly they played war. Again, the sad pre-conditioning. They were preparing themselves for a lifetime of aggression. We are soldiers Mistegan.

The war games took several forms. Spear throwing and dodging was a favourite. Using spear grass or the spears they made for Nandabida they would re-enact the *makarrta,* the trial by ordeal used in Arnhem Land to resolve disputes before ceremonies can be undertaken. One boy, or a group of boys would stand, unarmed at about 30 metres. The others would throw spears at them. The aim was to allow a spear to go as close to the body as one dared, without getting hit. It sounds dangerous, and it was, but they were of necessity all expert dodgers, and nobody was ever hit.

Defending, as they called it, was another game. One team would be the owners of, say, a big log that had fallen into the river. They would defend it against the rest, who would come at them from any angle, or from the water, to try to take control of the log. It was very physical, and yet I never saw any boy lose his temper. Occasionally a smaller boy would get hurt, and would cry, briefly, but it was cool, professional stuff. They were good soldiers, if you like that sort of thing. But it was a different sort of aggression they were fostering. It was personal. It wasn't like a military academy where the system is taking impressionable young people along the road of combining together as a unified force. They formed into sides for the game, but they never trusted one another, never formed a self-congratulory ring after the victory. Victory was never joyous, a means to conciliation. Victory was something you had to achieve to survive.

I didn't like it all that much, but it was essential to give them alternatives rather than just orders to stop the aggression. We got some other games going, board games, draughts, football, hoppo-bumpo, release, but they preferred war.

One game of theirs that I loved to watch related to their superb swimming skills. A boy would volunteer to climb to the top of a particular dead tree, about 10 metres above the river, at a wide spot where the banks were lined with reeds going down into the water. The boy would dive in — most of them were skilled, fearless divers. He would not surface, but would swim underwater to somewhere among the reeds. It was his job to stay underwater, drawing air through a reed, until he was discovered, spotted by the others. When they spotted him a stone would be thrown, with deadly accuracy to hit the water near him. At that point the swimmer was required to come to the surface to acknowledge capture. It was known that some boys 'cheated' in that when the stone was thrown to capture them they would embark on a tremendous feat of underwater swimming to reposition themselves, often 30 metres away. It sometimes took ten minutes to complete a game. Dead-calm water, not a sign of the hunted, the hunters prowling and watching for a telltale bubble. The levels of concentration, the alertness of the spotters on the bank, gave an insight into the potential of we frail human beings if only we weren't encumbered by all the stupid rules, conventions, systems and religions in our lives. Those kids were as smart as birds and animals.

At night around the campfire we sang, and their tongues loosened. They could not be so easily shamed in the dark. I did a reverse number on 'You teach us singing Mistegan'. I made them teach me a song. I still sing it as a party piece. It is called *'Ngiri Intamari'* — The Brolga is Flying:

Ngiri intamari ngiri intarr mari
Yagila, inagaria ngarawali yagila
Ugu kantara warla yagila
Ngiri intamari ngiri intarr mari

An incident I considered a victory at the time may not have been, now that I have spent years of review. We were playing volleyball when a big boy — whose name I must not mention, for he is still alive and might be mortified even now to be reminded of the occasion — lost his temper and punched the ball way out of court, necessitating somebody going to retrieve the ball, or else the game was over. Everybody stood stock still. The others were looking for a chance to jeer at him, but he was a tough kid likely to inflict some sort of injury if provoked. I knew he had a huge intellect, and in all my dealings with him he had displayed a determination to try to get above the system that held him back. He was always polite, helpful, cheerful in everything he did with me. I knew he liked me, and he was without a doubt my favourite pupil.

Nobody moved. I walked quietly alongside him, and manoeuvred our position so that nobody else could hear what I said to him, and nobody could lipread or interpret my body language.

'You can show that you're a man here. OK, you lost your

temper. All you have to do is go and get the ball, and I'll deal with anybody who has a go at you.'

He looked at me, and weighed up the consequences. He was trembling with emotion. He didn't say a word. He walked towards the ball. I fixed the others with a glare that threatened something dreadful if they made a sound or a gesture. He picked up the ball, walked back, and handed me the ball. I thought we'd won a major victory. But he refused to rejoin the game and went and sat on his own. Our eyes met. His were full of tears. Mine are now as I write this 30 years later. Because the system got him. Ten years later he killed his brother. Same old Groote Eylandt stuff, an argument over who would marry a particular woman. Out came the spears. Life sentence.

Criticism of the traditional Aboriginal way of life is treated with suspicion in these sensitive times where political correctness is much valued. That lifestyle is often hopelessly romanticised. It's dangerous to generalise and my comments are made with specific reference to Groote Eylandt. But if there's an upside to male Groote aggression, I fail to see it. That boy could have become anything. Their lifestyle should change for the sake of all the people of that lovely island. It's hell in paradise, and I'm sure Groote women must be sick of it. They are still living in *inugwamba* land.

The introduction of decimal currency provided a wonderful opportunity to teach maths. Against all advice I got $200 in cash and left it in a jar on my desk. It was never locked up, even at night, and we never lost a cent. Someone had the job of 'balancing the cash' by counting it every day. There were coins and notes sufficient for the game I introduced. I look back on it and shudder at the racist overtones of it all.

I set up a little 'shop' called Sun Cheong Loong, after the well-known Darwin store that they had heard about but never seen. I sat behind the counter and played the role of Chin Gong, the old man who was the proprietor. I would give a boy or girl or a group of children the jar of money and they did 'the shopping'. We had clothing and food lines, quite a variety, and prices were displayed. Sometimes I cheated them, sometimes not. I patronised them, talking down to them, in pidgin, which I knew they hated.

'Ah, you from Groote Eylandt, blackfellow? You like buyim something, anything?'

'You pretty Groote Eylandt girl. You like dress, nice one?'

'Ah, you little Groote Eylandt boy. You like trouser shirt? Salty plum? Anything? What colour shirt you likim? Red one. Any colour, long as he red. Ha Ha Ha. Funny eh?'

'Ah, he good country, Groote Eylandt? You got plenty money bring my shop? We got everything here.'

'You like docket, paper? You read and write, you Groote Eylandt blackfellow?'

'That $25 altogether. You happy? You give me this one note I give you change.'

'Don't forget you change. You satisfy?'

They would have fierce discussions among themselves, in language, and they were giving me heaps, I could tell that much. Furious with me. Although I did set them up as primitives capable of exploitation, and the Chinese shopkeeper as tricky, both unforgiveable, I'll bet there is one group of Groote Eylandt adults who don't get cheated with money.

Given the Groote Eylandt social taboos the biggest single difficulty was in conducting spoken English classes. The school curriculum tied us all into the assimilation policy, and the idea of first making people literate in their own language was anathema. We did not actively discourage traditional languages, but we did not encourage their use in class: it was held that fluency in English was going to be a pre-requisite for societies that would see value in becoming 'like whites'. The standard of English among Groote Eylandt people was good, if they would talk to you. Those who could read and write had high standards, a tribute to some of the teaching skills of missionaries along the way, but at the same time an indication that there had been a concerted attempt to wean people away from pagan language and beliefs.

My pupils had a built-in radar system of spotting when I was taking them into spoken English classes, based on role-playing. I tried to be subtle, but they picked me every time. We beat you again Mistegan. Round two to us. I learned to recognise 'the Groote Eylandt turnoff' whereby their faces would not change but they switched their minds into another world. We have gone Mistegan.

As a handcraft exercise we made some *papier mache* heads. We had balloons of all shapes and sizes, and these were blown up. We layered strips of glued paper onto the balloon to create heads, all sorts of heads, monsters, animals, birds, people. The glued paper set hard. The balloon was deflated, and the head was capable of being worn. We painted the heads in bright colours, ready for the Mardi Gras. The Groote kids were very good with their hands and the standard of heads made was very high. I noticed that in fitting the heads over their own, the kids lost their inhibitions and would talk freely as Mr Crocodile, Brother Buffalo, Sister Wallaby or Mrs Horse. They would sing as 'The Animals' choir, tell me of their environment, lifestyle, chances of survival, unaware of the structured lessons I took them into. Fulfilling. Speaking English became just another game.

It was exhausting, but it was a challenge, and in some instances it was fun. But not often. It was more like war or an armed truce at best. They were soldiers. I didn't have the heart for it. In 1958 I had studied Groote Eylandt aggression in the confusing half-western system that had been imposed on them by missionaries. In dealing with the kids in 1966 I could see them developing into the same adults, and there didn't seem much I or any other outsider could do about it. This not you island Mistegan. This my island. I born here. This my sitdown country.

14
The Way of Wuyal

At the end of school year 1966 we all went to Darwin for holidays, but I was immediately told to cancel mine, and go back to Groote Eylandt. Rae and the kids stayed in town. We were allocated a new government house at Rapid Creek. Colonel Mike Casey, who was the District Welfare Officer at Groote Eylandt, was going on long-service leave and I was sent to relieve him. It meant living at the embryonic town of Alyangula, and taking over as government representative in the district. I was familiar with the workings of the island, and knew everybody, so it was an easy transition into the new job, and simple after the exhausting work as head teacher.

I was not aware at the time, but my superiors in Darwin had me under consideration for something else, and wanted to see how I handled the District Welfare Officer's job. I must have convinced them I could handle things, for in February 1967 I was appointed on a permanent basis to the newly-created position of District Welfare Officer of the Flinders District, based on what was becoming known as the Gove Peninsula in northeast Arnhem Land, where a subsidiary of Alusuisse, Nabalco, had been granted leases to mine bauxite and establish a huge alumina plant.

One of the most important things in Aboriginal Affairs in 1967 was the referendum concerning Aboriginals. Many years later there is considerable misconception about the terms and result of that referendum. A referendum proposal is usually rejected in Australia, as voters follow their normal party political bias for or against the particular issue, with the result that the vote is split. To change the constitution in Australia by referendum there has to be a 'for' vote by a majority of voters in a majority of states, plus an overall majority. There has never been a referendum response like that of 1967, where there was bipartisan support for the constitutional change, and 90 percent of voters said 'yes'. I have always urged people to consider that 10 per cent of Australian voters said 'no' to being asked, in effect, 'Do you consider Aboriginals to be human beings?'

The 10 percent 'no' vote came from polling booths in places where there were sizeable Aboriginal populations, and the worse the reputation of the place for race relations, the higher the 'no' vote. In Wilcannia (NSW), Townsville (Qld), Roebourne (WA), Port Augusta (SA), Orbost (Vic), King Island (Tas) and the many similar places where there had been racial conflict or antipathy over many years, whites had a chance in the secrecy of the polling booth to show what they thought of the blacks. In the Northern Territory there was no vote given, for it was not a state. There were angry demonstrations by whites in Alice Springs, who would have registered a hefty 'no' vote if given the chance.

Many people think that the 1967 referendum waved a magic wand and gave Aboriginals 'citizen rights'. Wrong. Queensland was the last state to bestow voting rights for Aboriginals, in 1965. So from 1966 all Aboriginals could enrol to vote for all Commonwealth or State elections. Enrolment was not compulsory for Aboriginals, but once they enrolled they had to vote. The right for Aboriginals to drink alcohol, regrettably seen as the most prized component of 'citizen rights', was granted in 1964. The referendum of 1967 provided that henceforth Aboriginals would be counted in the official census figures, something specifically denied by Section 127 of the 1901 Constitution of the newly-federated Australian states. The 1901 denial was not as sinister as it seems: it was felt in 1901 that it would not be possible to get an accurate count of Aboriginals, as many of the regions where they lived in a tribal state had not even been 'explored' by whites, and it was whites framing the constitution. The 1967 referendum also paved the way for the Commonwealth government to 'make laws in respect of' Aboriginals. Previously states had framed their own 'protectionist' laws in respect of Aboriginals: now the Commonwealth had a concurrent role.

The Commonwealth Council for Aboriginal Affairs was set up, consisting of Dr H C (Nugget) Coombs, noted anthropologist Professor Bill Stanner, and Barrie Dexter, a career diplomat who became Director of the Office of Aboriginal Affairs, based in Canberra. It was agreed that there would be no confrontation with the states, but the council felt it had a positive and active role to play in the Northern Territory, where Commonwealth laws were the only laws. I was about to become embroiled in the huge clash of personalities and attitudes of my employers, the Northern Territory Administration, a branch of the federal Department of the Interior, and the Council for Aboriginal Affairs, responsible to and based within the Prime Minister's Department. Two federal agencies at each other's throats was a revelation to someone as naive about politics as I was at that time.

My role was to act as go-between in issues affecting the Aboriginal people, the Methodist church which controlled Yirrkala mission, the Commonwealth government's many agencies, and the mining company Nabalco. My place of residence was symbolic, half way between the Nabalco headquarters and the Yirrkala mission. I lived at a place called Gunyibinya, an old mining camp set up by a previous mining company, Pechiney. The camp consisted of a couple of big sheds, a lighting plant, toilets and showers. Sharing the camp with me were three government school teachers posted to the Yirrkala mission school in much the same way as I had been sent to Groote Eylandt. They were head teacher Bob Morrish, and two fine young blokes, Neal Stewart and Gil Warman. We knocked out a lot of fun together.

A lesser role for me was to effect liaison between Commonwealth agencies and Eldo, the European Launcher Development Organisation that had set up a tracking station on the Gove Peninsula to track rockets fired from Woomera. It was a very sophisticated set-up at Eldo. Among other gadgetry and intricate technology they had amazing new things called computers. Five

European nations plus Australia were working together at Eldo, and Bob, Neal, Gil and I plus other government teachers at Yirrkala were made honorary members of the Eldo mess and social club. Very nice too, mixing with around 60 talented Belgians, Italians, French, Dutch, and English, as well as some beaut Australians. Eldo residents lived like lords, with five-star facilities. They had a very clever role-reversal structure in place whereby those most important at work became the lowest-of-the-low at the social gatherings. It took the form of the Carlsberg Fusiliers. The cook — sorry, master chef — Roy Linnett, was a tough little Lancashire bloke who stood no nonsense from anybody. He had been known to produce the meat cleaver if there were complaints about his food. That was a rare occurrence, as the meals at Eldo were superb. In the Fusiliers Roy was a field marshal, our commander-in-chief. Geoff Wood, the boss of Eldo by day, became OIC Garbage around the bar at night. I was appointed an honorary general, later promoted to field marshal.

There was a very hairy Australian chap named Geoff Arnold who gave the European technicians hell. He was a general in the Fusiliers, a diesel fitter by day. Because his entire body was covered with a rug of thick black hair he was Ranga to his mates, or Mr Tang to the lesser mortals. When new technicians from Europe arrived in Arnhem Land by DC3 from Darwin, straight into an Australia that must have seemed as remote as the Amazon, Ranga would be ready for them. The communal bathrooms were stainless steel cubicles full of unfamiliar plumbing. You had ten reflections of yourself in every direction. Just as the new chap sorted himself out and exposed his pale body to the first shower in this strange land, the door of the cubicle would open and alongside him, looking him straight in the eye but saying nothing was Ranga, soaping his hairy body, unsmiling. First to talk loses. Welcome to Australia.

The country now called the Gove Peninsula by whites is pure bauxite, to a depth of about 8 metres, an immense deposit covering thousands of hectares. Peter Gove was an Australian airman killed in a crash in the region during the war, when a big bitumen airstrip was constructed for the RAAF. The airstrip was definitely named after him, but Nabalco sought to name the region after him, and proposed that the new township to service the mine be called 'Gove'. That was to provoke one of many battles.

Nabalco was part of the huge international consortium Alusuisse. The international supervisor of the company was Dr Bruno Sorato, the Australian managing director was David Griffin, at one time also lord mayor of Sydney. Griffin had decided to take a very hard line on Aboriginals. He had heard the rumbling new words 'land rights' and was not impressed. He was aware of previous agitation over land by Aboriginals in north-east Arnhem Land, and determined to pretend that Aboriginals did not exist. He would speak only to government: his line was that Nabalco were tenants on Crown land, they paid their rent, they were there to mine bauxite and look after their employees. He had a deplorable propensity for bestowing, with a great 'I hereby name thee' flourish, names on places that already had them. Town Beach and Wallaby Beach are unimaginative compared to the real names, Lombuwuy and Burulilipa. Most of Griffin's dull and uninspired names remain in common usage. But the Aboriginals dug their toes in over the new town. He wanted to call it Gove: they insisted on Nhulunbuy, their name for the little hill called Mount Saunders by Matthew Flinders. Nhulunbuy, pronounced Noolanboy, is one of the names the Dreamtime hero Wuyal bestowed as he travelled the country creating the people and leaving his sacred dilly bags as reminders of his travels. The Aboriginals won.

I had never been exposed to 'land rights' issues before, but quickly became involved *totus porcus,* boots and all. I surprised myself at how strongly I aligned with the Aboriginal camp against my own employers, the government, but on reflection I wonder how anybody could take up an anti-Aboriginal stance when their claims were so obvious, so real. I tried to sum up their attitudes to land in a song I wrote called 'The Tribal Land', recorded for RCA in 1969 by a handsome young bloke named Galarrwuy Yunupingu:

There was no fight,
And when the white man came
We welcomed him as a friend
But that didn't mean he could take our land
For that would be the end.

Methodists have never shied away from politics, and there was strong support within that church for the Aboriginal cause over the issue of who owned the land, the government or the Aboriginals. In 1963 the superintendent of Yirrkala was the redoubtable Reverend Edgar Wells. I had met Edgar at Milingimbi when I walked overland from Maningrida in 1957. I respected and liked him. At Yirrkala Edgar was quick to point out to Aboriginal leaders that the government was shafting them by granting mineral leases all over their country. He organised the famous Bark Petition, whereby Aboriginal leaders listed their grievances in their own language and in English, and sent these with a symbolic bark painting to the Commonwealth Parliament in Canberra. A parliamentary committee of inquiry visited the region and heard evidence on the ground. The upshot was that one mining company, Pechiney, left the region, but the government issued leases to Nabalco. The Aboriginal Benefits Trust Fund was established, and royalties paid by Nabalco and other mining companies like Gemco at Groote Eylandt were paid into a fund administered by the government for the benefit of all Aboriginals. This rankled with the Yolngu, as the people of north-east Arnhem Land call themselves: they felt they had nothing in common with 'those other blackfellows' and less with 'the yellerfellers', the mixed–race people down south. So much for the pan-Aboriginal movement. To prove political points union is strength: when the dollars are down, forget it.

There were meetings every other day at Yirrkala where people aired their grievances. Legal advice was coming from supporters in the south, and a very clever lawyer named John Little was in the forefront for the issue of writs to challenge the government in court. My dilemma was that I was sympathetic to the Aboriginal cause, but working for the government which directly opposed the Aboriginal legal action and the very question of ownership. Nabalco was the meat in the sandwich: 'We will do as we are told.' But they had to share the costs of the expensive litigation. As with all the other hotly-contested land issues, the mining company or pastoral company became the *bete noire* when the government was in fact the principal opponent of the Aboriginals.

Munggurawuy Yunupingu, Mawalan Marika and Daymbalipu Mununggurr issued writs against the Commonwealth government and Nabalco, asserting ownership of the land over which mineral leases had been issued. As the three sides worked out their strategies local life went on. Nabalco continued its exploration of the bauxite deposits, and began work on the conveyor line, the port at Melville Bay, the new township of Nhulunbuy and the mine itself. Mining of bauxite is very straightforward. You simply take 8 or 9 or 10 metres of bauxite off the top, and move it to the alumina plant, or stockpile it at the port for bulk shipment to wherever. The company's attitude was that this was a normal process, capable of being done cleanly, and they went to great pains to establish nurseries to enable trees to be planted when the land profile was 8 to10 metres lower than before.

I was able to establish good relationships all round. Dr Alec Somm was the local Nabalco boss during the exploration period, and Leigh French came in for the construction stage. Both were experienced men in international mining, and had an assured sophistication that made them easy to work with. They were quick on the uptake, and good friends socially, although there was always the recognition that business was business. Rev Wally Fawell was the superintendent at the mission, and he, too, was a straight shooter. Roy Marika was the principal contact for the Aboriginal people, and he was a charming man, but resolute to the point that sometimes he came across as unreasonable. But it was his country, and he wasn't going to give an inch without a battle. Two very impressive young men were wonderful as intermediaries, for most of the old people at Yirrkala spoke no or little English, and all meetings were slow and laborious as every point was translated backward and forward. The young men were Wally Wulanybuma and

Galarrwuy Yunupingu. They had both been to Brisbane to attend bible college and receive quite good secondary education.

I met scores of politicians during my three-year stay in the region. Politicians are famous for deserting the chilly wastes of Canberra and heading north during the winter months. I formed a very low opinion of politicians in general: I resolved never to employ any of them. The banal questions, the big-headed airing of so-called knowledge, the patronising behaviour towards Aboriginals, the sheer rudeness were characteristics I did not expect, but now realise are common. There were two notable exceptions, and I am talking about the human being stakes here, not to any political bias or skills. Lance Barnard and Malcolm Fraser were lovely to meet, kind, considerate, intelligent, both great men. The rest? Forgettable.

Government officials from Darwin were the greatest single problem on the Gove Peninsula. Floods of them came to and fro, members of a team determined to sell out the interests of the blackfellows, and ingratiate themselves with the mining company. The Aboriginals could not compete with the big seafood and booze lunches the company cleverly put on to win the hearts and minds of the public servants. I was fighting a losing battle, trying to put forward Aboriginal interests, and suggesting things like Aboriginal participation in the day-to-day activities of the new town and the construction period. When I suggested that Aboriginals be given the licences over concrete and fuel, which they would then have been able to lease to people like Pioneer Concrete, BP or Shell, I was laughed to scorn. Why would you bother? I was asked. If you don't give them a slice of the action they or their supporters will get all morose and litigious, I replied.

I will never forget one occasion when a big dinner was being organised for Dr Bruno Sorato on one of his visits. Sorato was an Italian, a charming bloke, but with very little English. His major input was a beaming smile and constant bursts of 'Pleasa gentlemen, pleasa helpa Nabalco' and the response of the government boys was to do just that. Pass the chardonnay, Bruno. David Griffin and a senior government bloke were drawing up the list of locals who would attend. I was present at the meeting.

I suggested that it would be good sense and good manners to invite Roy Marika and Mungurrawuy Yunupingu. The government man blushed and said to me, 'Come on, Ted, those people would never make it through the door into Mr Griffin's office, or the Nabalco boardroom in Sydney. Why invite them here?' Griffin nodded his head in support. 'Up to you, gentlemen, it's your party,' I said, and manufactured reasons to prevent my own attendance. I should have said 'It's your funeral,' for the land rights pot was boiling. So many issues that became confrontationist on principle could have been avoided if there had been a bit of sensible dialogue rather than the determination by officials to put the blackfellows down.

Nugget Coombs was different. This tough little fighter became a regular visitor to the region, and I started to wonder what was going on. Here was I, working for the Northern Territory Administration in the belief that I was paid to represent the best interests of the Aboriginals. My employer, the Commonwealth government, seemed desperate at the local level to sell the blackfellows down the drain and completely ignore their traditional rights. Yet here was Coombs, a household name in Australia, working for the same government, using socialist terms like 'struggle' in respect of Aboriginal land, and diametrically opposed to all other government people I dealt with. Nugget would sit for hours at meetings with Aboriginals, his beady eyes roving from one speaker to another, listening intently to the interpreters, occcasionally himself saying something supportive. I could not help contrasting his respectful behaviour to a senior government man from Darwin who used to fly out regularly, and bring a big bag of Minties. I am not kidding. This bloke, every time he saw any Aboriginals, would throw a handful of Minties up into the air for the blackfellows to catch. No wonder I became a Coombs man!

As well as all the liaison capers — I won't call it work — I was responsible as the District Welfare Officer to travel around the Flinders region and report on all matters concerning Aboriginals. I made regular visits to Elcho Island (Galiwinku) Methodist mission, and visited the outstations that had been encouraged by the Methodists when the government made noises about mining exploration and wood-chipping.

Most of the problems Aboriginals now have, at core, emanate from the time when they were either encouraged or forced to leave their tribal land and go to missions or government settlements for proselytisation or education or assimilation or — regrettably in some cases — protection in the real sense of the term. That enabled government and other interested parties to call the Aboriginal land Crown land, later 'unalienated' Crown land. So the land is empty. *Terra nullius*. As I say in my song 'Bullocky Joy and Jesus':

> The miners said: 'We'd like this land.'
> The government said: 'We'll give you a hand.
> It's government land, didn't you know?
> The blackfellers left there long ago.'

I was also required to get involved in disputes among Aboriginals that could not be resolved by the local councils. There was a feud between two clans at Yirrkala that had been going on for many years, perhaps centuries. Occasionally there would be a fight, the spears would be rattled, but more often than not it was a talkfest and parties would go away mumbling, 'You wait. One day I'll get you.' Things got out of hand in 1968, and a man was killed, speared through the heart. A car raced up to my place, and I was called to Yirrkala mission. Wally Fawell was away on holidays, and none of the mission staff seemed to have any idea what to do. The two sides were strutting around, trading insults, waiting for somebody to throw the next spear, and she'd be on. I arrived and heaved a sigh of relief. Narritjan Maymuru was there. One of the great conciliators of Arnhem Land, Maymuru was taking them all on. He had a handful of spears, a woomera, and a dilly bag hung around his neck. The dilly bag, a little container made of woven pandanus fibre, told me it was Very Serious Business. Narritjan was marching up and down, yelling at both sides, sometimes running. He was magnificent. He was from a clan with connections to both of the opponents. Every ten seconds or so he would pause, hook a spear into his woomera, put the dilly bag in his mouth and clench his teeth on it — in the bag were the *maraian* (sacred) objects that made him bullet–proof and ten metres tall. He adopted the classic fighting pose. He beat his chest and removed the dilly bag from his mouth, leaving it swinging like a necklace.

'If you want fight, fight me,' he said. 'You've been fighting one another too long. It's time to stop.'

He saw me. We were good friends. Suddenly I was in the act. Clever feller properly, old Narritjan.

'My friend, Ted Egan, he here now. You mob go home. Me and Egan will find the killer man, and we'll lock him up for the police.'

Thanks, champ.

The others drifted off. Narritjan turned to me.

'Come on Egan, he's down in the beach camp.'

'Who is it?' I asked. He told me. I know it sounds melodramatic, but I must not record the bloke's name, for it could have repercussions to this day. I was apprehensive when I heard the name. He was a big, brooding, unpredictable joker, just the type manipulated in situations like this to keep the feud going.

We went to the beach camp. There was our man, standing by a little shed, a handful of spears and a woomera. Ominously, he too was wearing a dilly bag. Susceptible people like this man, the type chosen for a killing, are often given a *maijabala*, something like a relic, to remind them of the contract in hand. The *maijabala* is placed in a dilly bag, hung around the executioner's neck, and the magic is woven. We walked to him. It was disconcerting, but of all things he was wearing sunglasses. I had never seen a bush blackfellow with sunglasses. He did not adopt a threatening pose to us. Narritjan stuck his own spears upright in the sand to indicate peace, and nodded to me. Your turn, white man. I've done my bit.

Confidence, Ted. Look confident. I walked right up to him. I hoped I looked braver than I felt.

'OK, I'll have the spears,' I said, and held out my hand. I tried to eyeball him, but couldn't make contact because of the sunglasses. His grip tightened.

'The spears,' I said. He handed me all of the spears except

one. He had a woomera and he half-hooked that spear into the woomera.

'Would you like to take that dilly bag off?' I thought that was important. His body language showed relief, as he disrobed himself of the dilly bag and gave it to me. As I took the dilly bag I spotted it. The tomahawk he had gripped between his toes. He was moving his leg ever so slightly. This bastard is going to split my skull open. Help!

I forced myself deliver a fierce right–hook look, deep into the sunglasses, tried to keep my voice calm:

'And I'll have the tomahawk.'

It probably took only 15 seconds for him to decide to lift his foot, still gripping the tomahawk, remove it from between his toes, and hand it to me. Fifteen lifetimes more like it.

'Thank you,' I wheezed. 'Now, Narritjan is going to look after you until we get the police out from Darwin. Aren't you?' My turn for the flick pass. Narritjan composed himself, and became the elder statesman.

'*Yo, manymag,*' he said. Yes, good one.

The relieved assassin had one more shot to fire. He hooked up his last spear, and hurled it, full force, at the little tin shed. It cut through the galvanised iron like aluminium foil, the shaft shaking. He came with us.

Later Narritjan and I looked at the contents of the dilly bag. We expected to find a finger bone, or some other relic of a dead person being avenged. But no, there was a photograph. A photograph of a very flamboyant fellow who had been killed a couple of years before. The feud was as old as time: the *maijabala* was state of the art.

The list of plaintiffs for the court case changed when Mawalan Marika died. Mawalan is known throughout the world as an artist. Picasso once saw his paintings and said, 'Ah, if I could paint like that.' Some people more knowledgeable than I about art say they can detect Aboriginal influences in Picasso's work from about the time when he saw Mawalan's paintings. I consider myself fortunate to have Mawalan's last painting, finished about three days before his death. It depicts a Macassan *prahu*.

A Macassan prahu arrives, Malawan's last painting. Turn it upside down and note the slight deviations from horizontal symmetry.

Power passed to the next senior member of the Riratjingu clan, Mawalan's brother Mathaman. Like Pope John XXIII Mathaman's seniority proved to be short, as Mathaman well knew it would be. Mild little Mathaman wielded power for the first time in his life, and seized the opportunity to paint on bark the principal stories of the Riratjingu. Mathaman lived only one more year, but during that time he was wisdom itself in the discussions about land and mining, and he painted like a man certain that time was both valuable and in short supply. Mathaman's few paintings are bringing astronomical prices in world art circles. I have two of them, and will bequeath them back to the Riratjingu people, along with Mawalan's, when I die: while I live I want to be reminded of those two dear friends.

One of Mathaman's paintings that I reproduce here — the old man gave me permission — concerns a series of unfortunate incidents largely attributable to David Griffin's hard-nosed attitudes. I started a local liaison committee, consisting of a representative of the mission, the Yolngu, and the mining company, plus me as chairman. We met weekly and relationships were good. The aim of the exercise was to keep one another posted on what was happening. But Griffin specifically ordered the company not to disclose its hand even to its own liaison committee representative when some big bulldozing work was scheduled for the new town and the alumina plant site.

One day there was typical coastal scrub and creeper-covered dunes behind the beach. The next day it was cleared and flattened. Old Mathaman came to me and said, 'My heart is broken.' Just that. In English, which he didn't speak well. 'My heart is broken.' His eyes were full of tears, not the tears that Aboriginals can summon when required to express sorrow on a formal level. The tears of a man whose heart was broken. His wife, Yinitjuwa, who spoke excellent English, told me of the clearing. We drove to Melville Bay, 30 kilometres. Sure enough, the flattened ground, the big scar up the side of the Nhulunbuy hill, where a road had been cut. The bastards. In the face of opposition from his own people, in the spirit of compromise, with sheer logic, Mathaman had organised permission for Nabalco to put a water tank on the top of the hill as long as there was minimal interference to trees. It would have been easy. But no, you can't let savages call the shots. Not savages who wouldn't be invited into the boardroom.

When the other Yolngu heard of the desecration they were furious, frustrated. They took their spears to the top of Nhulunbuy and performed a ceremony, swearing retribution. Mathaman was still prepared to compromise, to be a bloody sight more reasonable than I was. I wanted to take them to court. He said, 'No. The trees will grow again. The stringybark trees. They'll grow again in two years time and it will look good again. But it's the Wuyal tree I'm worried about. It is Wuyal himself. And they have killed him. The *balanda* court can't bring Wuyal back.'

I already knew that Wuyal was the creator of the Nhulunbuy hill. Mathaman now told me that there were three other places that Wuyal had created, Dimbukawuy — a cluster of rocks; Dhanburama — a banyan tree on the alumina plant site; and another banyan tree, actually called Wuyal, at the construction camp site. The Wuyal tree had been bulldozed. I told Mathaman he must show me Dimbukawuy and Dhanburama in order that I could get them gazetted as sacred places.

We went that day. Dimbukawuy was easy. Some rocks near, but not on the conveyor line that would take the raw bauxite 20 kilometres from the mine to the port. Nabalco had asked me to design a notice to indicate to Aboriginals dangerous places around the mine site. After consulting Roy Marika and the Yolngu council we decided the sign should depict a red snake with the words *'Dhuwala madakaritj warnga'* which means 'This is a dangerous place.' Many of the Yolngu were literate in their own language but not so good in English. We now put the signs all around Dimbukawuy — to keep the whitefellers away — and I arranged for it to be surveyed and fenced, pending gazettal. It was fortunate that we were told of Dhanburama, the banyan tree at the alumina plant site, for when we got there clearing had started. Mathaman identified the huge banyan tree. I asked Leigh French, the local manager, to come with us and explain to all his staff that no matter how it inconvenienced the construction of the alumina plant the banyan tree, quickly fenced, was to be protected. And it was.

Mathaman saw me two days later, and said, 'I've done a painting for you.' In the painting there is a huge banyan tree and Wuyal, travelling around the country with his spears. Wuyal is the sugar–bag man, responsible for creating all the native bees and the wild honey so prized among the Yolngu. At each of the sites he created he left one of his dilly bags, full of wild honey, to last forever. Until the vandals arrived. The tree in the painting is Dhanburama. Tucked away in the corner of the painting is a little animal.

'Did Wuyal have a dog?' I asked Mathaman.

'No. That's a wallaby,' the old man said. 'You know that white man who gives the new names?'

'Yes, I know the arrogant old bastard,' I replied.

'Well, where they killed the Wuyal tree is the place the white man calls Wallaby Beach, so I thought I'd paint a wallaby for him.'

Just like that. Generous of spirit in spite of such arrogance and meanness. What a man.

And then Mutty, as we called Mathaman, died. He was buried with full honours in the land of his fathers, the land of Wuyal. The next brother Milirrpum became the senior member of the Riratjingu clan, and thus the famous case is known as *Milirrpum* v. *Nabalco and the Commonwealth of Australia.*

Preliminary hearings had just started in Darwin when Mutty died. I was disgusted at the vehement approach taken by the defendant, my employer, the Commonwealth of Australia, as their haughty, professionally insensitive QCs ridiculed the Aboriginal case. Yet there was the incongruous component of the court proceedings where the same Commonwealth, via Coombs, had organised the funds for the Aboriginal plaintiffs, and Professor Bill Stanner was briefing the Yolngu's lawyers.

I had just about taken the decision to resign in protest when Nugget Coombs said to me:

'Would you like a job working for my mob? The other government mob? The ones who care.' He gave one of his rare, wry smiles.

'Where?'
'Based in Canberra, but reporting to me on places like this.'
'You're on.'

Wayul, the sugar-bag man. For the heart-breaking but uplifting
background to the painting, see pages 244–6.

15
Poor Bugger Me

Again, I travelled alone to the new posting. Rae and the kids stayed in Darwin until I could organise a house in Canberra. I stayed at a Canberra hostel, Acton House, a short walk from the Office of Aboriginal Affairs in London Circuit, right in the centre of the many concentric rings that make up inner Canberra, the national capital. It was spring of 1969, and Canberra looked good, with all the blossoms and new growth, and the bracing weather that was one of many shocks to my system.

Research Officer, Office of Aboriginal Affairs was going to be an exciting job. That was obvious from my first meeting with my workmates. The council extended a formal welcome to me. Barrie Dexter, Director of the Office of Aboriginal Affairs was a former career diplomat, a wartime commando with an illustrious war record, a very intelligent and charming bloke, one of those myopic, mild-mannered men who win Victoria Crosses when the chips are down. I'd had lots of dealings and talks with Dr Coombs in Arnhem Land, and I felt good that we were officially on the same side. I had seen in court and now met for the first time Professor Bill Stanner, the third member of the Council for Aboriginal Affairs, an eminent anthropologist, a quaint, scholarly little koala, who smoked a fragrant pipe. I was to discover that pipe smoking was an art form in Canberra, *de rigeur* in the many games of 'Let's look knowledgeable, even if we're not', that are played in the panelled conference rooms. Unlike my old Alice Springs boss Bill *puff puff* McCoy, and the other pipe smokers I was to meet in Canberra, Bill Stanner did have a huge brain and a lot of common sense. The council was a delightful combination of three great minds that often thought alike, but in very different ways. They enjoyed one another's company.

There were only nine other staff members in the engine room. Frank Moy, former Director of Native Affairs in Darwin, was Barrie Dexter's deputy. I met the famous Charlie Perkins for the first time, and had the chance to tell him I admired his Freedom Rides in the early 1960s. Charlie was one of four Aboriginals on staff, the other three being Reg Saunders, the first Aboriginal to attain a commission in the Australian armed forces, Phillip Roberts — an old mate from the Top End — and Margaret Lawrie, formerly a nurse, from South Australia. Working on different projects around Australia were three white research officers with better academic qualifications than me, Jan Cooper, Kevin Martin and a good mate of mine from the old Native Affairs Branch of Darwin, Jeremy Long. It was a close-knit show, and there was that dynamic mood that prevails in a prestigious, small, uninhibited new unit.

It was clear that I would have the chance to see more of northern Australia than I had in the 20 years I had lived Up North. Barrie Dexter said he wanted me to concentrate and report to Council on four regions — the Northern Territory, north Queensland including Torres Strait, the Kimberley and Pilbara regions of Western Australia. Yes, please.

I visited each of the regions. It was heady stuff. Prime Minister's Department. The feeling in some quarters that the Coombs group was going to wave the wand that would finally resolve all those nagging Aboriginal problems. Disillusionment and the realities of politics were not on the agenda. The power of Coombs within government circles was paramount. In Canberra.

But not in the specific places where the Aboriginal issues were to be fought out. In Queensland Coombs was regarded as a dangerous little communist. In the Northern Territory he was one of those bastards from Canberra held responsible for all the Territory's ills and shortcomings. In Western Australia they were prepared to take federal money, but were certainly not going to relinquish any control over the blackfellows to 'the wise men from the east', as anybody on the wrong side of Kalgoorlie is vilified.

The Yirrkala Land Rights case, as *Milirrpum v. Nabalco and the Commonwealth* came to be known, commenced in the Northern Territory Supreme Court. The case was heard by Justice Blackburn, and it was obvious from the first day that it was going to be tedious and protracted. I was to have no more involvement — not that I had done very much, except declare my support for the Yolngu — but I followed it intently, for I could see the ramifications of the case no matter which way it went.

I did get very involved in the other land rights battle being fought on the streets, on university campuses, at trade union meetings and in the bush. This concerned the Gurindji, the people from the Wave Hill station in the Northern Territory, who had walked off the station in 1966 to demand better rights. That provoked levels of laughter from all quarters, from people who believed that the Gurindji would be starved into subjection in about one week flat.

Their leader, Vincent Lingiari, a simple stockman, could not read or write, but he had dignity and a cause. He got some help from the North Australian Workers Union in Darwin, and declared that his people were 'on strike' for better wages and conditions. As well they said that they wanted to get title to some of their own land, held under pastoral lease by the Vesteys organisation, the British meat barons. It was through the Gurindji that the words 'land rights' came to have real meaning in Australia. There were demonstrations in Melbourne and Sydney, concentrating on the Vesteys offices in those places. At one of these a large group of university students shouted slogans and carried banners. One young girl had a banner that read:

LAND RIGHTS FOR THE GURINDJI.

'Get out, you idiot, you wouldn't know a Gurindji from a barramundi,' an irate heckler shouted to her.

'And I don't care,' replied the student, 'as long as they both get their land rights.'

The real villain was the Commonwealth government, determined not to hear the ominous 'land rights' words.

Phillip Roberts and I went to Wave Hill, and then to Daguragu, where the Gurindji were sitting down. They had been on strike for over two years, and had built a cosy little camp, a bush timber shelter with a spinifex thatch roof — 'bough shed' in the Territory — that was headquarters for the

       MURRAMULLA GURINDJI CATTLE COMPANY

as the sign announced. Some symbolic stockyards. They had fenced their bank of Wattie Creek, as white people called the permanent water at that pretty spot, Daguragu.

Vincent Lingiari was very much in charge, yet he was a softly-spoken kind old man, very gracious to Phillip and me. Vincent was courteous to everybody, and patiently answered the million questions thrown at him by journalists and visitors. At all times the dignity shone through and the message was clear. It's our land. We're happy to share it with anybody as long as we are treated like human beings, not dogs. The Gurindji had been given a lot of support by the trade union movement, and also ABSCHOL, a dynamic student group led by Tony Lawson — a very skilful operator, and Tom Roper, later a Victorian Minister. Frank Hardy worked hard for the Gurindji and had written his excellent book, *The Unlucky Australians*. An Aboriginal bloke named Dexter Daniels deserves a lot of admiration, for he virtually put his life on the line as a union rep for the North Australian Workers Union. It was dangerous for any union rep to go on a cattle station in those days, but a blackfeller! There's courage.

I was surprised to find that the Director of Welfare in Darwin had sent my old boss and good mate, Ted Evans, to ride shotgun on me, for I had switched allegiances within the Commonwealth and was now working for 'that bastard Coombs'. Ted and I had a good laugh, and promised not to come to blows: it showed how silly the situation was. But the two Commonwealth agencies were deadly serious. My brief was to try to develop tactics to enable the Gurindji to have their ownership of their land recognised. Ted Evans was very supportive of the Gurindji, but had to follow the Department of the Interior line, which was not to encourage land rights claims. They proposed 'a government settlement' on the Wave Hill Common, thereby offering the Gurindji an alternative to working on the Vestey's station, Wave Hill. In the past they had no option other than to live and work for Vestey on the station if they wanted to retain contact with their land, which they must. For 80 years since the unheralded invasion of white settlers they had been enslaved on their own land, forced labour paid flour, tea and sugar.

The government had built twelve houses on the Wave Hill Common, and the original name, Kalkeringi, was being used for 'the new town'. The Gurindji knocked back the dangled carrot of three-bedroom brick homes, all facilities, good views. The houses were empty, a temporary embarrassment to the government. The houses were eventually occupied by Warlpiri people, moving north like Caesar. I have to conceal a smile nowadays when Warlpiri people tell me they were on strike with the Gurindji in the 1960s. The myth becomes the reality. I don't seek to disabuse them. Nor do the Gurindji, for the blackfellow way is to tolerate others' foibles.

Not much happened in the strike camp at Daguragu, except a lot of pipe-dreaming about 'getting our land back'. I was a good listener as I tuned in to Vincent and Ted Evans reminiscing about events and personalities in the region. Ted had been the patrol officer there from 1946 to 1954. I took on board the important date, 1953, in the life of the Gurindji. Vincent vividly recalled the day at the Negri Races when, after working for the white bosses on Wave Hill since 1888, the Gurindji stockmen touched money for the first time. Each Gurindji stockman was given a £5 note. Not bad deferred pay for 65 years in the saddle, working daylight to dark, getting belted around the ears with hobble chains.

I no sooner returned to Canberra when the Minister for the Interior, Peter Nixon, spoke in parliament about the Gurindji. It must be recalled that part of the portfolio of the Minister for the Interior was to promote the best interests of Aboriginals in the Northern Territory. He was paid a huge salary to do the job. Nixon got up in parliament and said that if 'these Gurindji' want to get some land they should do what any decent Australian would do — work hard, save their money, and buy some land! Yes Minister.

I was so angry. That night I wrote my song 'The Gurindji Blues', which has as its final verse:

> Poor bugger me, Gurindji,
> Peter Nixon talk long we,
> 'Buy you own land, Gurindji
> Buyim back from the Lord Vestey,'
> Oh poor bugger me.
> Poor bugger blackfeller, Gurindji,
> S'pose we buyim back country,
> What you reckon proper fee?
> Might be plour, sugar and tea
> From the Gurindji, to Lord Vestey
> Oh poor bugger me.

I decided to ring RCA and remind them that Sam Hordern (I think) had sent them the tape of me singing around the campfire at Brunette Downs. Were they interested in a song? Yes, talk to us. My mate Jenny Isaacs at the Aboriginal Arts Board organised funds for Galarrwuy Yunupingu — who's a fine singer — and Vincent Lingiari to come to Sydney and Galarrwuy and I recorded the song, preceded by a short archival statement from Vincent. Through Chicka Dixon we eventually sold thousands of copies of the recording, and that was one of the main means of financing the Aboriginal Tent Embassy that had been set up on the lawns of Parliament House. An aftermath was that George Warwick-Smith, the secretary of the Department of the Interior, rang Dr Coombs demanding that I be sacked for this attack on the government. I heard Coombs take the call. Nugget replied, 'Listen George, I don't propose to do anything about this. Firstly, I think it's a bloody good song, and secondly, I think it's a succinct appraisal of the government's pathetic performance.' Goodonyer Nugget.

Vincent and Galarrwuy came to Canberra first: their travel was funded on the basis that there were to be talks on their land issues. The Gurindji were holding on, and looking good: they had the support of the Australian people. Galarrwuy's people, the Yolngu, had taken their case to the Supreme Court, and they lost. It was an irony that they were tried under the British legal system. Under the same system their land had been declared *terra nullius* by the British, so it was understandable that Justice Blackburn would reaffirm that the Crown and not the Yolngu owned the land.

At a meeting of the Council for Aboriginal Affairs convened after the loss of the Yirrkala court case, we felt that the plaintiffs would be shattered, so we brought Roy Dadaynga Marika and Daymbalipu Mununggurr, with Galarrwuy as interpreter, to see the prime minister, to let him know that, although they had lost the case, they would continue to fight for recognition of their land ownership. It was very poignant. We encouraged the two older men to talk only in their own language, in order that Galarrwuy could then remind the prime minister that they had been talking in Australian, the 'language of the land', and he would then translate into the prime minister's foreign language, English. The point seemed to be lost on McMahon. Galarrwuy addressed the National Press Club, where he spoke first in Yolngu matha, then English. The press gallery responded positively.

Vincent, too, was feted by the press, and in Sydney, in a memorable interview, Lenore Nicklin asked the old man, 'What do you think of Sydney, Mr Lingiari?' In his typical, measured style, Vincent looked around, up and down at the skyscrapers, and said, 'It's a bigger place altogether: more big than Wattie Creek.' We took the opportunity to have Dr Fred Hollows examine Vincent's eyes. The old bloke had bad trachoma, common among bush Aboriginals who live outdoors and are subject to strong sunlight, heat, dust, smoke and flies. It was miraculous. Galarrwuy and I were in the studio recording a couple of other songs. Vincent left us at 11 am. At 5 pm he returned to us, his face beaming, his eyes clear, a couple of stitches in each eyelid, the weeping gone, his vision as he told us, 'Good enough I can hunt kangaroo again.'

Galarrwuy stayed on for two months. I had written a play about land rights and Dr Amy McGrath had agreed to produce it at her Australian Theatre, Newtown, as long as I could get two Aboriginal men, one young, one old, to play two of the main four parts. I chose Galarrwuy and a good old friend, Albert Barunga from Derby in Western Australia. After only two weeks of rehearsals they were ready to perform their difficult roles. The director, Peter Williams, was astonished at their natural ability as actors. Amy McGrath was good enough to provide accommodation for the two men at her Centennial Park home. The play ran for the scheduled month to packed houses, and received top reviews. It was called *No Need for Two Blankets*. I re-read my play recently, post-Mabo, and it's dated, but the issues were very relevant in 1970.

The mining boom started in Western Australia and Poseidon fever hit the country. Reg Saunders and I went to the Laverton-Leonora region to seek to assist the many Aboriginal prospectors who were handicapped in not having the finances to take out exploration licences. Reg was a great travelling companion, impeccably tailored, worldly, a tough man who had fought with distinction in Greece, Crete, New Guinea and Korea, a man who did not hesitate to pull army rank and his status as a Life Member of the RSL in some of the tricky situations we found ourselves in. The story has become legend that he visited Wilcannia shortly after being appointed as a liaison officer with the Office of Aboriginal Affairs. He took an Aboriginal mate of his to the RSL club for a beer. The steward said:

'I'm sorry, Major Saunders [Reg did not seek to be called Major, and was long since out of uniform, but he was regularly called Major Saunders]. I can serve you of course. But your companion is not a member.'

'But he's my friend, and I have signed him in to the club.'

'Well . . . ,' said the steward, 'local Aboriginal people are barred.'

'Is that so?' said Reg, and stormed to a telephone. Speaking at a level to enable all club members to hear him he rang a mate in the Transport Workers Union in Sydney and arranged for the club's beer supplies to be black-banned, in the true sense of the term.

Reg and I were impressed at the calibre of most of the Aboriginal prospectors around Laverton and Leonora, and were able to stake a few of them to take out quite valuable licences. They in turn did deals with the bigger gold and nickel companies. It was a very satisfactory experience.

I had heard for many years of the legendary Don McLeod in the Pilbara region. Milanka, as Aboriginals call old Don, was a wharf labourer in Port Hedland in the 1940s and organised a strike of Aboriginals, even though he was a white man. He derived his authority, he said, from a 1942 meeting attended by 'thousands' of Aboriginals at a place called Skull Creek. McLeod had written to Dr Coombs on a personal level for many years, so I was sent to see what I could do to help McLeod's Mob, as they are known in Western Australia. The group had maintained a commendable independence of government agencies for many years, mining and running cattle. They were fiercely loyal to McLeod, although on the face of things it looked as though McLeod himself was something of a hindrance to the group in latter years, as he became a bush lawyer and frittered away a lot of the group's earnings in litigation. They had once owned Yandeyarra station, but lost it. McLeod must have done a wonderful job in the early years to keep the group together and get them working free of government and mission control, but he was set in his ways when I met him, and I made the mistake of telling him so.

McLeod's Mob had quite a few mining leases in the Pilbara, mainly mining tin. They obviously could do with an injection of funds, and we had access to money for deserving causes like this. But I fell out with McLeod very early in the piece, when he demanded that I write out a cheque made out to Don McLeod.

'I don't actually write the cheques,' I said. 'If I recommend a project you can rest assured it will be funded. But I work for the Office of Aboriginal Affairs. You're a whitefeller.'

'And don't you bloody well forget that I'm the appointed spokesman for 8000 Western Australian blackfellows. Appointed at Skull Creek in 1942,' he snapped.

'Good on you, Don,' I said, 'but I can't deal direct with you. You're not one of my clients.'

That ended our relationship. I wasn't just going to walk away, so I decided to spend the next month visiting various groups in the region. I had been asked to make preliminary inquiries about the purchase of Strelley station for McLeod's Mob, so I needed to talk to different groups, including some of his people, working at a place called Coondinna, out from Marble Bar. They were yandying tin.

To yandy is to use a traditional skill whereby Aboriginal women winnow seed from the stalks and husks of edible grasses to enable them to make seedcakes. This is done by a circular arm motion, using a wooden coolamon as a dish. As with all winnowing the material is tossed around as part of the process to enable the wind to blow the rubbish away. The heavier seed is retained. Aboriginals in the Pilbara demonstrated that they could clean heavy tin from other, lighter waste dirt better than any white man's machine. The best test to see if you can yandy is to mix tea and sugar, and then separate the tea from the heavier sugar. Give it a go.

There were about 40 men, women and kids camped at Coondinna. They had a mining lease issued in the name of Clancy, one of Don McLeod's famous 'lieutenants'. They sat in little groups cleaning tin-bearing ore by yandying. Their basic unit of economy was what they called a 'fruit' — an empty fruit can full of cleaned tin ore. At the end of each day they went to a little shed that was their communal food store and in which were kept the 44 gallon drums that they slowly filled as they tipped each 'fruit' into the drum. Clancy could not read and write, but he kept his own tally by a series of strokes with a piece of charcoal. He had different spaces for each person. 'Bessie, three fruit. Tommy, two fruit,' he would say as he did the books.

On a memorable day (for me at least) they received a cheque for their previous consignment of tin (I almost wrote fruit). The payment was $2000 plus. Clancy asked me to drive him to the bank at Marble Bar where he cashed the cheque in $2 notes. That evening they divvied up the money. They sat in a ring and the pile of money was placed on a towel in the centre, on the ground. The genial Clancy paid out all the 'fruits' first, then an allottment to 'woman gottim picaninny'. Next were the 'old flourbags' (flourbag is code for grey hair) — the pensioners. At the end of the distribution there was still about $500 left. Clancy sat down. This needed some serious thinking.

'What we going to do this one?' he asked the group.

'Well, old Bill, that tent belong to him he bugger up,' said Molly. Right, a new tent for Bill.

'My car needs two tyres,' said Barney. Done.

'We got that sorry business for that old dead woman,' Bessie reminded the group. Cash to Bessie. $100.

I have never forgotten that evening in that dusty, ugly, scarred little tin mine. Never will. Never should. That was economics stripped of all the bullshit.

I had quite a few trips to Torres Strait and the mainland of north Queensland. I did not get to know either region well, but I had some interesting things to do. I had heard for many years the constant clamour for kangaroo farming, but always felt it was impractical and difficult, and conjured constant visions of stockmen in a furious chase after kangaroos, only to see the roos jump the fences and escape to freedom. Nowadays, with the strong demand for lean meat it might be time for kangaroo farming on a large scale. Sheep and cattle farming involve lots of international competition, but there is only one country with kangaroos. At the moment. But I was not interested in kangaroo farming in 1970. There were bigger and better fauna to fry.

I had for many years espoused the benefit to Aboriginals and Islanders of emu, crocodile and green turtle farming. In every case an animal capable of being kept in easy captivity, an animal that laid a lot of eggs, an animal that could provide valuable commodities like meat, oil and leather. The council was enthusiastic about this idea, particularly as it would help us get a footing in Western Australia, the Northern Territory and Queensland. We started in 1970 a little company called Applied Ecology. That enabled us to employ a Scottish scientist, an expert on reptiles from the Australian National University, Dr Bob Bustard. His name was interesting, for the bustard, the bird that was our staple diet at Newcastle Waters during the flood, could also stand some investigation with a view to farming: if nothing else, it might prevent the extinction of the bustard.

Emu farming, which we started at Wiluna, Western Australia, crocodile farming which we started at Porumpuraw, Edward River, Queensland, and turtle farming, which we started in Torres Strait were and are a great idea. The emu and crocodile farming notion has spread slowly and meaningfully across the appropriate areas in remote Australia, but the turtle farming went sour when that dreadful additive, politics, was put in the pot.

In April 1972 Rae and I went overseas on long-service leave. When I left Australia in April there were six experimental turtle farms in Torres Strait, all under close supervision, just establishing the point that turtles could be raised and fed in captivity. When I returned in October there were 110 turtle farms. Dr Bustard had got the taste for politics, and envisaged himself with great economic control in Torres Strait, where he had a high profile. He had captured the ear of Peter Howson, the minister, who allocated funds sufficient in Bustard's mind to enable him to be the entrepreneur of a total new economy in that depressed community. Alas, there was no established market for turtles yet. Control went astray, and wild stories emerged about thousands of turtles in bath tubs starving, eating one another to survive. It was exactly the bizarre story the media love. The Queensland government, still in draconian control over Torres Strait, seized the opportunity to attack that interfering usurping interloper Coombs. The council finished up with very scrambled turtle egg all over its face. Turtle farming was disbanded. A pity. It still has a place, as a conservation device as well as an economic one.

I spent a lot of time in the Territory, keeping in touch with the Gurindji, trying to establish the principles whereby we could buy some cattle stations on behalf of worthy Aboriginal groups. I took Dr Coombs on extensive tours to the most remote places, including a drive through Arnhem Land visiting vital little groups living on outstations. Nugget became very keen on the idea of supporting lots of little groups living on their own land, rather than have large numbers of Aboriginals on settlements and missions. I guess I had some influence on him in that respect, for I kept extolling the virtues of Fred Gray, and telling him of my own efforts to create outstations at Yuendumu.

He was a good travelling companion, Nugget, with immense energy. He would be up and alert at 5 am, usually electing to run a few miles while I packed up the overnight camp. I picked him up along the bush track. He was a sparkling conversationalist, and around the campfire at night we had Mozart in the background on a little cassette recorder as we sat on our swags sharing a bottle of fine red wine. Our arrangement was that I bought the tucker, he supplied the music and the wine. He was a good judge of both and I'm a good bush cook. I went into my good listener mode, and plied him with questions, for I was only just starting to learn the depth of the man's experiences. He told me of working direct to all the prime ministers since Curtin, and felt that Ben Chifley had no peers. He had been Governor of the Reserve Bank for 20 years, and had headed up the Department of Post-war Reconstruction. He gave me three good clues on life which are worth passing on.

Never resign.

Try to keep a report to one page.

It doesn't matter who attends the meeting, as long as you write the minutes.

Nugget asked me to organise meetings of Aboriginals in different centres. One of these was at Alice Springs. The usual subjects were discussed. Health, land, education, employment. I could have written the minutes in advance. But there was a difference. On each topic a genial little Warlpiri man, Stumpy Martin, would get to his feet and say, 'Doctor Coomb, I'm not talk for the health business. I'm talk for the Willowra cattle station.' On education: 'Doctor Coomb, don't worry the education, more better we talk for that Willowra cattle station.' Nugget gave me the nod to check Stumpy out. I knew him slightly from my Yuendumu days: he certainly knew me.

Stumpy told me that the Willowra cattle station, owned by Edgar Parkinson, was on the market, and he wanted the government to finance its purchase for the Aboriginal residents, for it was their traditional country. Here was the lever we needed, and Stumpy was the perfect medium for our campaign, a tough resolute little battler, with plenty of savvy about the workings of the white man's world. Edgar Parkinson, in ill health, would prefer to sell to the Aboriginals rather than the Americans who wanted to purchase the place. Stumpy told me of the visit of the American prospective buyer. He gave me a graphic picture of the Yank. 'He got that big one cigar and him reckon: "Parkinson, three thing wrong you station. You price too high. You gottim no more nuff cattle. But you gottim too much nigger."' We started to get organised to buy the place, against hefty opposition from my old employers, the Northern Territory Administration. Their solution was that the government would buy the station from Edgar, and then turn it into a government-run settlement, along the same lines as Yuendumu. I had visions of the Warlpiri as owners, raising and selling cattle, and then cashing their cheque in $2 notes and divvying it up, as McLeod's Mob did. Real economics. We had the funds to engage management consultants, and hefty negotiations commenced. Big national principles were at stake. We felt we must not lose this chance to establish the precedent that viable, worthy groups of people should be assisted to attain economic independence.

While travelling with Dr Coombs in Arnhem Land I got a lesson in the workings of government. We were on the Blyth River, in about as remote a spot as one could get in Australia. An Aboriginal walked into our camp with an envelope, addressed to Dr Coombs. The bloke had driven a Toyota four-wheel-drive from my old stamping-ground, Maningrida, to bring him as close as possible to our camp, and had walked the last 5 kilometres. Nugget opened the envelope. It was a telegram, in code, from Prime Minister John Gorton, advising Nugget of the challenge for Liberal Party leadership, and thereby the prime ministership, issued by David Fairbairn against Gorton. The guts of the message was: return to Canberra immediately. Nugget told me we would travel with the messenger to Maningrida, where I was to organise a charter flight to Darwin, and ongoing travel to Sydney by the first aeroplane available.

We got back into Darwin later that day. Nugget was tired so I took him to the house of my friends, Rhonda and Mick Gray, and they put him to bed. I checked out available flights. The only aeroplane going through Darwin was a BOAC flight, London-Sydney. I went to the booking office, and yes two seats were available. What class? First class. Names? My name's Ted Egan, the other passenger is Dr H C Coombs. I noted that the clerk wrote H C Coombs, VIP, without being told. Booking confirmed.

I went back to Mick and Rhonda's house, had a shower, changed into some clean clothes, and the Grays and I had a few drinks. Nugget slept through until I woke him at midnight. He was still in his daggy old bush clothes, and I mean daggy. As we got on the BOAC flight the young lady took our tickets — we had been given the VIP seats — and said graciously to me: 'This way, Dr Coombs,' and put me in 1A. She turned a withering look on my scruffy companion and put him alongside me. When the steward asked, 'Can I get you a drink Dr Coombs?' I said, 'I'll have a glass of Bollinger, and we'll have a red wine for my friend.' Nugget gave a bit of a grin and said, 'You'll keep, you bastard.' The taxpayer paid for that entire exercise, just because Gorton needed support at his time of crisis. The challenge by Fairbairn fizzled, so we may as well have stayed in Arnhem Land. But I had my first taste of Bollinger: that was a real fizzer.

When McMahon successfully challenged Gorton and became prime minister in 1971 it was obvious that Labor would win the next election. The Vesteys people in England did the political sums and realised that they should take some initiatives about the Gurindji land claim at Wave Hill. Lord Vestey sent Colonel Patrick Montgomerie of the Anti-Slavery Society in London, at Vestey's expense, to visit Wave Hill and Wattie Creek, and then have talks in Canberra. I went to Wave Hill with the colonel, who was a very affable clear-thinking Irishman. It took this experienced man about two minutes to decide that Vestey must offer to surrender a sizeable portion of the Wave Hill lease to give the Gurindji the opportunity to establish a viable home base. Coombs supported Montgomerie and pressed for the transfer of the land, but the battle was not over yet. McMahon dug his heels in; for the government still shuddered every time the words 'land rights' were uttered. The Gurindji issue was still unresolved at the time of the 1972 Labor victory.

While I was at Wattie Creek with Colonel Montgomerie, Ralph Hayes, the manager of the Wave Hill cattle station, drove in to see Vincent Lingiari. This will be interesting, I thought. I knew Ralph, not all that well, but I liked him, and could recognise that he was in an awkward position, manager of the station and thereby required to toe the company line, but at the same time friendly to Vincent Lingiari, for he knew of the many selfless years Vincent and other Gurindji stockmen had given to Vesteys.

Vincent and Ralph went through a bit of small talk, and their rapport was obvious. I could sense that there was some important reason for the visit, so I withdrew, but not too far. Be a good listener, Ted. 'Listen, old man, I've got a problem,' said Ralph. 'I've got 600 head of cattle on Such-and-Such [he named it] Bore. The windmill's busted and the cattle are going to perish unless I move them. But I've got no men.' Wow, I thought. The strike had been going for four years. Here's your chance to stick it up Vestey's, Vincent. But no. Without hesitation, old Vincent swung a look around the Gurindji camp. 'You, you, you,' he ordered three young blokes, 'get a saddle and bridle each, and go with Ralph. You got cattle to shift.'

'Thanks, old man,' said Ralph, and drove away with three helpers.

'That was interesting,' I said to Vincent. I felt I had no right to say anything more provocative.

'Yeah,' said Vincent, in his slow soft voice. 'We gotta look after the whitefellers in this country.'

When the definitive books are written about Australia in the twentieth century, say a hundred years from now, there will be many a prime minister who'll barely rate a mention. I hope and think that Vincent Lingiari will.

Speaking of prime ministers we were due for a new one, the first ever to mention Aboriginals in his policy speech, and that in the opening paragraph! The 1972 election, held in December, had as its aftermath the 19-day Whitlam-Barnard government. During that time Nugget Coombs went every day to Parliament

House with a pile of files. Right, I've signed this: here is where you sign — that was the basic message. One of Whitlam's many portfolios was Aboriginal Affairs. Willowra was purchased, the principle of land rights was established, the regionalisation of Aboriginal Affairs was approved, a Department of the Northern Territory was created, a federal Department of Aboriginal Affairs was instituted (although Coombs was only lukewarm about that idea he had to go along with ALP policy), the framework of the Woodward Royal Commission into Land Rights was set up, the Coombs Task Force into Public Spending was mooted. Never resign, keep it on one page, and let me write the minutes.

My mid-life crisis was upon me. I needed room to move, time to think. I left Canberra, and Barrie Dexter was good enough to suggest that I set up the Aboriginal Artists Agency in Sydney. It was to be part of the Aboriginal Arts Board and was to concern

Plaque telling of the handover of 1250 square miles of the former Wave Hill pastoral lease

itself with the encouragement of Aboriginal participation in the arts through sound management and the protection of their copyright.

I like to think I created some desirable initiatives. We put out a couple of recordings of traditional music, and they sold well. At the same time I was aware that my own recordings were good sellers. Via my 'Gurindji Blues' association I had recorded two albums of my own songs with RCA, and both went gold, something almost unheard of in Australia at that time. I knew that the main outlet for my records was to tourists visiting Alice Springs, mainly because coach drivers were playing the songs on the coaches. I decided to do a drive around Australia to clear my head. Along the way I checked out the Alice and felt confident that I could do shows there for the many thousands of tourists visiting The Centre. As part of the trip I went for a few days sitdown with old Vincent at Daguragu. He had won his battle: the Gurindji were recognised as the owners of their own land, and Gough Whitlam would soon make formal recognition. The place was looking good, morale was high, and I sang 'Gurindji Blues' especially for Vincent. The old bloke laughed, then cried.

I travelled on towards Katherine. On a lovely morning I stopped the car, got out, took a notepad from my briefcase, and wrote a three-line letter of resignation to the department. I posted the letter in Katherine. I never went back. I had decided it was time for a white bloke like me to step aside and leave Aboriginals to sort out their own problems. The obstacles seemed to have been removed, and I had played a minor part: they still had my support.

I would sing songs and tell lies for a living.

Index

Abala, Steve, 25, 34
ABC Radio 35, 63
Aboriginal Affairs, Dept of, 265
Aboriginal Artists Agency 265
Aboriginal Arts Board 254
Aboriginal Inland Missionaries 111
Aboriginal Tent Embassy 254
Aboriginals Ordinance 25–7, 61, 62, 65
ABSCHOL 252
Aerial Medical Ser 156
Ahmat, Ali, 34, 67
Ahmat, Cyril, 20–2, 32–4
Ahmat, Jaffa, 22
Ahmat, Jane, 20
Ahmatt, Ankin, 67
Ahmatt, Michael, 51
Aileron Hotel 160
Alexandria 160
Alice Springs 8, 9, 139–158, 174, 266
Alusisse 231
Alyandabu 187–189
Alyangula 231
Amagula, Nandjiwarra, 220
Amateur Hour 194
Amoni, Tony, 52
Anamayera 87
Anderson, Andy, 105, 108
Anderson, Lenin, 108
Anderson, Stalin, 108
Anderson, Trotsky *later* Hector, 108
Angeles, Jacko, 75
Angeles, Tim, 19
Angurugu 119–39, 219–29
Angus 214
Annear, Col Frank, 14, 15
Anthony's Lagoon 69
Anti-Slavery Soc 263
Applied Ecology 259
Apuatimi, Luke, 76
Apuatimi, Raphael 'Uncle', 18, 39, 75–9
Armburst, Bill, 16, 78–9
Arnold, Geoff 'Ranga/Mr Tang', 234
Atkinson, Carl, 37
Australia, HMAS 33
Australian Halfcastes Progress Assoc 25, 167
Australian School of Pacific Admin 85,182
Australian Theatre 256
Bailey, Jack 'Silver Fox', 102, 103
Baker, Margaret, 145
Bangtail Muster 174
Banka Banka 8
Baraltja 92–3
Bark Petition 236
Barnard, Lance, 264, 238
Barrow Crk R C 160
Barunga, Albert, 94, 256
Bates, Bullwaddy, 208
Bathurst Is 18, 38–9, 51, 54–5, 64
Becker, Paul, 37
Bennett, Br Ed, 37
Bessie 170
Beswick Crk 94
Betaloo 215
BHP 119, 137, 220
Bing Bong 104, 168
Bismarck 56
Blackburn, Justice, 251, 255
Blackmore, Tim, 53
Blowes, Maureen, 24
Blue Mud Bay 130
Blyth R 83, 88, 93, 262
Bombing of Darwin 10–11, 68, 194–6
'Bombing of Darwin' 68, 69
Bond's motor coach 8–10, 43
Bonson, Don, 75
Booroloola 97–115, 149, 165
Bostock, Peter, 208
Braitling, Bill, 146
Braitling, Doreen, 146
Braitling, Wally, 146
Brennan, Bill, 33, 41
Brennan, Bob, 41
Brennan, Cecil, 41
Brennan, Dot, 41
Brennan, Frank 'Frunner', 33–40, 203
Brennan, Len, 41
Brennan, Leo, 33
Brennan, Mick, 41
Bridgett, Joe, 43
Bridgett, Ron 'Cuddles', 14, 43–5, 52, 74
Brisbane Tonight 204
Briston, 'Sabbo', 20, 34
Brock's Crk 192
Brooks, Fred, 149
Broome 21, 40–41
Brown, George, 145–6
Brunette Downs 160, 164, 254
Brunker, Col, 220
Buffalo Lodge 36
Buffaloes F C 9, 20, 28, 34, 48, 75–8
'Bullocky Joe and Jesus' 121, 240
Bundubunda, Jockey, 88
Bungawuy 69, 70, 92
Burera people 87–8
Burns, Jacky, 32 -3
Burns, Ronny, 79
Burrell, Frankie 'Fatman', 29
Burrinjuck, Tommy, 34
Busbridge, Beryl, 141
Busbridge, Don, 14–8, 151,158, 173, 179
Bustard, Dr Bob, 259–60
Butler, Dick, 19, 25
Byers, Wason, 99
Byrnes, Jackie, 74

Caledon Bay incident 134–36
Calwell, Arthur, 108
Campo, Teddy de, 49–50
Campbell, Basil, 79
Capricornia 188–9
Cardo 56
Cardona, Martin, 51
Cardona, Peter, 23
Cardona, Primo, 51
Casey, Col Mike, 220, 231
Chan, Albert, 20, 75
Channel Is 57–8, 63–4, 89, 194
Chapman, Kevin, 77
Chin, Cedric, 75
Chin, Eric, 36
Chin Loonga Pak 11, 12
Chin Mook Sang
Chin, Ossie, 36
Chin, Robert, 32
Chin, Ronny Chui Hoong, 23, 24, 195
Chin, Sam, 29
Chin, Sue Wah, 11, 36
Chin, W G, 11
Chin, Wellington Patrick 29, 74–5
Chisholm, Scott, 79
Church Missionary Soc 119, 121–39, 219
Clancy 258–9
Clarke, Billy, 19
Clarke, Gilbert, 34
Collins, Fr Aubrey, 50
Commonwealth Council for Aboriginal Affairs 233
Coniston Massacre 149, 180
Continental Hotel 40–41
Coolibah 30, 31
Coombs, Dr H C 'Nugget', 233, 239, 246–54, 257–62, 265

Index

Coondinna 258
Cooper, Jane, 250
Cooper, Merle, 20
Cootamundra, HMAS, 93–4
Cora 119
Cornelius, Brian, 204
Cornelius, Dee, 204
Cosgrove, Fr, 38, 39, 55
Costello, Joe, 193
Cresswell 160
Cubillo, Benny, 19, 51, 55
Cubillo, Dolph, 23
Cubillo, Murray, 51, 55
Cubillo, Steve, 51

Daguragu 251, 253, 266
Dajarra 164
Daly Waters 8, 9
Damaso, Babe, 22
Daniels, Bob, 34
Daniels, Dexter, 252
Darcy, George, 171
Darwin Basketball Assoc 73
Darwin Chinese Recreational Club 20
Darwin Club 36
Darwin Hotel 10, 11, 17, 21, 48, 101
Darwin Police Court 59–60
Darwin Rifle Club 48
Darwin Town Acquisition Act 46
Davies, Neil, 79–80, 203
Day, Jack, 8–10
Dexter, Barrie, 233, 245, 249, 265
Dhanburama 245–6
Dimbukawuy 245
Dixon, Chicka, 254
Djaparri 134–36
Djaylama 73
Dodd, Mrs, 94, 96
Dodson, Mick, 186
Dodson, Pat, 186
Dowler, Jack, 161
Driver, Johnny, 56
Drysdale, Dave, 85–7, 91
Drysdale, Ingrid, 85–87, 91
Dulverton 33, 40
Duncan 205
Dunn, Rolly, 14
Duntroon 41, 42

Eagles B C 20
East Alligator R 46
Edwards, Roy, 210, 212
Egan, Brian, 196–99
Egan, Grace, 8, 42, 50–57,122, 182–3
Egan, Greg, 75, 95, 98, 211, 214, 219

Egan, Jacki, 182, 204, 213, 219
Egan, Margaret, 94, 98, 210–11, 219
Egan, Mark, 175, 211, 219
Egan, Rae, *nee* Pierssene, 46, 53, 55, 67–8, 75, 94, 97–8,114–15, 175, 201, 204, 260
Elcho Is 239–40
Elizabeth, Queen, 69, 70, 72, 92
Elkin, Prof, 120
Elliot 213, 215
Ellis, Tom, 182–3
Ellis-Kells 16
Elsie 205, 210
Emu, HMAS, 84
Entrance Is 84
Erice 214
Eucharia, Sr, 63
Eurabo Association 25
European Launcher Development Org 233–4
Evans, Ted, 84, 85, 114, 119–29, 205, 252–3

Fagan 134–36
Fairburn, David, 262
Falwell, Rev 237
Farley, Deaconess Norma, 219
Federal Hotel 41
Fisher, Betty, 194
Fitzer, *m* Gribbon *nee* Styles, Eileen, 191–4
Fitzer, Tas, 194
5 DR 77
Fleming, Pat, 141
Fleming, Rev Tom, 141, 158, 159
Flinders District 231
Flying Doctor—*see* Royal Flying Doctor Ser
Flynn, Fr Frank, 67
Flynn, John, 146
Flynn, Tom, 196
Flynn, Tommy, 36–7
Fogarty, Peter 'Fogue', 14, 24, 199
Fong, Albert, 76
Fong Yuen Kee 19
Forrest, Peter, 105–6
Fort Dundas 39
Fortiades, George 7
Fortiades, Leo, 74
Foster, Horace, 105
Fraser, Malcolm, 238
Fremantle 40, 41
French, Leigh, 237, 245
Fry, Tommy, 86, 92

Gaden, Ada, 46, 53–4

Gaden, Frank 'Frong Kee', 54
Gaden, Hazel, 46, 53–4
Gaden, Hazel, d, 54
Gaden, Neil, 54
Galahs B C 20
Galiwinku 239–40
Gallacher, Jim, 200, 219
Gallacher, Ron, 208–209
Galora, Goorie, 49
Ganley, Dinny, 34
Garajama Crk 90–91
Garden Point 39–40
Garrett, Bertie, 14, 28, 29
Gasiunas, Rimgaila 'Bluey', 51–3, 74–5
Gaupangu 93
Gemco 119, 220
'Gibby' 14, 15
Glass, Don, 76
Goldfields Hotel 43
Goldner, George, 19
'Goodbye to You, my Nona Mani' 23
Gordon's Don Hotel 10
Gorle, Tommy, 197, 198
Gorton, John, 262–3
Gove Penin 231, 234
Government Gazette 57
Governor Broome Hotel 40
Gowrie, Lord, 194
Grand Central Hotel 43
Gray, Fred, 119–36, 141, 147, 173, 184, 218, 261
Gray, Mick, 263
Gray, Rhonda, 263
Green Ant Paddy 60
Green, Cmmdr Arnold 'Noic', 61–2
Greenhalgh, Dr, 202
Gribbon, Harry 'Mad Irishman', 192–4
Griffin, David, 238–9, 244, 246
Groote Eylandt 114, 115, 116–39, 219–30, 231–46
Groote, Gerhard, 119
Gsell, Fr francis Xavier, 38
Gunderson, Ted, 34
Gunn, Ian, 220
'Gurindji Blues, The' 254, 267

Haast Bluff 58, 71
Hagan, John, 164–5, 171
Hagan, Norman, 53, 146, 147, 160–5, 172, 199
Haines, Norm, 14
Hales, Jack 'Borrie', 15–16, 48
Hardy, Frank, 252
Haritos, George 'Noondi', 66

Harney, Bill 'Bilarni', 65, 105, 122–3
Harney's War 105
Hart, Kevin, 133
Harvey, Musso, 100–3, 115
Harvey, Roddy, 115
Hasluck, Paul, 57, 71, 167
Hassan nee Lee, Selina, 189–91
Hatch, Murray, 34
Hayes, Ralph, 264
Herbert, Francis Xavier, 188–9
Hickey, Leo, 66, 169
Holden, Danny,19
Hollow, Tom, 60–63
Hollows, Dr Fred, 255
Hollows, Tom, 29
Homestead, The, 8–9
Hordern, Sam, 171, 254
Hot and Cold Bar 101
Howson, Peter, 260
Hughenden 204
Hutchins, Arthur, 174

I, the Aboriginal 96
Ingrid Drysdale Hosp 87
'Isa Lei' 214
Isaacs, Jenny, 254

Jabada, Terry, 214, 215
Jabaljari, Nosepeg, 69
Jabaljari, Wally, 180–181
Jabananga, Sandy, 144, 147, 151, 158
Jabangardi, Tim, 141, 144, 156, 185
Jajapun, Barney, 88
James, Doug, 74
Janajanakanu, Dick, 69–70
Jangala, Peter, 175
Jedda 34
Jessop, Keith, 15
Joes, Roger, 116
John Stubbs & Co 45
Johnson, Dick, 48
Johnson, Edmund, 75, 79
Jolly, A E & Sons 36
Jones, Alan, 12
Jones, Norm, 15
Jose, Roger, 105–115
Joseph, Terry, 79
Juburula, Anzac, 158, 159
July 56
Jungarai, Johnny, 144, 147, 151, 175
Justice All Their Own 134

Kahlin compound 189
Kalkeringi 253
Kantilla, David, 79
Kantilla, Felix, 18, 38, 39
Kantilla, Saturnius, 75
Katherine 9, 94, 215, 266

Kee, Charlie See, 51
Keighran, Jack, 105
Kelly, Tony, 31
Kelvin Grove Teachers' College 202–203
Kerinaua, Walter, 79
Kevin 213
Khungarukung 187
Kidman, Sidney 'SK', 161
Kingsford Smith, Charles, 48
Kookaburras B C 20
Koolinya Kool Store 16, 48
Kooltong R 130
Koosey, Ernie, 196
Kriewaldt, Judge Martin, 15
Kumamoto, Aki, 84–5

'*La Marseillaise*' 214
Lane, Jack, 112
Larrakeyah, Bill, 72–3
Lathbury, Col, 32
Laverton 256–7
Lavington, Bill,145–6
Lawrie, Doug, 15
Lawrie, Margaret, 250
Lawson, Tony, 252
Lee, David, 55
Lee, Henry 'White Chinaman'/Kim Hoong 'Fung Quee Doy Hoong' 189–91
Lee, Tommy, 105, 110–112
Lewfatt, Terry, 75
Lim, Alec Fong 'O'Lim', 30, 197
Lim, Arthur, 30
Lim, George, 30, 36, 70
Lim, Richard, 30
Limerick 165, 166, 170
Lingiari, Vincent, 251–5, 264, 266
Linnet, Roy, 234
Long, Brian, 79
Long, Jeremy, 250
Long, Michael, 79
Lorna Lim & Sons 11, 26
Lowe, Beulah, 92, 216
Loy, Granny Lum, 31
Ludwig, Sadie, 20
Luna Park 72
Lyons, Tiger, 74

Macarthur R 97, 100, 102
Macassans 120, 123
MacLeod, Colin, 114
Macrides, Peter, 20
Margaret Mahy 37–8
Maher, Jack, 14
Main, Charlie, 112
Major, Smiler, 167–9
Makuljar, Jack, 63
Mallapunyah 171

Maningarida 84, 87, 91
Mannion, Sgt Jim, 31
Maranboy 95
Marble Bar 258
Marika, Mawalan, 237, 243
Marika, Roy Dadynga, 237, 243, 245, 255
Marion, Mother, 63–4
Marrenah B C 20, 46
Marrenah House 24
Marshall, Jim, 168, 170
Martin, Kevin, 250
Martin, Leo, 146, 160–63
Martin, Stumpy, 261–2
Martin, Thelma, 146
Mataranka 8, 9
Mathaman 'Mutty' 244–246
May, Alfie, 20, 34
Maylgura, Frank 'Kapula', 89–90
Maymuru, Narritjan, 240–42
Mayo, Johnny, 19, 75
McCaffery, Reg, 73
McColl, Cnst, 134–35
McCoy, Bill, 139–42, 175–6, 183
McDonald, Jack 'Mac', 206–207
McGill, Billy, 196
McGill, Geoff, 54
McGinness, Barney, 188
McGinness, Jack, 25, 188
McGinness, Joe/ Pumeri, 188, 189
McGinness, Lucy, *see* Alyandabu
McGinness, Margaret, 188
McGinness, Stephen, 188
McGinness, Valentine, 188, 189
McGowan, Scotia, 74
McGrath, Dr Amy, 255–6
McKay, Jack, 94–6
McKay, Mrs, 95
McKay, Sandy, 14
McKee, Bluey, 34
McKinnon, Don, 58, 59
McLaughlin, Phil, 75
McLean, Molly, 210
McLean, Viv, 210
McLeod, Don Milanka, 257–8
McMahon 255, 263–4
McNab, Sandy, 63
Mellifont, Dot, 55, 76
Mellifont, Mick, 76
Melville Bay 244
Melville Is 38, 39, 65
Methodist Church 233, 236, 240
Methodist Overseas Mission 92

Index

Mildura 8
Milibgimbi Mission 84
Milikins,Trevor, 85
Milingimbi 91–2, 93
Milirrpum 245
Milirrpum v *Nabalco and Cmwlth* 245, 250
Millers & Sandovers 32
Minaham, Mona, 193
Mirera 135
Montgomerie, Col Patrick, 263
Moo, Charlie, 30
Moose Jaw 79
Morcom, Albert 'Tower Flash', 104
Moreen, Ginger, 34, 69, 70
Morgan, Edna, 24
Morrish, Bob, 233
Mosek 35
Mosman 85
Moss, Reg 'Burlington Bertie', 14
Mt Allan 146
Mt Denison 146
Mt Doreen 146
Mt Doreen 147
Mt Isa 43
Mt Wedge 146, 172
Mountford, Charles, 65
Moy, Frank, 57, 65, 250
Muir, Billy, 25
Mulholland, Jack 'Mull', 105
Mulumbuk, Harry 'Left Hand', 81, 83, 88–91, 93
Mungatoi, Stanislaus, 79
Munsell, Jack, 36
Mununggurr, Daymbalipu, 237, 255
Murphy, Carmel, 24
Murphy, Josephine, 24
Murramulla Gurindji Cattle Co 252
Murray, Cnstb, 149
Myilly Pt 45

Nabalco 231, 233–8, 244–5
Nabulaya, Jacky, 81, 83, 88, 91
Nakara 87–8
Naliba, Johnny, 86–8, 91
Namatjira, Albert, 69–72, 128
Nambijinba, Uni, 141
Nandabida 224–5
Nango 116, 123, 220
Nanindjurra 224–5
Narkaya 135
National Press Club 255
Native Affairs Branch 57–65
Natjemla 135
Negri 253

Neidji, Bill 'Kakadu Man', 66–7
Neptuna 33, 196
New Guinea 11, 66, 85, 182–3
New Zealand 73
Newcastle Waters 204–15, 218
Newell, Jessie, 199
Newell, Jim, 199
'Ngiri Intamari' 227
Nguiu 18, 38–9
Nhulunbuy 235, 237, 244–5
Nichols, J W 'Fatty', 28, 59–63
Nicklin, Leonore, 255
Nightcliffs F C 33
Nixon, Peter, 253–4
No Need for Two Blankets 256
'No One Will Ever Know' 204
North Australian Workers' Union 19, 35, 59, 251, 252
Northern Standard 16, 35, 58, 78
Northern Territory Admin 46, 53, 57, 233, 239, 262
Northern Territory, Dept of, 265
Northern Territory F L 28, 50–51
Northern Territory News 59, 80, 104
Number 3 Hostel 13–16, 18, 36, 45, 49–50, 68

'O Mariana' 117–18
O'Callagahan, Johnny, 76
O'Donoghue, Steve, 34
O'Dwyer, Charlie, 14, 43
Oenpelli Mission 84
Office of Aboriginal Affairs 96, 249–90
'Old TI' 22, 76
O'Loughlin, Bis, 50, 52–3, 63–4
Olympic Games 51
On, Charlie, 54, 60, 74
118 Camp 20
O'Neill, Tom, 37
Oodnadatta 161
Ough, Mavis, 219

Palais 36, 67, 76
Papunya 172–3
Parap B C 20
Parap Camp 36
Parkinson, Edgar, 261–2
Paspali/Paspalis, Mick, 31–2, 74

Paspali/Paspley, Nick, 31–2, 74
Pechiny 233,236
Pedersen, Pete, 85
Peel, Yorky, 25
Perez, Frank, 34
Perez, Josie, 20
Perez, Rusty, 23
Perkins, Charlie, 250–51
Petrov, Mrs, 51
Picasso 242
Pierssene, Bert, 46–7, 94
Pierssene, Eunice, 46–7, 53–4
Pierssene, Marie, 46, 80
Pilbara 257
Pine Crk 9, 192
Pirlangimpi 39–40
Pitts, Alan, 94
P&O Hotel 41
Point Sampson 40
'Pokare Kare Ana' 214
Pon, Leo, 34
Port Hedland 40
Portley, Coll, 202, 204
Portley, Margaret, 202
Postmaster General's Dept 46
Pott, Brucie, 34, 35
Priestly, Anne-Marie 'AMP', 219
Prime Minister's Dept 233, 249–50
Puantulura, Aloysius, 55–6, 68, 69, 72, 185
Puantulura, Mena, 55–6, 68
Purvis, Bob 'Sandover Alligator', 160

Queensland, Univ of, 181–2, 200
Quong, Eddie, 19
Quong, Lester, 74

Radomi, Paul, 32, 74
Randall, Gerry, 37
Rapid Creek Hotel 30
RCA 254, 266
Redmond Causeway 212
Reid, Lois, 219
Rendezvous Cafe 7, 12, 30
Rieff, Sonia, 145
Rioli, Manny, 79
Rioli, Maurice, 79, 186
Rioli, Sibby, 79
Riordan, Jack, 14
Roberts, Phillip Waipuldanya/Watjarr Watjarr, 96, 250, 253
Roe, Billy, 19, 51, 74–9
Roe, Gordon, 51, 55
Roebuck Bay Hotel 41
'Roger was No Death Adder' 113–4

Roper, Tom, 252
Rose, Fred, 127–8
Ross, Barney, 100, 115
Ross, Kathleen, 100, 115
Rostrover College 219
Rotary Intern 175
Rotorua 73
Royal Doctor Flying Ser 67, 145–6, 167, 175
Rusty Valley B C 20
Ryall, Sgt Greg, 51, 74
Ryan, Baylon, 59
Rynne, Kathy, 20

Sacred Heart Order 37–8
Saint Mary's 18, 67
Saint Mary's B C 50–53, 73, 74
Saint Mary's F C 50–51, 54–6, 75–9, 186
Salonika 53
Sam, Chin, 74
Sammy Going South 221
Samson 132
Sang, Chin Mook 'Mooky', 32, 74
Sariago, Maxie, 32
Sarib, George, 75
Sarib, Joey, 20, 34, 74, 75
Saturninus, Joe, 77, 78
Saunders, Reg, 250, 256
Scarborough 41
Seaman's Union 40
Secretary, Bob, 63
Secretary, Frank, 58
Services F C 18
Seven Emus 105
Shadforth, Willy, 103–5
Shawn, Ted, 35
'She's on again in Darwin' 13
'Shuffle off You Buffaloes' 76
Skull Crk 257
Sliver Fox—*see* Bailey, Jack
Smith, David 'Did', 146–7
Smith, Dawn, 146
Smith, Ron
Smith, Ron 'Smithy' 7–14, 17, 46, 199
Snape, 'Bingo', 20, 34
Snape, 'Froggy', 20, 34
Somm, Dr Alec, 237
Sorata, Dr Bruno, 238
South Fremantle F C 76
South Pacific Festival 73
Splinter 112
Stanner, Prof Bill, 233, 249
Star Pictures 36, 37, 46
Starlight Hotel 10
Stawell, Michael, 105
Steam Laundry 76
Stewart, Neal, 233
Stinson, Mick, 19

Stokes, Col, 34
Stokes, Judith, 219
Strelly 258
Stroude, Rowena, 20
Sun Cheong Loong 11, 19
Swanson, Nelly, 94
Swanson, Tiny, 94–5
Sweeney, Gordon, 57, 65
Sweeny, Jack, 55, 78

Talbot,'Kanga', 20
Tanjin Pera 21–2, 76
Tardif, Johnny, 34
Tasman 119
Tatz, Colin, 175–6, 181, 200
Taylor, John, 79
Taylor, Rev Jim, 220, 225
Temora 85, 92
Tennant Creek 43
Thursday Is 21–2
Timber Crk 194
Tipett, Dr George, 175–6
Tipiloura, Urban, 75
Tipperary (stn) 194
Tipungwuti, Dermott, 75, 79
Tiwi 38–40,
Toby 86
Tom Brown's Schooldays 221–2
Torres Strait 118, 259–60
Townsville 43
Traeger, Alf, 145
Traynor 134–36
Trenowden, Beryl, 173
Trenowden, Max, 173, 174, 179
'Tribal Land, The' 235–6
Tuckiar 134–36
Tudawali, Robert,34
Tungutalum, Hyacinth, 79

Ulamari, Lena, 213, 218
Ulamari, Tim, 218
Umbakumba 147
Umbakumumba 119–39
United Nations 152
Unlucky Australians, The, 252
Uraputway, Ali, 76, 77
Urgers B C 20, 74

Vaughan family 219
Vaughan, Johnny, 55
Vestey, Lord, 254, 263
Victoria Hotel 12, 24, 30, 37, 51, 73
Vigona, Benny, 79

Wagin 41–2
Walker, Wendy, 24
'Wallaby Hunt, The' 68, 69
Wallaby Crk 123–4, 126
Walter R 130

Wanderers 28, 34, 57
Waratah F C 24
Waratahs 28, 34, 48, 49–50
Warlpiri 253, 172–185
Warman, Gil, 233
Warren, Rev Rix, 119–20, 123
Warwick-Smith, George, 254
Waters, Fred, *also* Nadpur 58
Wattie Creek 252, 263
Waudby, Bill 'Wallaby', 146, 161–2, 172
Wauby, Bob, 146
Wauby, Pat, 146
Wauchope 193
Wave Hill 251–2, 263– 6
Welfare Ordiance 128, 167
Wells, Rev Edgar, 92, 236
West Australian State Ships 33
Whiteman, Frank, 17, 28, 29, 33
Whitlam, Gough, 264–5
Wilcannia 256
Wilkinson, Clarry, 53
Willowra 261–2, 265
Wilson, Bob, 34
Wokulgari 158
Wood, Geoff, 234
Wood Green 160
Woods, 'Deadly' Dallas, 20
Woodward Royal Commission 265
Workers' Club 19, 73
Works and Housing Dept 12, 15, 17, 24
Works and Housing F C 28–9, 33
Worms, Fr Stephen, 183–4
Wu, Jocelyn, 20
Wu, Marian, 20
Wulanybuma, Wally, 237
Wurramurra, Mark, 224
Wüyal 235
Wyndham 40

Yates family 53
Yee, Ray, 75
Yirrkala mission 233, 236, 240
Yuen, Jamesy 'Mad Chinaman', 195–6
Yuendumu 140–159, 173–85, 261
Yunnupingu, Galarrwuy, 235, 238, 254–5
Yunupingu, Munggurawuy, 237, 239

Zapopan mine 192
Zena 66